DEBATING AMERICAN IDENTITY

Debating American Identity

Southwestern Statehood and Mexican Immigration

LINDA C. NOEL

THE UNIVERSITY OF ARIZONA PRESS
TUCSON

The University of Arizona Press
www.uapress.arizona.edu

We respectfully acknowledge the University of Arizona is on the land and territories of Indigenous peoples. Today, Arizona is home to twenty-two federally recognized tribes, with Tucson being home to the O'odham and the Yaqui. Committed to diversity and inclusion, the University strives to build sustainable relationships with sovereign Native Nations and Indigenous communities through education offerings, partnerships, and community service.

First paperback edition 2022

ISBN-13: 978-0-8165-3045-8 (cloth)
ISBN-13: 978-0-8165-9893-9 (ebook)
ISBN-13: 978-0-8165-5033-3 (paper)

Library of Congress Cataloging-in-Publication Data
Noel, Linda C., 1966–
Debating American identity : Southwestern statehood and Mexican immigration / Linda C. Noel.
pages cm
Includes bibliographical references and index.
ISBN 978-0-8165-3045-8 (cloth : acid-free paper)
1. Mexicans—Arizona—History—20th century. 2. Mexicans—New Mexico—History—20th century. 3. Arizona—Ethnic relations—History—20th century. 4. New Mexico—Ethnic relations—History—20th century. 5. Arizona—Politics and government—To 1950. 6. New Mexico—Politics and government—1848–1950. 7. Ethnicity—Political aspects—Southwest, New—History—20th century. 8. Immigrants—Southwest, New—History—20th century. 9. Southwest, New—Emigration and immigration—History—20th century. 10. Mexico—Emigration and immigration—History—20th century. I. Title.
F820.M5N64 2014
305.8009791—dc23
2013034058

Printed in the United States of America
♾ This paper meets the requirements of ANSI/NISO Z39.48-1992 (Permanence of Paper).

To Larry

Contents

Acknowledgments

Acknowledgments are often written in a rush as the deadline looms for publication, and this one is no different. Or at least that is my excuse for writing acknowledgments which may forget important folks who helped along the way and do injustice to my friends, family, and professional contacts that deserve much more thought and praise than they are going to receive.

Professionally I have received much help. Gary Gerstle got me started with some of my initial questions in his graduate course at the University of Maryland long ago and has remained a valuable resource; Ira Berlin and David Sicilia asked tough questions that helped me to refine my work and have provided ongoing support. Mary Kay Vaughan shared her enthusiasm of my project and guided me around Mexico City. Barbara Weinstein provided key support at a critical moment, as did Daryle Williams. University of Colorado professors Ralph Mann, Virginia Anderson, Lee Chambers, and Patricia Limerick welcomed me into the field long before this project began. And it was in Virginia Anderson's class that I first became interested in New Mexico. Laura Muñoz read and commented on an earlier version of one of the chapters. Anonymous reviewers corrected some mistakes and helped to improve the book's flow. Librarians at the various archives I visited also deserve thanks and appreciation, as well as all the staff at the University of Arizona Press who guided me through the publication process.

Current and former colleagues (and friends) at Morgan State University have *all* been very supportive of this project, but especially Frank Brown,

Susanne Deberry Cole, Mary Ann Fay, Robert Morrow, Jonathan Robins, Sarah Smiley, Glenn Smith, Sebastian Swann, and Brett Berliner who closely edited one chapter (several times!) and gave generously of his time to answer innumerable questions and provide much advice.

In addition to all the professional support, my friendships are very important to me and have helped enormously to sustain me through this process. I regret that in this process I lost two friends last year: one of whom first introduced me to the question of Spanish-American identity (Mark Allen) and the other a Latin Americanist (Rebecca Lord) who inspired me, by example, to persevere. They will be missed, but definitely not forgotten.

Several friends should be mentioned more specifically due to their greater involvement with this project: Tom Castillo, who is not only a dear friend, but should be on anyone's list as the *very* best person to consult for advice on writing, research, and history, due not only to his willingness to share his time, but because his advice is sprinkled with outside-of-the-box humor that has made the whole process a lot more fun. Herbert Brewer first suggested that I go to Mexico, and ever since then has been a good friend and colleague who helps to keep me current on international events. Long-term friend Jeff Coster gets a special plug for being an all-around nice guy whose ongoing support and sense of humor I value greatly. Shari Orisich read one chapter and greatly improved it, but far more than that she helped me through some rocky times. Keila Grinberg, Flavio Limonic, and Laura Lenci introduced me, through their friendship, to Latin America, and Laura helped me with Spanish. Other historian friends who provided support and companionship include Patricia Acerbi, Claire Goldstene, and Sarah Sarzynski. Matt Clark, the one nonhistorian in this paragraph, deserves a special mention for tackling the entire manuscript, cleaning up the prose, and at least feigning much interest in the prospective book! Big thanks to you, Matt!

Friends outside of the field of history provided a very welcome respite from working on the book and include: Laura Allen, Stephanie Clark, Sevgi Erdogan, Lisa and Jamie Gleason, Dave Griffin, Carla Herbig and Chris Walker, Lincoln Kallsen, Susan Kallsen, Terry Harris and Jim Rowader, Jeff McKinney, Maria Morocco and Mike Worth, Janice Popowich, Erica Rapier, Aruna Sannuti and Mohan Tatikonda, Jon Shurberg, Patty Tuttle and Darek Newby, Nancy Shay, Steve Sparks and Elia Burgos, John Sprovieri and Regina McNulty, and Chris and Lauren Weiland. I would be remiss if I forgot to thank my coffee shop friends at Tryst Coffeehouse in Washington, DC, where I wrote most of this book, thanks especially to "Sam" and Rodney Leeper.

I consider my family friends as well and am grateful for their support, especially my father, Don Noel, who read and commented on the entire draft and my brother, Doug Noel, who sustained me with weekly phone calls as well as other family members including Virginia Noel, Glen Noel, Nancy Noel, Sue Eastes, Sally O'Connor, and the extended and growing O'Connor family (too many to name them all!) as well as Dorothy Nagl, Nannette Nagl, Debbie Nagl, and Camille, Bob, Nikolai and Misha Auskalnis, Del Noel, Red and Carol Noel, and Edith and Bob Wiechel and their families as well as my now deceased grandmother, Susan Reynolds Noel Allin Steineke, a gifted storyteller who inspired me to study history.

And finally, deep thanks to my very best friend of all, Larry Nagl, who has suffered through far too many drafts and will be happy to have it all done and get his wife back.

Note on Terminology

The United States has appropriated the word *American* for its citizens. While many people living in North, South, and Central America object to this—and I understand why—I use the word *American* to signify citizens of the United States because that is the commonly used term in the United States. Other terms, such as *North Americans*, seem too cumbersome or equally problematic. I use *Anglo Americans* or simply *Anglos* to refer to persons considered to be "white" Americans—regardless of their actual ethnicity—during the time period studied. While it is becoming more common to use *Euro American*, I avoid this term to eliminate confusion since a part of my argument involves people of Mexican descent claiming a Spanish or European identity. I use *people of Mexican descent* to signify people who have that ethnicity, regardless of their citizenship. Sometimes I make further distinctions, such as *immigrant*, or *Mexican American*, when the need to differentiate is particularly relevant. I use the terms *Mexican* or *Mexican national* to refer to someone from Mexico; depending on the context this could include Mexicans still residing within Mexico or Mexican immigrants in the United States. I sometimes use *nativos* (natives) to refer to people of Mexican descent, regardless of citizenship status, since this was a word commonly used in New Mexico during the statehood debates. I also use *Americans* when I mean Americans more generally, including Anglo and Mexican Americans.

DEBATING AMERICAN IDENTITY

Introduction

Today's Americans struggle with the meaning of American identity as they debate how many immigrants to admit, the extent to which civil rights and benefits should apply to newcomers, and whether or not there should be a guest worker program or a path to legalization. To those who study the history of immigration and national identity, these questions are eerily similar to those of a century or more ago when Americans like Theodore Roosevelt grappled with earlier variants of these same questions: who was an American, who could become one, and who should enjoy the full rights of citizenship.

In June 1899 during the first anniversary celebration of the Battle of Las Guasimas, Theodore Roosevelt, then governor of New York, gratefully accepted a diamond and gold medal from the Rough Riders of New Mexico to commemorate his leadership in Cuba during the Spanish-American War. Roosevelt was reportedly so moved that he extemporaneously proclaimed his regiment and the gathered audience of 10,000 plus to be Americans, just like himself: "I am an American, as you are Americans." In his enthusiasm, he went further still and added: "All I shall say is if New Mexico wants to be a State you can count me in, and I will go to Washington to speak for you, or do anything you wish." But a few years later, as the newly anointed U.S. president, Roosevelt had apparently forgotten his spontaneous pledge and become more circumspect in his allegiance to New Mexico.

Nearly four years later, in May 1903, Roosevelt returned to New Mexico for the christening of his eponymous godson, Theodore Roosevelt Armijo, who was the offspring of Sergeant George Washington Armijo, a New Mexican of Mexican descent and one of Roosevelt's illustrious Rough Riders. In contrast to Roosevelt's previous visit, in which he had toured the territory for three days, the president did not spend the night, making only a hasty trip to attend the baptism, lunch with the governor, and deliver brief speeches in Santa Fe and Albuquerque. While Roosevelt remained popular in the region, the invitation may have been designed to remind him of his former promise since statehood advocates wasted no time in subtly reminding him of New Mexico's uncertain status. Situated directly across from Roosevelt's podium, at the Alvarado Hotel in Albuquerque, stood a tableau of forty-five girls—each representing one of the states in the Union—while an "Uncle Sam" prevented a forty-sixth girl from joining the assembled group. Upon noticing the display, Roosevelt allegedly remarked that once New Mexico developed a more extensive system of irrigation, the forty-sixth girl need not stand alone. Roosevelt's earlier speech in Santa Fe likewise reflected these sentiments, but his private remarks conveyed that he had serious reservations about New Mexico's Spanish-speaking population and its denizens' readiness for statehood.

A few years later, Roosevelt supported the creation of one enormous state by merging the New Mexico and Arizona territories—which neither territory had called for or desired—thereby reducing the political power of the area's Spanish-speaking population. Regardless of this proposal, neither territory became a state, combined or otherwise, during Roosevelt's presidency. According to one newspaper account, Roosevelt's new godson, Theodore Roosevelt Armijo, behaved very poorly at his christening, "emitting yells of rage and disapproval."[1] Perhaps his anger—and the newspaper's telling of it—reflected displeasure that the newborn Armijo would be nearly ten years old before New Mexico became a state.

Roosevelt's ambivalence about the prospective inclusion of New Mexico was part of a larger debate in the United States over who could be an American, and what the boundaries of that America should be.[2] At the very same time that Americans weighed statehood and belonging for the residents of Arizona and New Mexico, they were entangled in debates over immigration: between 1865 and 1900 at least 15 million immigrants legally entered the United States, and the stream of entrants showed no signs of slowing. Moreover, the annexation of Hawaii in 1898 and the subsequent treaty with Spain for the Philippines, Puerto Rico, and Guam exacerbated tensions over the meaning of *American* and how national unity might be achieved if all the new peoples were to be included.[3] While many Americans of the era then believed that a homogeneous population was necessary for national unity and identity, they differed in their understanding of just *how* Americans needed to be homogeneous, and specifically if they needed to share the same class, race, and/or culture.

These debates about U.S. identity held consequences for *all* Americans, not only because of how the political map might change but also because the questions raised were part of the national discourse over whether and how to incorporate "others" into Anglo-dominated America, and at a time when the various strategies for doing so were still evolving. Matthew Jacobson explains how Americans in this era created distinct ways for incorporating new places into America's expanding empire without necessarily granting full rights or a "political voice" to the residents within them.[4] Likewise, Anglo and Mexican Americans debated whether people of Mexican descent should fit within the nation in the context of statehood, and the extent of their incorporation as Americans in terms of full citizenship as well as social recognition and equal treatment. But the disagreements over these questions did not cease once Arizona and New Mexico became states in 1912, because Americans then turned their attention to the growing debate over Mexican immigration.

This book focuses on four national debates over statehood and immigration during the first third of the twentieth century. It was during these years that the United States greatly expanded its "gatekeeping" role in determining and codifying who—and which places or territories and peoples within them—could formally enter the boundaries of the country and become American.[5] Specific events in this period brought questions about the status of people of Mexican descent to the foreground: the proposed statehood of the Arizona and New Mexico territories in the early twentieth century, the creation and extension of a temporary worker policy around the time of the Great War, efforts to restrict Mexican immigration in the 1920s, and the push to "return" many of these same immigrants, and some Mexican Americans, to Mexico during the 1930s. In the course of each of these events, heated discussions arose over whether the door to American society should be open to people of Mexican descent and how such an opening might affect U.S. national identity.

While historians have studied each of these four debates separately, this book adds to this literature by linking the discussions over expansionism and statehood with those concerning immigration and guest workers. Juxtaposing these histories helps to expose the connection between the initial debates over statehood and later ones concerning immigration. Comparing New Mexico with Arizona showcases the differing strategies each territory relied upon to incorporate people of Mexican descent, reveals how the varying perspectives influenced debates at the national level, and explains why New Mexico was less of a factor in the later debates.[6] These comparisons also highlight how the voices of people of Mexican descent influenced discussions over national identity, emphasizing the ongoing significance of class status, race, and culture in determining who could be an American.

As the title suggests, *Debating American Identity,* concentrates on the debates among people within the United States over what they thought being an American meant, and who could become one; it is *not* a history of Mexico or of the U.S.-Mexican borderlands, or a transnational history. Although Mexico and the borderlands influenced U.S. identity, this work aims only to elucidate the aforementioned national debates that were discussed widely in the American press, among U.S. policy makers, and/or within the halls of Congress. Likewise, this book focuses on the years 1898 to 1935, a period during which the definition of national identity was of much concern. In short, this book covers four debates concerning people of Mexican descent and American identity in the first three decades of the twentieth century. As it is, the subject is still quite large.

Because of its broad scope, this book synthesizes extant historians' arguments and uses an extensive number of primary sources to pull together the story of the contested and changing views of American identity. By using a wider lens than related works—including local newspapers and archival materials from both New Mexico and Arizona, as well as national newspapers and congressional records—this book makes clear the principal views that Anglo and Mexican Americans held regarding how, whether, and to what extent people of Mexican descent should fit within the nation, how these views changed, and which perspective dominated at a given time.

During the course of the statehood debates, several perspectives—exclusion, assimilation, pluralism, and marginalization—emerged regarding how and whether people of Mexican descent should be incorporated into the nation-state.[7] The perceived class standing of people of Mexican descent mattered greatly in each of these views or strategies for incorporation. Class status entailed not only a certain standard of living, which included having a permanent home with a "modern" design and conveniences, but also the ability to exert a certain political clout as a consequence of economic power, and the social respect that came from having such a standing in society.[8] Exclusionists, who favored denying statehood or closing the border to those they deemed incapable of becoming American, weighed the class and racial background of people of Mexican descent and, in determining that they were lower class and of mixed African, European, and Native American heritage, used these arguments as a rationale for excluding or limiting their participation in the United States. Pluralists and assimilationists also assessed the racial and class status of people of Mexican descent but arrived at very different conclusions. Primarily, they perceived people of Mexican descent as having a pure European background and therefore as holding, or capable of attaining, a respectable class position in society; consequently, they argued that people of Mexican descent should be admitted into the nation with all the rights of citizenship. The difference between the two was that assimilationists demanded conversion to an Anglo American culture, whereas pluralists believed no such change was necessary for becoming American.[9] Those touting marginalization attempted to avoid the awkward questions regarding incorporation, arguing instead that such talk was irrelevant since people of Mexican descent either performed low-wage work under the authority of their employers or did not remain in the country for long.

While all four strategies, in a sense, were white nationalisms—rooted in ideologies of white supremacy—people of Mexican descent who could plausibly claim a European or white heritage did so because this was the recognized path to power and advancement during the first third of the twentieth century.[10] A few people of Mexican descent suggested other ways of becoming an American, one based more upon a state of mind and their long personal history of living and working in the United States—a kind of "cultural citizenship" as posited by other scholars. But during the first third of the twentieth century, few who held socioeconomic power, or had the chance of attaining any, advanced a claim solely on this basis. Although Gabriela Arredondo uncovered a short-lived pan-American identity in the 1920s among a few Chicago Mexicans and Latin American intellectuals, this was not widespread or discussed much in national newspapers or congressional debates about immigration. It was not until later in the 1930s that the descendants of immigrants or Mexican immigrants themselves openly asserted other kinds of identities as Mexican Americans or promoted a more "flexible" or "cross-border" nationalism.[11]

This book argues that, in the course of early twentieth century disputes over national identity, Americans first relied upon familiar strategies of exclusion and assimilation (strategies previously applied to Asian and European immigrants, respectively) when facing the incorporation of people of Mexican descent in significant numbers. Later, they turned to the less common strategies of pluralism and marginalization when the former constructs proved unsatisfactory. A strategy's predominance at any given time depended upon the socioeconomic clout of those espousing it, the class background and perceived race of the new arrivals, newcomers' interest in becoming full members of the United States, and employers' demand for laborers.

The participants of the day did not use the terms *exclusion*, *assimilation*, *pluralism*, or *marginalization*, but their writings and speeches suggest that they generally coalesced around or provided support for one of these four positions. Although the names and components of the strategies are not fully original, they offer a useful and familiar vocabulary for understanding the competing views of the day and the variation in how people perceived what it meant or took to become American. This grouping, however, does not mean that Americans who held one view never changed their minds and did not overlap with other strategies, or that no other perspectives existed. Instead, they exemplify the primary strategies then being debated regarding the place of people of Mexican descent in the nation-state. The strategies themselves also morphed, as the following chapters show, during the first third of the twentieth century.

The adherents of exclusion, assimilation, pluralism, and marginalization also were not necessarily wedded to any one set of policies. They adjusted their rhetoric and their strategies to conform to the political context of the times and to achieve their varied goals related to statehood, temporary exemptions, immigration restriction, and/or repatriation. At times they made statements that they did not themselves condone in their effort to win support for a desired policy. Regardless of their individual beliefs, their arguments in the public sphere contributed to the national conversation about what it meant to be American and the place of people of Mexican descent within it. This discourse had a powerful influence upon policy decisions and laws related to the four debates discussed in this book.

Background on Expansion and Statehood

The issue of incorporating people of Mexican descent first arose as a consequence of American expansionism and the resulting Mexican-American War (1846). During the war, a few Americans proposed to expand the country's geographical boundaries to include all of Mexico and its people. But as the common trajectory for new territories had previously involved a quick transition to statehood and parity with existing states, other Americans worried that the infusion of eight million Mexicans—whom they regarded as primitive peoples of mixed race (whose lack of racial "purity" connoted degeneracy) or Indian heritage—would impair the nation. Consequently, the U.S. government rejected the idea of conquering all of Mexico and instead wrested "only" the less populated northern half, which included approximately 100,000 Mexicans widely dispersed throughout the region. In the 1848 Treaty of Guadalupe Hidalgo ending the war, signers agreed that anyone who decided to remain within this ceded territory would be automatically granted U.S. citizenship unless they opted otherwise; only a few thousand chose to remain Mexican nationals. The treaty further stipulated that the U.S. Congress would incorporate the region into the nation-state as several states "at the proper time."[12]

In the fifty years following the Mexican-American War, there were few significant debates concerning statehood for New Mexico or Arizona, or much discussion or recognition that the people of Mexican descent in this region were actual American citizens. Two years after the Treaty of Guadalupe Hidalgo, the U.S. government officially organized New Mexico as a territory, which spurred a brief campaign for statehood among some of its inhabitants. Once that effort fizzled, few legislators tried subsequently due to the imminent threat of civil war. Even after Arizona formally separated from New Mexico during the Civil War (1863), residents of both territories remained skeptical about the benefits of statehood. These internal divisions continued throughout the more serious drives to join the union in the 1870s and 1880s, making it very easy for the U.S. Congress to reject all such petitions and deny it being "the proper time" for statehood.[13]

Following the Spanish-American War (1898), questions of empire and belonging arose with renewed vigor, resulting in awkward comparisons between the territorial residents of the American Southwest and those of the newest acquisitions. Julian Go finds that the continental and island territories comprised a "chain of empire," in that they all influenced and were affected by the disputes of the others.[14] Some legislators of the day declared that the U.S. Constitution did not necessarily follow the flag, thereby insinuating that the rights it bestowed might not apply to new *or* existing territories. Other commentators openly wondered why the new possessions should be treated any differently from existing ones and suggested that if they were, then those restrictions might be applied to the extant territories as well. Initially, the U.S. attorney general argued that "there is no difference between the status of Porto [*sic*] Rico and Oklahoma, New Mexico and Arizona" and that "Congress has the right to govern, tax and alienate any of its territories." The commissioner for Puerto Rico concurred, remarking, "We have kept New Mexico out forty-nine years, Arizona thirty-seven years; the islands can be kept out until everybody agrees that they ought to be admitted." Ultimately, a set of U.S. Supreme Court decisions referred to as the Insular Cases, and specifically *Downes v. Bidwell* (1901), determined that Puerto Rico, Guam, and the Philippines should follow a different trajectory from the "incorporated" territories—Oklahoma, Arizona, New Mexico, Hawaii, and Alaska—which were all eligible for and on the path to statehood.[15]

Although the *Downes* decision clearly differentiated the southwestern territories from the newest possessions, it pushed the residents in Arizona and New Mexico to press for statehood. The U.S. House of Representatives' Committee on the Territories reported that those in the Southwest had become "more keenly" aware of their limited rights and status as "newcomers to the national fold—the Hawaiian, the Porto [*sic*] Rican, and the Filipino—are placed side by side as to the political rights with the pioneers of American civilization." Partisan bickering in the territories ceased as the local Republican and Democratic leadership, along with the Spanish- and English-language papers, united in favor of self-government and statehood. The year following the *Downes* decision, residents of the southwestern territories combined their efforts to support an omnibus bill for separate statehood.[16]

Years ago Howard Lamar emphasized the importance of territorial history in the context of America's expanding empire and suggested that more scholars study it. Some historians then heeded his call, although they concentrated more on the political arguments over statehood than on connections to the empire or the role people of Mexican descent played in the statehood debates. More recently, various historians have examined the place of people of Mexican descent within New Mexico or Arizona, although they have not always focused on statehood or empire.[17] This book differs from those works by examining the two nascent states together, illuminating differences between them and showing how people of Mexican descent and the other inhabitants of the territories contributed to the debates over statehood and empire.

Background on the Temporary Worker Policy

The establishment of a temporary worker policy during the First World War—in actuality exemptions from existing immigration laws—allowed Mexicans to continue entering the country and helped to define the nation in terms of who would be granted admission as potential permanent members of the United States, and who would not. Of course, temporary workers or contract laborers lived in the United States long before the Great War: Chinese immigrants in the mid-nineteenth century had arrived through various arrangements, many of which mandated their return. Frequently these workers did leave, especially after the 1870s when few Chinese women were permitted to emigrate due to fears that they would bear Chinese-American children via *jus soli*—birthright citizenship, as stipulated by the Fourteenth Amendment to the U.S. Constitution—and threaten America's presumed racial homogeneity. By 1882, however, new restriction laws prohibited Chinese entry per any type of contract.[18] Likewise, in the late nineteenth and early twentieth centuries, Italians and Greeks immigrated temporarily as indentured workers to *padrones* or labor contractors and returned home upon completion of their terms. But once the U.S. government imposed strict restrictions in 1921 and 1924 upon these and other European immigrants, it effectively ended any tradition of their temporary immigration to the United States.[19]

Although Americans at the time were broadly aware of the circular peregrinations of many immigrants—and in some cases expressed dismay over those who they saw as taking American resources back to their native homelands without trying to become Americans—the implementation of Asian exclusion and European restriction laws between 1882 and 1924 limited Americans' concerns about those groups. In the 1920s it was people of Mexican descent who became explicitly connected to this temporary image as Americans began to accept the idea that Mexicans were in the United States only temporarily, or that if not, they should be.[20]

Major questions about Mexican immigrants first arose over naturalization and whether or not they could be considered as free white persons, in accordance with U.S. naturalization law, so that they could become U.S. citizens. In 1897 Judge Maxey, a federal judge in Texas, designated Ricardo Rodríguez, a Mexican immigrant, as "white" for naturalization purposes, relying on the precedent established under the 1848 Treaty of Guadalupe Hidalgo, which had granted the inhabitants of the territory U.S. citizenship. So unlike Asian immigrants, Mexican immigrants were eligible to become naturalized Americans. Despite this legal ruling, discussions concerning the belonging of people of Mexican descent had scarcely begun since Americans barely noticed their growing presence and continued entry until after the Mexican Revolution and the outbreak of the First World War.[21]

As early as the first decade of the twentieth century, Mexicans entered into short-term contracts with U.S. employers, but this practice was not common and was primarily coordinated by the Mexican and U.S. governments to aid in railroad construction. Years later, after the United States entered the

First World War, agricultural employers demanded relief from recently imposed immigrant restriction laws—a literacy test plus a tax on entry—and requested exemptions from them, especially for Mexican and Canadian immigrants who could be more readily returned once their contracts expired.

The initial restrictions, exemptions, and the later debate to end them were all part of the nation's evolving understanding of who could enter the country and become American. Only in recent years have historians begun to explore the second *bracero* (migrant worker) program during and after the Second World War, but few mention or address this first *bracero* or temporary worker program to any extent. Those historians who have addressed it have primarily done so from the standpoint of describing the policy and how it affected immigrants, rather than on how it contributed to the developing image of Mexicans as only temporary residents and reflected dominant understandings of U.S. national identity.[22]

This book explains how Mexican immigrants came to be defined as temporary immigrant workers rather than as permanent immigrants and potential Americans. While many historians have noted how growers promoted the idea of Mexicans as only temporarily in the United States, *Debating American Identity* shows how this notion of them as only "temporary" developed, grew, and spread in the years following statehood. This mental image of Mexicans in the United States only as "sojourners," to borrow language from Lawrence Fuchs, was part of a concerted strategy—referred to here as marginalization—to balance the demands of capitalists who desired open borders and an ongoing stream of workers against those who favored more restrictive policies aimed at preserving the nation's presumed racial homogeneity and the retention of jobs for existing Americans.[23] The growth of this temporary image in the late 1910s and early 1920s precedes and fits with Mae Ngai's argument (see below) concerning the construction of Mexicans as "illegal" in the late 1920s.

Background on Immigration Restriction

In deciding who could enter the country permanently and become naturalized citizens, Americans defined and shaped their nation and themselves. Recent works on the Mexican restriction debates of the 1920s all point to a clear pattern of increased racialization and characterization of Mexicans as illegal aliens, as well as a hardening of border controls and related restrictions. Mae Ngai explains how these processes developed in the 1920s to affect Mexican Americans and immigrants alike. As European immigration subsided and Mexicans became more visible and associated with migrant and unskilled labor, Mexicans came to be seen as alien in ways that they had not been before. Various policies and laws contributed to this development: increased enforcement of existing laws that rarely had been applied to Mexicans before (e.g., the exclusion of those "likely to become a public charge" and collection of a head tax), demeaning inspection procedures, the creation of the Border Patrol, and deportation of immigrants who were in the country illegally. These policies contributed to the public image of Mexicans as foreign and nonwhite and thus unassimilable and altogether different from the dominant Anglo population. It was an image that effectively stripped them of membership in the nation-state. As Ngai shows, the newly enforced policies reduced Mexican immigration by 76 percent from 1925 to 1930, offsetting the failure of restriction bills.[24]

The failure to officially restrict Mexican immigrants was primarily due to fears of angering Mexico, the belief that other forms of restriction—short of closing the border entirely—could be effective, and the strength of the employers' lobby.[25] Yet in addition to these former arguments, frequent references to Mexicans' temporary status made it easier for Americans to avoid passing restriction laws that would offend Mexico and frustrate U.S. agricultural interests. This notion of Mexicans as only temporarily present in the country mollified those who had been influenced by exclusionists and eugenicists, who perceived Mexicans as of mixed race and inferior to white Americans and worried about how the immigrants' presence would affect U.S. national identity.[26]

This narrative differs from other books on restriction by emphasizing how people of various backgrounds contributed to the construction of an image of Mexicans as only temporary workers. It was not only employers who had a vested interest in fluid borders but also, at times, Anglo American journalists and academics, the U.S. and Mexican governments, Mexican Americans, and even Mexican immigrants themselves. Debates over the temporary or permanent status of Mexicans also contributed to the broader society's definition of what it meant to be an American. Because if Mexicans were temporary, migratory, and in the United States to do only the lowliest jobs that no Americans wanted to do, then naturally Americans must be stable, permanent, and of a higher class standing.

Background on Repatriation

The repatriation of approximately 500,000 Mexican immigrants and Mexican Americans in the 1930s was another nation-defining project in which some Anglo and Mexican Americans demonstrated their understanding of their national community as one that did not include Mexicans. Repatriation, according to Abraham Hoffman, included the massive roundup and deportation of Mexicans, as well as tactics designed to encourage them to leave. Interestingly, the federal government did not play the predominant role; instead, local governments initiated and organized most of the repatriation activity with only limited support from the U.S. and Mexican governments. Such campaigns occurred nationwide with drives taking place all over the Southwest as well as in the Midwest, Seattle, New Orleans, and New York.[27]

As other historians make clear, the large-scale expulsion of the Mexicans did not last much beyond 1934 because the proclaimed cost savings to other Americans never materialized and business owners and bankers recognized that a significant portion of their customer base had disappeared. Antagonism to the policy also developed as voices inside Mexico, along with various community organizations and the Spanish-language press in the United States, increasingly decried the actions as racist since a significant number of Mexicans, the dominant immigrant group affected due to European immigrant restriction, faced expulsion.[28] Although it soon ended, repatriation contributed to the growing notion that lower-class people of Mexican descent were not American and belonged only temporarily in the United States.

Several historians study Mexican repatriation from the United States and suggest a link between their temporary status and the ease of removal. This analysis builds on the works of Abraham Hoffman, Francisco Balderrama, Raymond Rodríguez, and Camille Guerin-Gonzales to emphasize how the temporary worker image—created and bolstered by many Americans at the time—was used to bring about Mexicans' removal.

Book Overview

Debating American Identity argues that during the first third of the twentieth century, in the context of the national disputes over statehood and immigration, Americans developed and altered various strategies for incorporating people of Mexican descent into the United States; in doing so, they demonstrated what they thought being an American meant. Part 1 of this book examines four strategies used for handling "others"—exclusion, assimilation, pluralism, and marginalization—and how they were applied to and/or used by Anglo and Mexican Americans during the battles over statehood.

Anglos outside of Arizona and New Mexico reacted to the turn-of-the-century attempt at statehood—and proposed incorporation of people of Mexican descent—in ways reminiscent of those strategies applied to the extant immigrant groups, and favored exclusion or assimilation. At the same time that Anglos continued to worry about the ongoing influx of immigrants from southern and eastern Europe as well as Asia, they expressed concern about the presence of "foreigners" of Mexican descent, despite the fact that most of the territorial residents with such heritage were natives who had either been born in U.S. territory or had "the border cross them" as a consequence of the Treaty of Guadalupe Hidalgo or the 1854 Gadsden Purchase from Mexico. Regardless, these exclusionists argued that the southwestern residents could not be admitted without seriously damaging the cohesiveness of the United States due to what they perceived as their mixed Spanish, African, and Indian heritage. Viewing them as "off-white," to use Laura Gómez's term, and of a lesser race—much as they perceived southern and eastern Europeans—exclusionists understood people of Mexican descent as unfit to belong in what they perceived to be an otherwise pure, white, and Anglo-Saxon nation.[29] In contrast, assimilationists claimed that the territorial residents should be included in the nation because, like other European immigrants, their Spanish or European heritage meant that they possessed the capacity to conform.

While many Anglos outside of the territories continued to adhere to the dominant strategies of exclusion or assimilation, territorial inhabitants increasingly found these stark poles to be unacceptable. During the first decade of the twentieth century, residents and their allies began to cluster around two distinct strategies—pluralism and marginalization—for incorporating people of Mexican descent into the United States.

Pluralism evolved and flourished in New Mexico, which had a sizable community of middle-class people of Mexican descent. These "pluralists" rooted their beliefs in a Spanish or European background and called for those willing and able to claim such a heritage to enter the nation as full American citizens who would retain aspects of their ancestral language and culture while claiming the same social and political rights as Anglo Americans. Like assimilationists, pluralists asserted that people with this Spanish heritage embraced modernity, pledged their allegiance to American institutions, and shared a middle-class rank or aspiration, educational level, and history with other European Americans. Although not all of the people who met these criteria spoke English, pluralists argued that they could unite with other Americans on the basis of their European background and shared history of colonization. In doing so these *nativos*, or people of Mexican descent in New Mexico, included themselves along with Anglo Americans on the top rung of a racialized hierarchy, even as people of the same Mexican heritage in Arizona found themselves increasingly relegated to marginal citizenship.[30]

Marginalization began to dominate in Arizona. Adherents of this strategy were generally of Anglo descent and included major employers and their allies along with politicians and others with a vested interest in statehood. Since they controlled the territory's politics and economy, they had few concerns about the presence of people of Mexican descent of a lower class standing and thus promoted their incorporation as quiescent laborers. These marginalizationists did not concern themselves much with the racial heritage, class status, or culture of people of Mexican descent; instead, they were sensitive to how high the workers might rise. Ideally, these workers would remain safely under their employers' control, neither threatening the status quo through the organization of unions or strikes nor attempting to transform the national culture. They would be expected to accept their low-wage jobs, segregated schools, and English as the dominant language. Marginalization allowed for the physical inclusion of people of Mexican descent as second-class or marginal citizens, but excluded them from full rights and belonging in the nation.

By 1912, the year in which both territories attained statehood, pluralism and marginalization had become the primary strategies for understanding how people of Mexican descent could fit within the nation without harming national unity. To some extent, this resulted in more inclusion for people of Mexican descent since the strategies provided them with either a marginal space in the United States, or full rights and maintenance of their culture by expanding the definition of American to include anyone who could claim a European heritage. But these strategies had been designed to maintain national homogeneity and unity in the presence of people of Mexican descent, some of whom held a high socioeconomic standing, and many of whom had been long-term residents within U.S. territories. Following statehood, there was a dramatic increase in the number of Mexican immigrants (due to the Mexican Revolution and its aftermath) who had no former affiliation with the United States and were generally of a lower-class standing. This change resulted in a re-evaluation of the extant strategies for their incorporation.

While part 1 has a geographic focus on Arizona and New Mexico, as well as the United States as a whole, the emphasis throughout the rest of the book is on Arizona, and the United States more generally, as Mexicans immigrated into Arizona as well as other parts of the West or Midwest. Despite New Mexico's proximity to Mexico, there were few economic opportunities for unskilled workers in the new state; consequently, few Mexican immigrants migrated there and thus debates about people of Mexican descent moved elsewhere.

The chapters in part 2 address how Anglo and Mexican Americans modified the previously developed strategies of incorporation in the new context of war and revolution. Demography was central to the change. Because the recent immigrants came from the lowest classes in Mexico, and moved into areas where Anglos already dominated the political and economic landscape, it was easy for the latter to marginalize the newest arrivals. These Anglos were joined by other European immigrants who—as Katherine Benton-Cohen and Linda Gordon explain—saw opportunities for boosting their own status by separating themselves from Mexicans.[31] Despite this strategy's growing appeal, it faced serious challenges from Americans' heightened fears of immigration and radicalism, and so advocates of marginalization shifted from their original emphasis on incorporating the newest Mexican arrivals as second-class Americans to highlighting their temporary status and lack of permanent belonging in the nation-state.

Part 3 demonstrates how the popularity of assimilation and pluralism waned as the marginalization strategy gained credence as a plausible way in which Americans could benefit from Mexican labor without having to worry about how the newcomers would influence national identity. George Sánchez shows how Americans lost faith in efforts to Americanize immigrants as they increasingly viewed the latest arrivals, many of whom were of a lower-class standing than former Mexican immigrants, as unlikely to have a European heritage and thus incapable of assimilating into the dominant Anglo American mold or asserting a Spanish American identity. As the voices clamoring for assimilation or pluralism diminished, those in favor of exclusion or marginalization grew louder. Advocates of marginalization were especially successful in promoting their views due to the socioeconomic clout of the agriculturalists and other employers who favored this strategy to permit a steady inflow of immigrant labor so that they could continue to maximize profits. Thus, this revised strategy of marginalization—in which employers and their political allies emphasized Mexicans' temporary status—spread rapidly throughout the 1920s. At times the Mexican government, and even some immigrants themselves, did much to bolster this image of Mexicans as temporary workers who would soon return to Mexico. This shift in emphasis, from second-class citizen to temporary worker, enabled those favoring marginalization to balance their own interests in retaining a pool of laborers against exclusionists' concerns of how Mexicans might subvert the nation. They presented their strategy as one which resolved the struggle between employers who wanted to expand the economy through the continuous infusion of new workers and those Americans who wanted to exclude newcomers so as to preserve their class and cultural dominance.[32] According to its advocates, marginalization—in the form of a temporary worker—could provide the former without threatening the latter.

But as part 4 makes clear, the marginalization strategy proved to be enormously elastic. For while the transnational creation of a temporary worker pool made it easy for Americans to open the door for Mexicans when they desired more laborers, it also made it easier to send them back out the door when they did not. This unofficial policy of entry and eviction affected not only the Mexican immigrant experience—setting forth the pattern of a "swinging door" for the future *bracero* (migrant worker) programs during and following the Second World War—but also reflected changes in Americans' self-perception.[33] The expulsion of Mexican temporary workers during the Great Depression, having previously viewed themselves as being of European heritage, middle class, and permanently settled, showed that when such a calamity occurred and affected an even larger group of Americans, contesting Americans' vision of themselves as a middle-class nation, Americans were then willing to re-envision their national identity as one of all class backgrounds, but not all races, and as a people who performed all types of jobs, including migratory ones.

Over the first third of the twentieth century, the marginalization strategy became the dominant way in which Americans perceived how Mexican immigrants would fit within the nation-state. It was during these years that those favoring marginalization perfected their strategy to persuade a sufficient number of Americans during times of economic boom that their policy of admitting allegedly temporary workers was sound and, as such, open borders should be retained. When poor economic times came, Americans, who had accepted this strategy for the limited or marginal incorporation of Mexicans, lobbied to push those who they perceived as only temporary back through the "swinging door" into Mexico. The fluidity of this strategy—created and promoted by people with varied backgrounds and interests—ultimately proved difficult to contest, resulting in devastating consequences for people of Mexican descent. Marginalization remains the core of American immigration policy and incorporation to this day.

Immigration today, especially the entry of undocumented immigrants, is a daily subject in the national news, with the state of Arizona front and center in these debates while its neighbor New Mexico is mostly silent on the topic. This book did not set out to explain these conditions, yet in the end it provides some historical background for why immigration is so hotly contested in Arizona and much of the country even as it remains peripheral to the lives of most New Mexicans. These two states, entwined from the beginning of their association with the United States as the New Mexico Territory, share much in common: their distance from the seat of governmental power, first in Mexico and then the United States; their native inhabitants who persisted despite Spanish and then Anglo encroachments; an arid climate; economies based on farming, ranching, and mining; and parallel entry as two distinct states in 1912. Over time, the changing economy and resulting demographics produced divergent results in terms of how the two territories ultimately entered as states, and in how or if they played any role in the ongoing debates over immigration and related issues in the 1920s and 1930s.

PART ONE

The Late Territorial Years, 1898–1912

CHAPTER ONE

The Closed Door

Exclusion Reigns

Miguel Antonio Otero Jr. considered himself an American and he was one. Born in St. Louis, Missouri, in 1859 to a father and mother of Mexican and Anglo descent, respectively, Otero moved with his parents to the New Mexico Territory when he was two years old. Well educated, bilingual, and raised in a political family, Otero was bound to do well, and he did. Like his father before him, Otero chose a career of business and then politics, whereupon he befriended no lesser known a figure than that of President William McKinley. McKinley liked Otero so well that in 1897 he appointed him governor of New Mexico. In this position, Otero ardently fought for statehood and recognition that his territorial constituents were full Americans entitled to self-rule.[1]

Like Otero, Carlos Corella Jácome believed he was an American. Born in Ures in Sonora, Mexico, in 1870, Jácome immigrated to Arizona as a young boy and later became a U.S. citizen. After working in various low-end jobs—including hauling mud for adobe bricks—Jácome eventually met and worked under the tutelage of a local businessman, Emilio Carrillo. Sponsored by Carrillo, Jácome set up shop and became one of Tucson's most successful businessmen and one of the community's leaders as he fraternized with other such men through his membership in the Arizona Historical Pioneers' Society, as well as the local philharmonic band, in which he played the brass horn. In 1894 he helped to found the Alianza Hispano-Americana, an organization devoted to improving conditions for people of Mexican descent, and immersed himself in local and territorial affairs, including the quest for statehood.[2]

This matter of statehood, which both Otero and Jácome supported, raised anew the question of who could be an American. Although most New Mexicans and Arizonans were already U.S. citizens, they held fewer rights as a consequence of their territorial standing: they had no direct representation at the national level, save for one nonvoting delegate in the House of Representatives; could not vote for president or select their own governor; and faced the threat of a congressional veto on territorial legislation.[3] Furthermore, as the Supreme Court weighed the status of the islands acquired during the Spanish-American War, Arizonans and New Mexicans increasingly worried that they might become associated with the inhabitants of these isles and limit their chances for statehood.[4]

But if the territories did become states, then the residents within them would have their rights secured and the votes and representation to influence national politics. This possibility worried Anglo Americans from outside of the territories, especially given the significant number of people of Mexican descent who resided within the disputed region. For this debate over the territories' status—similar to the ongoing disagreements over America's expanding empire—was in large part one of whether or not people of Mexican descent could fit within the nation without harming national homogeneity and unity. Consequently, Americans re-evaluated the dominant strategies for excluding or including newcomers—exclusion and assimilation—to see whether and how they pertained to people of Mexican descent. In the first years of the twentieth century, exclusion reigned.

The final years of the nineteenth century were a time of great uncertainty due to high levels of immigration, disputes over territorial expansion, and continued problems between capital and labor. During these years, the United States accepted an enormous number of people from Europe and Asia and the stream of immigrants showed no signs of slowing. This ongoing migration caused many Anglo Americans to wonder just how long they could continue to absorb and assimilate such a diverse group of people without jeopardizing national cohesion. These same Americans had similar questions and concerns with regard to the people residing in the territories recently acquired through the Spanish-American War.[5] In addition, labor unrest in the 1890s, and within the territories themselves, brought more attention to the unresolved problems between the ruling- and working-classes, with many Americans fearing that more working-class newcomers would exacerbate class conflict and undermine the nation. As scholars

William V. Flores and Rina Benmayor have argued, "Homogeneity is assumed to be the basis for political stability and growth," and Americans at the time saw anything but uniformity in their nation.[6] It was during this period of change and uncertainty that Arizonans and New Mexicans decided to press for statehood and full inclusion within the political boundaries of the country.

The deferred admission of Arizona and New Mexico, until 1912, was not unique in that other territories experienced significant delays before statehood. Few territories, however, waited very long and none involved as much debate over people of Mexican descent. The multilingual population of New Orleans, acquired as part of the 1803 Louisiana Purchase, troubled some Anglo Americans, but its growing Anglo population helped to mitigate this concern such that Louisiana achieved statehood in 1812. Other statehood battles concerned the institution of slavery more than demographics: Texas and California both included Mexican residents, but by the mid-nineteenth century Anglos outnumbered them and the major concern for admission was over how to balance sectional tensions. The Dakotas, Utah, and Oklahoma, as well as the newest territories of Hawaii and Alaska, spurred discussion over the fitness of indigenous people and Mormons, but none of these territories included many people of Mexican descent.[7]

Before statehood became a prominent national issue, most Anglo Americans gravitated toward one of two strategies for handling newcomers and maintaining national unity: exclusion or assimilation. Facing increased immigration and territorial expansion, those favoring exclusion—nativists and their political allies—pursued closing the borders and preventing the extension of the U.S. Constitution to areas outside of the continental United States. In 1882 they succeeded in limiting some arrivals with the passage of the first major restriction law, the Chinese Exclusion Act, which drastically reduced Chinese entrants, particularly those from the bottom sectors of Chinese society.[8] A few years later, exclusionists organized themselves into anti-immigration groups and strove to lessen the tide of Europeans as well, especially lower-class immigrants coming from southern and eastern Europe. One Republican senator from Massachusetts, Henry Cabot Lodge, worked actively with these groups to exclude such Europeans through the imposition of a literacy requirement. Although Senator Lodge and his allies initially failed (later succeeding in 1917), it was clear that the exclusionists had a strong and growing cadre of supporters. Their rationale for exclusion was closely tied to the perceived race and class of the newcomers because, as in the case of Chinese immigrants, exclusionists viewed the racial background of southern and eastern Europeans with skepticism. Although, as Thomas Guglielmo argues, they may have perceived them as white (for various legal purposes), they also saw them as members of a separate, distinct, and lesser race compared with Nordics or Anglo-Saxon Europeans from northern Europe. Other historians have suggested that southern and eastern Europeans were viewed as "inbetween peoples," neither white nor black. In either case, the immigrants' class status also mattered as exclusionists tended to view the southern and eastern Europeans as mostly peasants, forever locked into a feudal mind-set, who were incapable of improving their economic situation to become fully American.[9]

Late nineteenth-century assimilationists, whose ranks included reformers and educators as well as businessmen who desired a continuous supply of workers, promoted a broader vision for their ideal America; they argued that newcomers could become full Americans through education and their environment. Unlike exclusionists, they believed that anyone who claimed a European heritage—regardless of where in Europe their ancestors had originated from—could assimilate into an Anglo-American model providing that they agreed to forego their native language and customs. While class status was an important element of this version of American identity, those favoring assimilation thought that people of European descent had the requisite background to change their economic standing. At the close of the nineteenth century these assimilationists had staved off the first challenges to ongoing European immigration and successfully retained open borders. Yet this vision also contained exclusionary elements because, like exclusionists, few assimilationists believed that people who were neither European nor white could integrate successfully into the nation.

At the close of the century, neither exclusionists nor assimilationists thought much about people of Mexican descent: Mexican immigration was not a topic of discussion; most government agents neglected even to report their crossing.[10] The last time Americans had extensively and seriously debated what to do with people of Mexican descent was in 1848 at the close of the Mexican-American War. But by the turn of the century the disputes over the United States' island acquisitions caused the bickering to stop as the major political parties in both territories and the dominant Spanish- and English-language papers within them, all united in support of self-government.[11] In 1902, territorial residents succeeded in getting Arizona and New Mexico included as part of an omnibus statehood bill in front of the U.S. Congress. Their combined demand for statehood raised anew the question of what to do about people of Mexican descent.[12]

Statehood: Background

Traditionally, as stipulated in the 1787 Northwest Ordinance, a territory need only attain a population of 60,000 people and the support of the majority of its inhabitants to obtain congressional approval for statehood. Sufficient taxable wealth was later added as a criterion. By 1900 Arizona and New Mexico easily met these tests as Arizona had over 122,000 residents, and New Mexico, 195,000. Many states previously had entered the polity with far fewer people: Idaho and Wyoming became states in 1890 with approximately 84,000 and 60,000 inhabitants respectively. As other historians have shown, concern about the ethnic makeup of Arizona and New Mexico tempered legislators' enthusiasm for statehood, delaying it for over fifty years.[13]

The two proposed states did have a diverse population. The 1900 U.S. Census classified 180,207 of the approximately 195,000 New Mexicans as white, and noted that at least half (90,000) of these whites were of Mexican heritage. This statistic worried exclusionists, despite the fact that the territory had been a part of the United States for 52 years and that over 90 percent of the people of Mexican descent were native-born American citizens. The remainder of the population included just over 13,000 American Indians, 1,610 "Negros," and 349 persons classified as "Mongolian." Because many people of Mexican ancestry had voting rights and owned land, they retained substantial political power in the territory and a significant voice in the statehood debates. The Arizona territory also included many people of Mexican descent. David Berman estimates that by the end of the 1890s, Arizona's population of Mexican descent had declined from approximately 45 percent of the total residents in 1870 to 20 percent. In contrast to New Mexico, approximately one-half of these residents, 14,172, were Mexican-born, representing about half the foreign-born population in all the territory. The proportion of middle-class people of Mexican descent had also declined due to Anglo in-migration and the immigration of poorer Mexicans to Arizona for mining jobs or agricultural work. Consequently, middle-class Arizonans of Mexican descent had less influence in statehood politics than did their New Mexican counterparts. American Indians comprised another 20 percent (26,480) of the territory's population, but without voting rights they held scant political clout. Some native-born people of Mexican descent also found it difficult to cast a ballot as Anglos perceived them as "mixed" or "Indian," associating them with American Indians, who were not U.S. citizens. Few people of African or Asian descent lived within the territory.[14] It was this diverse population—especially the people of Mexican descent who comprised over one-third of the combined territorial residents—that caused exclusionists to balk at statehood.

Exclusion

Exclusionists sought to protect America's presumed homogeneity and did not want to bring anyone into the country who they believed would threaten national unity or harm their own class standing in society. Consequently, they sought to prevent the inhabitants of Arizona and New Mexico from attaining statehood, thereby excluding people of Mexican descent—whom they regarded as of mixed racial heritage and belonging to a "peon" class—from becoming equal members of the nation.[15] These exclusionists included nativists, who did not acknowledge the territorial residents of Mexican descent as native born and hailed from both major political parties and all regions of the country. They were joined by some eastern politicians who feared statehood would enhance the western states' strength in the legislature. Because it was not exactly clear which way the territories would vote—most suspected Arizonans would choose Democrats, and New Mexicans, Republicans—support along partisan lines was less apparent with significant Republican legislators on both sides of the debate.[16]

One Republican exclusionist, Senator Albert J. Beveridge of Indiana, held substantial sway over the fate of New Mexico and Arizona in his position as chairman of the Committee on Territories. While members of the U.S. House of Representatives approved statehood for the territories in May 1902, the bill then stalled in Beveridge's committee. Beveridge, an avid imperialist who had supported the acquisition of territories after the Spanish-American War and called for further expansion into Mexico and Central America, narrowly defined who could become an American: he did not favor granting statehood to any of the new possessions, much less those previously acquired during the Mexican-American War. Pressured to address the issue of statehood or see it removed from his committee, Beveridge concluded that he and his colleagues would make a better decision if they investigated territorial conditions firsthand.[17]

Beveridge's congressional committee quickly achieved notoriety in the territories as the committee members charged through the prospective states in two weeks, toured only the most dilapidated areas, and met primarily with people preselected by Beveridge to confirm the members' preexisting views against statehood. One newspaper alleged that the committee's characterization of the territories had done much to firm up local residents' support for statehood, convincing the few remaining doubters that it was essential. Another critic vividly described the event, writing that Beveridge "tore through New Mexico with his eyes under his coat" in order to avoid seeing anything that he might like. Not surprisingly, the committee drafted a report recommending against statehood for Arizona and New Mexico, concluding that only at some undetermined point in the future—when the "Mexican" population had "become identical in language and customs with the great body of the American people," and when English-speaking people from the other states had emigrated there to do their "modifying work with the 'Mexican' element"—would the territorial population "finally come to form a creditable portion of American citizenship" and be entitled to statehood. It was clear from the tone of the report that the authors believed it unlikely that this would happen any time soon.[18]

Beveridge and his fellow exclusionists perceived race as central to their definition of what it meant to be an American and believed that only those with the proper background could assimilate fully. They argued that most Americans had an Anglo-Saxon heritage and a northern or western European background, and that only those with a similar history should be added to the nation; otherwise, America would be in danger of losing its presumed racial homogeneity and national unity. When Senator Beveridge was asked whether people of Mexican descent were white, he baldly asserted that there was "no ground for such an assumption."[19] A Republican senator of New Jersey, John Kean, agreed and thought that people of Mexican descent would make undesirable Americans because they had a pliant trait—causing them to vote as they were told—which he believed was biologically inherent and associated with their mixed racial background.[20]

A few exclusionists briefly resurrected the "black legend" to disparage anyone who claimed a pure Spanish heritage. Perpetuated by northern Europeans shortly after Spain's settlement in the Americas, the black legend portrayed Spaniards as cruel, lazy, and despotic because of their aggressive Catholicism and dominance over Indians in the Americas.[21] While this myth had spread widely amongst people of English descent since the inception of the Spanish empire, its explanatory power had faded by the late nineteenth century as Spain ceased to be a significant threat to the United States, especially after the close of the Spanish-American War.[22] Nevertheless, one Republican senator from Wisconsin, Joseph Quarles, relied upon this dying concept to suggest that Spain, corrupted by its decadence, had lost its colonies, become inferior, and then passed this "racial infirmity" on to its descendants in New Mexico.[23] But Quarles was an anomaly and one of very few who raised this point; most exclusionists focused on the belief that people of Mexican descent were not acceptable because of their mixed racial heritage.

Exclusionists also entwined class with race, viewing those with the proper racial makeup as having the potential to rise to a higher-class status. The converse of this argument was that those who were not white did not have the capacity to improve their class standing beyond the level of a "peon." Senator Kean disparaged people of Mexican descent in both territories for their willingness to live "as a Chinaman," eating only "a few mesquite beans and a little bacon fat" to sustain themselves.[24] The implication was that no white person would or should tolerate such a low standard of living.[25] Members of the New England Shoe and Leather Association felt so strongly about the lower-class composition of the people in the territories that they submitted a resolution against statehood because "the population of New Mexico and Arizona is largely composed of miners and persons whose occupation is not conducive to permanent residence." They further added that census statistics showed that the territories had a racially diverse population and a significant number of illiterates, which proved the territories "so much below the standard" that they could not "be considered as states for many years."[26] As Pablo Mitchell suggests, a certain kind of "respectability" and "comportment" were also expected for people to be considered white and American.[27]

Due to the residents' race and class status, those favoring exclusion concluded that people of Mexican descent were incapable of assimilating since they lacked the biological wherewithal to transform themselves or to progress, characteristics that both assimilationists and exclusionists considered to be essential components of being American. The Beveridge committee condemned the adobe buildings in which many people of Mexican descent resided and compared them with the "common and usual homes of the Chinese people," by which they meant that they were primitive and un-American.[28] Senator Quarles believed that people of Mexican descent were so detrimental to the nation that they inhibited civilization—preventing ongoing progress and modernization—because "they think the same thoughts and sing the same songs as their fathers had for centuries before."[29] Senator Knute Nelson, a fellow Republican from Minnesota and a Norwegian immigrant himself, asserted that New Mexico was more backward than any other territory between the two oceans.[30] Outside of the halls of Congress, others repeated these arguments. Morris Watson, a journalist for *Outlook* magazine, reported that "the spirit of progress do[es] not appeal to them [people of Mexican descent]" after he observed the "common food" they ate and their lack of silverware and practical furnishings.[31]

Living what was then defined as a modern lifestyle was also an essential criterion for being American.

Mostly, however, exclusionists stressed language difference to persuade other Anglo Americans that people of Mexican descent could not assimilate. Exclusionists such as senators Beveridge, Quarles, and Nelson all believed that Americans *must* speak English; they perceived territorial residents' lack of use or knowledge of the language as evidence of their unassimilability, and a threat to national cohesion. Senator Nelson argued "homogeneousness in language and in fitness for self-government is one of the fundamental elements and essentials for the American Union."[32] In fact, Senator Beveridge and his entourage were so concerned about language that most of their questions revolved around this subject as they quizzed almost everyone interviewed about how many people spoke Spanish, which languages were taught in the schools, whether the courts used Spanish to maintain their records, and to what extent interpreters used this language to translate opening statements, cross-examinations, and jury instructions.[33]

Upon discovering that the New Mexican courts permitted use of the Spanish language in a variety of ways, exclusionists presented this as additional proof that the people of New Mexico had not, and should not, become American. Senator John Spooner, a Republican from Wisconsin, argued that if people of Mexican descent did not "care enough about our institutions to learn the language of the country, if the business of the courts must be carried through an interpreter" then the territory was not worthy of statehood.[34] Senator Nelson, the naturalized Norwegian immigrant, vociferously attacked New Mexico for its reliance upon interpreters. He added that he knew of no place where such a policy was followed except in the newer territories such as the Philippines and Puerto Rico.[35] In making this reference, Nelson unmistakably connected New Mexico—a territory he saw as failing to meet the essential language requirement for being part of America—with those unquestionably (at the time) foreign entities. In response, the territorial papers enjoyed lampooning Nelson with their characterization of his thick Norwegian accent, "'Ay tank does fellairs en Arizona not beene enofe Amaracaines. To bay goot seetyzain, a fellair moost bay Amaracaine.'"[36] Ironically, a few years earlier, Nelson had defended the idea of dual loyalties—with Norwegians in Minnesota able to maintain their allegiance to Norway as well as that of their new homeland—as posing no problem for America.[37]

Exclusionists on Beveridge's committee refused to accept any anecdotes or statistics demonstrating that people of Mexican descent were learning English and becoming American. When touring the territories, they seemed most interested in learning which language children spoke at home as well as on the playground. Georgia Murray, a Wisconsin transplant, reported that the children she taught in New Mexico did not speak "perfect English" and admitted when asked that they "drop the English" after school.[38] When a committee member persisted in asking if the children "relapse" into Spanish, a justice in New Mexico affirmed that the kids switched "right back to the Mexican."[39] Maggie Bucher, a superintendent of schools and a statehood supporter, valiantly tried to answer the same question with an assimilationist slant, emphasizing that the children seemed "very anxious not to give up their English" and that the Spanish-speaking kids mingled with other students and spoke a mixture of languages when they played.[40] Despite Bucher's best efforts, Beveridge's committee remained fixated on the fact that the children of Mexican descent continued to speak Spanish. In its official report to Congress the majority of the committee members rejected statehood, concluding that the residents of the territories, especially those in New Mexico, needed more time, if it were even possible, to become American.[41] It would prove to be a very damaging report for those favoring assimilation and statehood.

Assimilation

Although exclusionists succeeded in delaying statehood for another decade, their efforts were not uncontested. Statehood supporters—within and outside of the territories, and of both Anglo and Mexican heritage—argued that people of Mexican descent had a pure Spanish and European background, and therefore could become American. Those favoring assimilation belonged to both major political parties and all sections of the country, although people in the West were more likely to advocate for statehood and assimilation since the new status would result in greater political clout for their region. Assimilationists did not limit American identity to only those with a northern or western European heritage, but extended it to anyone who claimed ancestry from any part of Europe. A few noted that some residents held a mixed heritage, but justified this lack of European purity by asserting that they were overwhelmingly of European descent. Since assimilationists considered people of Mexican descent as mostly European and thereby white, they thought that they held the potential to improve their socioeconomic status and argued that they *could* learn, change, and merge with the dominant culture, just as other Europeans had done before them.[42] Consequently, assimilationists emphasized the territorial residents' white heritage in a variety of ways: by contrasting the inhabitants against others deemed not white, by pointing to the many people of Mexican descent who had attained a higher class standing, and by providing a barrage of evidence that the residents had already assimilated or were doing so rapidly.

One of the most prominent assimilationists, the aforementioned Governor Otero of New Mexico, considered himself to be Spanish (European), white, *and* American. Otero did his utmost to convince others that most *nativos* (a term used during the time period and one generally referring to native-born Americans of Mexican descent) or *nuevomexicanos* (New Mexicans of Mexican descent) in his territory held the same pure European heritage that he asserted. His class status made it easy for others to "see" his whiteness, but for other *nativos* this was not always the case. Otero avoided using the label "Mexican" since this then signified someone who held a mixed racial background, was of lower-class standing, and thus inferior to all white people.[43] When an interviewer pressed Otero with questions about "Mexicans" in his territory, Otero usually replied with "Spanish," or made it clear that the term was not one of his choosing by stating that "the 'Mexican' as you call him is a first class citizen."[44] Mostly, however, Otero downplayed ethnicity. Instead he embraced assimilationist rhetoric and stressed the fact that he and other *nuevomexicanos* already had become, or always had been, Americans.[45] On one Fourth of July, Otero congratulated fellow New Mexicans in a town on the national border for their ardent celebration of the country, wishing aloud that people from outside the territories had been present to witness their impressive display of patriotism.[46] In another incident early in his political career, Otero arranged to greet his guests in the new territorial capitol at Santa Fe by positioning himself directly under the folds of an American flag; his implicit message was that he, the territorial governor and a *nativo*, was an American; by association, all other *nuevomexicanos* were as well.[47]

Politically savvy, Otero recognized the danger in being connected to peoples whom other Americans considered nonwhite. Rather than working with such groups to improve the status and opportunities of *nativos*, Otero strove to make it very clear that New Mexicans were *not* like the racially questionable residents of the recently acquired territories. When the Spanish-American War erupted and the loyalty of Spanish speakers became a question, Otero quickly recruited New Mexicans to fight against Spain and then the Philippines. At the close of the war, Otero immediately dispatched bilingual teachers and officials to the overseas territories to assist with daily government and the Americanization of the people in the islands. In doing so he highlighted the Americanism of *nativos* compared with that of the racially mixed Puerto Ricans and Filipinos who needed America's tutelage. He was more than willing to take up Rudyard Kipling's "white man's burden" to show the newest members of America's empire the path to civilization, providing that he and his constituents received recognition as Americans entitled to statehood.[48]

Otero also adroitly manipulated symbols at the 1904 World's Fair to emphasize the intrinsically American qualities of New Mexico's *nativos*. The exposition, designed to commemorate the centennial of the Louisiana Purchase and the success of earlier annexations as well as contemporary ones, offered a unique opportunity in which Americans could visually compare New Mexico with the Philippines. In the fair's New Mexico building, Otero displayed a coat worn by Emilio Aguinaldo, the captured leader of Filipino resistance, to demonstrate New Mexico's higher status over the Philippines. Given to Otero's wife as a gift from one of the participating soldiers, this coat demonstrated not only that Otero's family and his territory supported the government's expansionist goals, but also that the only appropriate association between *nativos* and Filipinos—who were a focal point of the St. Louis exposition as curiosities and a people at the bottom of the racial hierarchy—was as conquerors over them. The coat ensured that visitors would see New Mexicans as effective colonizers who could be called upon to support and contribute to the nation's imperialistic adventures. In this way Otero helped to legitimate the government's empire-building enterprise, while at the same time boosting his territory's American standing.[49]

Governor Otero and other assimilationists also made it clear that when they spoke of the territory's *nativos* they did not mean American Indians, who they did not consider to be white like themselves, and who were literally and figuratively on the outskirts of mainstream American society. Otero complained bitterly of tourists who photographed a "worthless old Indian" as representative of his territory, suggesting that he found this representation to be completely absurd. He further explained in an interview that the Pueblo Indians' transition to "civilization" had been slow and difficult because they were not very bright, adding, however, that they would not harm New Mexico or the country because their population was both docile and decreasing in number. In one of his reports to the Secretary of the Interior, Otero further separated Pueblos and other American Indians by including a special section entitled "Indians," distinct from statistics for the rest of the territory's population.[50] The New Mexican delegate to the U.S. Congress Bernard Shandon Rodey, a naturalized American from

Ireland, followed Otero's lead in specifically distinguishing *nuevomexicanos* from Indians when he stated, "I object to having them compared with Indians."[51] Another resident of New Mexico explained to Congress that he did not consider the Pueblo people to be the same as "Mexicans."[52] A Republican senator from Ohio, Joseph Foraker, argued that territorial residents deserved statehood because it was in the nation's best interest to "subdue the forest, to drive out wild beasts, and to drive away the redman." Although seeking to remove or ostracize Indians, Foraker felt differently about people of Mexican descent who had political influence in both of the territories.[53]

With a fairly small African American population in the territories, assimilationists did not have to expend much energy in contrasting people of Mexican descent against African Americans. The few references to African Americans, however, indicated that assimilationists wanted no affiliation with them. Bernabé Brichta, a Mexican-born Arizonan of Mexican and French descent, argued that a local labor union should not put people of Mexican descent in the same low category as Asians or black Americans, criticizing the union's exclusionary policy only when it harmed people of Mexican descent.[54] When Governor Otero complained about a proposal to combine the New Mexico Territory into one state with Arizona, he disparaged those who liked the idea as people who were so desperate for statehood that they "would willingly accept jointure with the Jungles of Africa."[55] He also mocked the anti-imperialists who professed concern over the Filipino leader Aguinaldo and "his dusky minions," because they had not consented to U.S. control, while pointing out that these same voices denied the "dusky citizen" of the American South any say in the nation's government.[56] Otero himself did not take a public position on Jim Crow legislation in the South, but his willingness to accept U.S. control over the Filipinos and then compare it with white rule over blacks in the South suggests his low opinion of African Americans' capacity for full citizenship.

Assimilationists believed that people of Mexican descent could rise to a higher class standing due to their European heritage and pointed to many examples of their having done so. Harry Pierce, in a letter to the editor of the *Washington Post*, touted the fine citizenry in New Mexico and specifically named many who held a middle-class standing: Mariano Otero, the president of the Commercial National Bank in Albuquerque; Antonio Joseph, a merchant; Tranquilino Luna, a businessman whose son had died fighting in the Philippines and lay buried there in an unmarked grave; and J. Francisco Chavez, who fought in the Civil War for the Union before becoming an attorney.[57] New Mexican Judge A. B. Fall provided an equally long list of prominent *nuevomexicano* families, "the Lunas, the Chavezes, the Armijos, Oteros, Pereas, Romeros, and others," all of whom had the financial means to educate their children in the nearby state of Missouri.[58]

When assimilationists did acknowledge that some people of Mexican descent held a lower-class standing, they defended them by arguing that they also possessed the ability to improve their economic position and status. The former mayor of Albuquerque asserted that he had seen "a wonderful improvement in the Mexicans" since 1889, adding later that they liked "the American methods" and were "very rapidly adopting" them.[59] A few years later, Judge Fall reported that many of the sheepherders whom other Americans viewed as the "lowest classes of Mexicans" were actually literate, read newspapers, and kept informed on the political issues of the day.[60] In short they acted like middle-class Anglo Americans, or had the potential with the right kind of tutelage to become like them. Although assimilationists thought that people of Mexican descent could become American—since they had the requisite European and racial background—they also agreed with exclusionists that *nativos* needed to conform to the dominant Anglo-Saxon culture. They argued, however, that people of Mexican descent either already had "Anglo-Saxonized" or were doing so at a very fast rate. By this they meant that they were becoming literate, learning English, and rejecting traditional customs and lifestyles in favor of Anglo American ones.

Governor Otero touted the substantial improvement in New Mexico's literacy rate as proof of his residents' assimilation. He observed that while illiteracy had been as high as 44 percent in 1890—the year before a public school system was implemented in the territory—by 1898 it had fallen more than half to 21 percent.[61] Otero further argued that if the federal government gave New Mexico the same level of funding for education that it had provided to support "the Indians in indolence," then literacy in his territory would cease to be a problem.[62] Under the circumstances, he believed that New Mexico had performed admirably, with the residents themselves raising the additional money necessary to establish public schools. Delegate Rodey further charged that the government had not assisted the territory since the Mexican-American War and complained that, while it was sending revenue and teachers to Puerto Rico and the Philippines, it had never done so for New Mexico.[63] Clearly, assimilationists proclaimed, people of Mexican descent were making progress and becoming more like Anglo Americans in terms of literacy, education, and presumably class standing as well; only a lack of federal support and statehood continued to hinder them.

Other assimilationists emphasized how many *nuevomexicanos* already knew or were in the process of learning English. A Boston scholar informed the nation that "ten years ago English was an unknown tongue over most of the area of New Mexico . . . today it is taught to the children of every county."[64] A New Mexican poet, J. W. Knaebel, agreed and drafted a witty poem on the subject, including a stanza with the demand that Senator Beveridge and his ilk acknowledge "that the children you talked with were quite bright. And with few exceptions spoke English right."[65] Another assimilationist testified to the visiting congressmen that there had been so much success with teaching English that soon only the elderly, and perhaps women—who had begun to attend school only recently—would lag behind.[66] Delegate Rodey echoed this assertion, noting that *nuevomexicanos* already spoke "English as well as Spanish" and that one could travel through New Mexico for hundreds of miles and "probably not hear a word of Spanish." Furthermore, he noted how the Spanish-language newspapers regularly informed their readers that "it is the duty of every father to see that his children learn the language of the country, and that is English."[67] Republican Senator Porter J. McCumber of North Dakota charged that residents of New Mexico would have learned English even faster had it not been for their territorial isolation; statehood would have enhanced their facility with the language.[68]

Those favoring assimilation further promoted the inhabitants' American qualities by stressing how modern and progressive the territorial residents had become, by establishing institutions of higher learning, adopting the latest technology, and embracing civilized culture. The former governor of New Mexico, LeBaron Bradford Prince, noted how many institutions had been built in recent years: the capitol, a military institute, and various asylums for the blind, the deaf, and the insane.[69] Assimilationists from Arizona submitted petitions to Congress asserting that their territory was "as much civilized as Indiana," the state of the despised Senator Beveridge.[70] Delegate Rodey informed congressional representatives that the cities and towns of New Mexico exhibited the most recent technology and signs of modernity including "street cars, electric lights, waterworks, gas works, telephones, clubs, postal city delivery, etc."

Governor Otero complained repeatedly about visiting easterners like Senator Beveridge who remarked upon every adobe building while remaining oblivious to the region's modernization. Otero further expressed irritation toward camera-toting tourists who observed only what differed from the East as they "press[ed] the button upon every burro that they meet. . . . They photograph the oldest adobe building erected over three hundred years ago."[71] Otero's grumbling about the East's fascination with "difference" was apt, as magazine articles of the era visually depicted Arizona and New Mexico as places lacking modernity by showing only decrepit adobe structures, creating an image of the territories' backwardness and inferiority.[72] This image also annoyed former governor Prince, who lived in an adobe home, one that several members of Congress had admired, and found its mud bricks the best construction material for handling New Mexico's sunny and arid clime.[73]

Some people of Mexican descent already were like other Americans, so argued the assimilationists, through military service to their country. Governors Otero and Prince and Delegate Rodey all cited the soldiers who died in the Civil War battle at Glorieta and the number that volunteered for the Spanish-American War, and rattled off personal sacrifices that New Mexicans had made on the distant battlefields of the empire at "El Caney," "Santiago," "San Juan Hill," and elsewhere. They reminded Anglo Americans that a greater percentage of New Mexicans volunteered for service during the Spanish-American War than those who came from any other single state or territory. Furthermore, Theodore Roosevelt's Rough Riders owed much to the region since over half of his famed group called New Mexico or Arizona home.[74] Otero alone had energetically recruited an impressive number of soldiers for the conflict with Spain, later winning a medal for helping to organize Roosevelt's regiment.[75]

Finally, assimilationists argued that not only were the territorial residents capable of becoming like other Anglo Americans—due to their pure European heritage—but that they already *were* American due to their birth on U.S. soil or via the 1848 Treaty of Guadalupe Hidalgo. Former governor Prince regarded his territory as "a specially [*sic*] native American community" due to its low percentage of foreign-born residents relative to other states: only 7 percent of New Mexico's population had been born abroad compared with the populations of nine other states, each of which exceeded 20 percent; North Dakota topped the list with an incredible 45 percent of its population born outside of the country.[76] Delegate Rodey explained that most of the territorial residents of Mexican descent aged 56 or younger were born "under the American flag" of the New Mexico Territory. Judge Fall of New Mexico informed U.S. congressmen that former Mexican officials swore allegiance to the United States back in 1846, and stressed that "these people are not in any sense Mexicans."[77] He continued by noting that they "appreciate our Government, and not one of them would go down into old Mexico if he were offered in exchange for his American citizenship one of the princely cattle ranches of that Republic."[78] The *Denver Republican* opined that the nation should fulfill the promises it made under the treaty and asserted that people of "American or Mexican" descent made good Americans.[79] Arizona Delegate Marcus Smith colorfully summed up statehood supporters' frustration by sarcastically remarking upon the Beveridge committee's refusal to grasp the significance of nativity when he noted how the senators spent "one day and two nights in a strange land infested by native-born American citizens."[80]

Exclusion Reigns

Despite these arguments, many Anglo Americans remained skeptical about the heritage of people of Mexican descent and their ability to improve their economic situation and assimilate. Even with the activism of Otero, Jácome, and other assimilationists, New Mexico and Arizona failed to become new states in 1903. Beveridge and his Senate committee seriously damaged the cause of statehood with the publication of their negative report on the territories and their recommendation to reject statehood. Although assimilationists succeeded in pushing the omnibus statehood bill through the House of Representatives, the bill remained mired in the Senate and under the control of the tenacious Senator Beveridge until it died without ever coming to a vote.

Initially, as explained in the Introduction, Theodore Roosevelt had expressed utmost confidence in his diverse band of Rough Riders from the territories and considered them ideal Americans due to their patriotic service and valorous deeds during the Spanish–American War, as well as because of how they represented America's success in fusing and assimilating different peoples into a new American mold.[81] In 1899 he had gone so far as to declare himself in favor of statehood for the territories. But by 1903, upon reading Senator Beveridge's injurious report, then President Roosevelt worried about how people of Mexican descent might affect the nation and approved of Senator Beveridge's covert tactics to prevent statehood from coming to a vote. He avoided mentioning the topic at all in his annual message to Congress.[82]

Other Anglo Americans shared Roosevelt's nascent reservations. One reporter, while initially accepting some of Delegate Rodey's arguments about the wonders of New Mexico, questioned this view at the close of his article in which he pondered whether the territory was as ready for statehood as Rodey implied. Because, he noted, one may "see many things which sort of weaken his belief in the advisability of making New Mexico a full-fledged State."[83] Morris Watson from *Outlook* also doubted that people of

Mexican descent in either of the territories could become good Americans because he felt that their Spanish blood had "so degenerated and mingled with the Indian tribes" that they did "little credit to their intrepid ancestors."[84] The Philadelphia *Daily Evening Telegraph* opined under the title "Not Fit for Citizenship" that "less than either Indians or negroes do these mongrel Mexicans afford the material of which citizens are made."[85] These views suggested that Anglo Americans refused to accept the assimilationists' claim that people of Mexican descent were predominantly European, and so they were also disinclined to accept that they could become American.

Labor problems and a growing perception of the radicalism of workers of Mexican descent also hindered assimilationists' efforts. In 1897, miners of Mexican and Italian descent protested the attempts of Phelps Dodge Corporation to run a railroad through Slag Town (near Morenci, Arizona) without compensation to the landowners. Four years later, in Ray, Arizona, workers protested differential wages based on race. In 1903, approximately 1,500 workers—80 percent or more of whom were of Mexican descent (mostly native born) and the rest of Italian descent—walked off their jobs in the Clifton and Morenci copper mines of Arizona to protest a reduction in pay. Holding their own against an assembled group of 800, including members of the Arizona National Guard, the strike ended when a devastating flood killed over forty miners and destroyed their homes. Although the workers ultimately made few gains for their efforts—other than a modest raise and a slight improvement in working conditions—they proved themselves to be organized and committed strikers.[86] Yet their activism also showed, as historian Linda Gordon has explained, the hardening of racial lines in Arizona since both sides emphasized the participation of people of Mexican descent. The owners did so as part of their attempts to divide the workers, whereas the strikers highlighted their ethnicity to promote solidarity and continued support for their cause. After the strike, there were clearer delineations between who could be white and accepted into the dominant community and who could not: Italians were white Americans; in this case, people of Mexican descent were not. The next year when a group of Irish orphans arrived from New York to move in with their adopted families of Mexican descent, the newly expanded white community, based on the Italian additions, decided that Irish (or white) children should not live with people of Mexican descent because the latter were not white. The event made national headlines.[87] This story, plus the strike, likely led many Anglo Americans to wonder about the wisdom of bringing more people of Mexican descent, especially those in Arizona, into the nation.

The spread of labor activism across the border to Sonora, several years later, also did not help matters.

In June 1906, miners at the American-owned Consolidated Copper Company in Cananea, Mexico, rose up to protest a change in their pay as well as race-based wages and job assignments. Some of these miners apparently gained experience from the earlier strikes at Clifton and Morenci. When the owner, William Greene, refused to negotiate with them, they stopped work. Eventually, the standoff led to violence, leaving some Mexicans and a few Americans dead. The strike ultimately ended with the assistance of the Arizona Rangers who crossed the border to help the Sonoran governor, Rafael Izábel, quell the violence and assume control. The Rangers' involvement and the American deaths made more Anglos aware of the conflict and inclined to view people of Mexican descent as dangerous and working-class radicals who would be unlikely to assimilate and make good Americans.[88]

The exclusionists' success in raising concerns about people of Mexican descent—specifically with regard to their race *and* class—led to new proposals to merge the territories into one Anglo-dominated state. The theory was that the larger group of middle-class, white, and modern Anglo Americans would be able to counteract the influence of the lower-class, mixed-race, and primitive folks of Mexican descent. The proposals to unite the two territories came with various suggestions to re-name the combined territory, including "Montezuma," after the Aztec emperor, "Lincoln," an indisputably American name, and simply "Arizona" to appease the Arizonans while placing the new state government in Santa Fe, the capital of New Mexico.[89] This proposed merger, or "jointure" as it was then called, resulted in a shifting of alliances as Delegate Rodey later worked with Senator Beveridge—who by then had moved from his support of outright exclusion to a more assimilationist stance since he had given up on excluding both territories—and President Roosevelt in calling for one new, behemoth state.

The changing nature of the debate permitted other voices, who favored pluralism or marginalization, to become more audible. Although these pluralists and marginalizationists had not been mute during internal discussions over statehood, they now had a wider stage upon which to promote their understanding of what it meant to be American and to gain adherents. When the jointure movement first erupted in 1904 (and lasted several years), the country became aware of these alternate strategies for how people of Mexican descent could fit into the nation. During the movement for joint statehood and thereafter, the strategies of exclusion and assimilation did not disappear, but some supporters did adjust their beliefs in which strategy was most effective for attaining their preferred goals, or moved back and forth in their support for a given strategy, depending on the context, much as Theodore Roosevelt had done. Still, the trend toward pluralism and marginalization, as the most effective ways to incorporate people of Mexican descent into the country, grew throughout the first decade of the twentieth century.

CHAPTER TWO

The Door Swings Inward

Pluralism and Marginalization

Octaviano A. Larrazolo, a naturalized U.S. citizen formerly of Mexico and the Arizona territory, eventually settled in New Mexico during the 1890s. There the teacher turned lawyer ran for office unsuccessfully, several times. Despite his initial electoral failures—he would later become a Republican governor and then senator for the state of New Mexico—he was a well-liked and gifted orator who impressed crowds with his fluency in both the Spanish and English languages. Larrazolo took great pride in his ethnicity and argued for the preservation and extension of rights for people of Mexican descent, yet he did not embrace a "Mexican" or even "Mexican American" label. Despite his immigrant status, he and other people of Mexican heritage referred to themselves as *nativos* (native-born), *nuevomexicanos* (New Mexicans), and increasingly *hispanos* (Spanish) or *hispano-americanos* (Spanish Americans).[1] In other words, they advocated a pluralist conception of belonging in the United States as Americans of Spanish descent. Their strategy called for the full integration of people of Mexican descent into the nation via statehood.

The strategies of pluralism and marginalization in the Southwest evolved together, were applied to and developed by people of Mexican descent, and had profound effects on the definition of "American" during a critical period of nation-building. Although the people of the era did not use these terms, the words they used indicated their respective beliefs that people of Mexican descent either were or could become Spanish Americans, equal in status with Anglo Americans, or that they should become marginal citizens, permanently consigned to a lower-class status and under the control of their Anglo employers. *Nativos* in New Mexico who successfully argued for their entry via pluralism attained more rights and protection for their Spanish culture than did people of Mexican descent in Arizona who, because of their primarily working-class status and smaller population overall, became part of the nation via marginalization. While these strategies included elements of white supremacy, as did more common ones for dealing with newcomers, like exclusion and assimilation, they offered alternatives to the dominant strategies by opening a space for people who claimed European heritage to practice the culture and language they chose, and by providing at least a marginal space in society for those deemed as nonwhite.

Spanish Identity and Pluralism

The Spanish American identity that Larrazolo and his counterparts claimed contained a racial component: to be Spanish meant that one held a pure European ancestry. The significance of purity of blood claims, or *limpieza de sangre*, had a long history dating back to medieval Spain. Once in Latin America, Spaniards disseminated their belief that people with pure Spanish blood were superior to those with a mixed racial heritage or an indigenous one. Eighteenth-century family paintings, portraying the marriage and offspring of people of various *castas* (castes or races), were especially popular in Mexico and made these prejudices abundantly clear. Such artworks depicted an elaborate array of *castas*, from *indios* (Indians) to *españoles* (Spaniards), which categorized people into rigid groups and a hierarchical structure according to their parents' combined background. However, intermarriage, wealth, and other factors created a system more fluid than it appeared, making it possible for people to alter their caste, identity, and place in society. Certain jobs bestowed a high status regardless of one's heritage. All military men, for example, were identified as "*españoles*" (Spanish) in the census. Moreover, those who held power or desired to advance often appropriated an *español* identity. According to historian John Nieto-Phillips, people of Mexican descent vigorously denied any attempt to categorize them as *mestizo*, or of mixed racial heritage, and instead asserted their *limpieza de sangre* and Spanish ancestry. In 1901, six hundred people in Las Vegas rose up in the streets, Nieto-Phillips explains, to protest allegations in a local newspaper that they were of "mixed blood" and therefore inferior. A local attorney informed the then-assembled crowd that he was as "'Spanish American as are those who hear me'" and that he had no other heritage except "'that which was brought by Don Juan de Oñate,'" the Spaniard who in 1598 had claimed New Mexico for Spain.[2]

Nativos in the territories saw themselves not only as Spanish, European, and white but also as capable of rising to the highest class like that of Don Oñate. They saw no contradiction in becoming part of a nation in which many of its dominant members considered themselves white *and* middle class. From the *nativo* perspective, sharing the same language or culture was irrelevant to national identity. They did not believe that they needed to change or learn new customs in order to belong, for they already saw themselves as sufficiently American in the ways that mattered: in terms of their agreement with the nation's racial, political, and economic systems. In part, these seemingly confident assertions of belonging represented an effort to maintain political and socioeconomic power at the local and state levels, which was increasingly difficult to hold as more Anglos encroached on their land.[3] Yet these middle-class *nativos,* many of whom had been educated in the East, believed that they held much in common with their Anglo neighbors; what concerned them was that these Anglos might not view them in the same way. Thus, they emphasized their shared European ancestry, history, and class status while simultaneously highlighting the differences between themselves and others being defined as nonwhite and un-American. By the turn of the century, most *nativos* demonstrated a clear preference for a Spanish American or *hispano-americano* identity over a "Mexican" one, going so far as to correct those who made the mistake of referring to them as Mexican.[4]

This greater resolve in asserting a Spanish American identity paralleled an intensification of the debate over New Mexico's entry into the nation. As exclusionists attacked the racial, class, and cultural background of *nativos* who were attempting to gain more citizenship rights through statehood, people of Mexican descent became ever more adamant in asserting their Spanish heritage, and more intent upon proving their white racial status and ability to be American. Increased negative encounters with Anglo Americans, the growing popularity of pseudoscientific ideologies denigrating Mexicans as persons of "mixed blood," and the concomitant rise of the Spanish-language press all contributed to this self-identification as Spanish American.[5]

At the same time, those who previously espoused assimilation also began to use "Spanish American" as an effective way in which to encourage other Americans to accept the state of New Mexico. Helen Hunt Jackson's popular novel *Ramona* (1884) helped to undermine the unfavorable black legend, replacing it with a more romantic and nostalgic rendering of the

Spanish missionary era.[6] The 1898 American victory over Spain further spurred the legend's demise as the quick defeat demonstrated that since Spaniards no longer threatened the United States, there was no need to demonize them. Influenced by these changes, the territory's Bureau of Immigration began to tout the Spanish colonial history—and thereby whiteness—of *nuevomexicanos* in their attempts to entice more Anglos to move there.[7] Moreover, few people then emigrated from Spain, allaying any latent fears about Spaniards.[8]

Pluralism Expands

Larrazolo and his allies did more than just assert a Spanish American identity, they also advocated their own variant of a pluralist strategy for incorporating people of Mexican descent into the United States. Their pluralism was rooted in a Spanish American identity and called for the full integration of *nativos* into the United States through statehood. Most Americans at the time believed that there needed to be racial, cultural, and even socioeconomic homogeneity for national unity. Pluralists agreed with a part of this definition and argued that no conflict would result from including people of Mexican descent who, they claimed, shared the same race and history (based on their European heritage), and aspirations for a middle-class status with other white Americans. They differed, however, in that they did not believe sharing a common language and traditions were prerequisites for unifying a nation. In their view, the process of becoming fully integrated into the nation would be smooth.

As opposed to those advocating assimilation or, in Thomas Guglielmo's words, a "Caucasian strategy," in which people of Mexican descent emphasized their whiteness *and* English-speaking as a way to attain civil rights, pluralists, primarily in New Mexico, proudly asserted not only their European background but also their class standing, Spanish language and traditions, and historical belonging in the nation. Such self-assertive positions went far beyond those held by people of Mexican descent in Arizona who, historian Linda Gordon describes, attempted to boost their self-esteem and status through intermarriage or the adoption of children presumed to be white. Indeed, these pluralists already perceived themselves to be European and white and demanded that others recognize their status as well. Although these elite *nativos* did not have much in common with their working-class counterparts, they knew that they were being associated with them on racial grounds and recognized the need to make the case to bring all of them into the nation via statehood. They made this collective argument by emphasizing the wealth, education, and political connections of certain *nativos* while asserting that the others shared their ambitions and would eventually progress.[9]

In 1915, Horace Kallen, a Jewish immigrant and philosopher, coined the phrase "cultural pluralism" and identified it as a strategy used by immigrants to incorporate into the nation without losing their culture. Although it is unlikely that he was referring to *nativos* in New Mexico, since his work concentrated on recent European immigrants to the Northeast, this same concept was at work in the American Southwest. The *nativos* there did not label their strategy pluralism, but as Kallen would later theorize about other ethnic groups, they asserted that they were or could become good Americans even if they retained a language and traditions that differed from those of the Anglo majority.[10]

New Mexico's form of pluralism evolved from a confluence of factors: the growth of a Spanish American label among people of Anglo and Mexican descent, the exclusionists' recent challenge of *nativos* during the statehood debate, and the recognition among some people of Mexican descent that those advocating assimilation had failed to convince others that they were sufficiently American. Most pluralists were people of Mexican descent who were well educated, bilingual, and political and economic leaders in their communities: cattlemen, merchants, teachers, lawyers, politicians, and the editors and journalists of the Spanish-language press. Other pluralists included Anglos, within and outside the territory, who favored statehood.

Pluralists and assimilationists agreed on two key issues: the incorporation of people of Mexican descent based upon their European pedigree, and the potential for *nativos* to improve their class position. Assimilationists, however, also required that *nativos* fully adopt Anglo culture in order to become American. Pluralists, while explaining that most *nativos* wanted to learn English, did not think a specific culture or language essential to being American. Instead, they believed that those who held a Spanish heritage were every bit as American, and perhaps more so, as those with English forebears, and so they promoted their right to continue speaking Spanish and encouraged others to learn it as well. Although these strategies differed, not all advocates were rooted to them and changed their minds when needed to attain certain objectives. Governor Otero, for example, initially distanced himself from his cultural heritage and promoted assimilation. Once he recognized that other Americans refused to ignore his territory's roots, he adopted pluralism as the most effective strategy for achieving his goal of statehood.[11]

Some of the clearest examples of this emerging pluralism became apparent in 1902 when members of Senator Albert J. Beveridge's Committee on the Territories (see chapter 1) toured the Southwest to determine the fitness of Arizona and New Mexico for statehood. At one of the committee's formal hearings, the Republican Senator William P. Dillingham of Vermont closely questioned Isidor Armijo, a probate clerk, about his ancestry. Armijo assertively replied that he was "of Spanish extraction . . . but I was born in the United States and I am an American." When Senator Beveridge, chairman of the committee, responded testily that the committee was "just getting at the racial blood; that is all" and pressed Armijo on his Mexican heritage, Armijo retorted, "Yes [his parents were Mexican] . . . and yours were German, but that doesn't make you Dutch."[12]

Many New Mexicans shared Armijo's pluralist views and promoted a Spanish identity alongside an American one. Pablo Jaramillo, a census enumerator, referred to himself as a "Spaniard" even as he explained to the Beveridge committee that he had always lived in New Mexico. When the committee interviewed Clementa Ortíz about whom she had visited for the census, "and to what race did those inhabitants mainly belong, Mexican or American," Ortíz replied using her own terms: "Spanish; that is not any Indians." To her way of thinking, there were very few Mexicans in New Mexico since she likely understood "Mexican" to refer either to an immigrant, or to someone of a mixed racial background, people whom she did not see as present in New Mexico. When the senators then grilled the New Mexican justice of the peace, José Maria Garcia, about the language he used for recordkeeping, the justice responded that he maintained the files "in Spanish, because the people here are Spanish . . . and of course I like my own language better than any other, the same as I like the United States better than any other country in the world." Garcia's clever response made it abundantly clear that he considered himself American, but that this identity did not require that he record official documents in the English language.[13]

In reporting on the statehood hearings and subsequent debates, the Spanish-language press emerged as one of the foremost proponents of pluralism. After hearing of Beveridge's investigatory trip, *La Voz del Pueblo* speculated that if statehood was rejected, it would be solely because of the number of Spanish speakers within the territories. The editors wondered openly what this had to do with whether or not New Mexico was sufficiently prepared for statehood and strenuously denied the validity of any argument requiring a single language for national unity.[14] *El Labrador* (Las Cruces, NM) mocked Beveridge's observation that he had heard schoolchildren speaking Spanish and ironically remarked, "*Tremendo descubrimiento!* [Tremendous discovery!]" The authors reminded their readers that speaking Spanish was not a crime and did not threaten the health or safety of the republic.[15] *La Voz del Pueblo* further lamented the problems existing between English and Spanish speakers and stated that there should not be such differences between "*miembros de una misma nación* [members of the same nation]." The editors saw no heresy with having two languages in one country: speaking Spanish did not imply any lack of patriotism. Slowly, some of these pluralist ideas spread outside the region. The *Omaha World-Herald*, for example, questioned why New Mexico was being denied admission because of its Spanish-speaking residents when people in the states of Louisiana and Missouri continued to converse in French.[16]

Amongst themselves, *nativo* pluralists and the Spanish-language press continued to do much to encourage Spanish speakers to maintain their language skills and pass this heritage to their children. *La Voz del Pueblo* criticized those people of Mexican descent who discouraged their children from speaking "*mejicano*" and instead taught their offspring *not* to pronounce Spanish words like native speakers, such as when they advised eliminating the rolling sound of the Spanish letter "rr." They admonished those readers who promoted this and reminded them of the beauty of their language—a "jewel" from their ancestors that they should respect and admire. Reacting to pressure being brought on the peoples of the territories to learn English, *La Voz del Pueblo* published a clever poem which declared that statehood would not occur until such a time that "frogs grow hair, mules have children, and donkeys learn to read." Then no one would speak Castilian for it would have been abolished; instead, "all the neighboring donkeys" would "bray in English."[17]

Despite their self-interest in preserving the Spanish language, many in the Spanish-language press also supported learning English, recognizing the opportunities that such a skill would bring in the United States. These pluralists adopted what Spanish scholar Arturo Fernández-Gibert identifies as a "dual discourse." They encouraged *nativos* to learn English while they simultaneously promoted the use of Spanish as a community language, one tied to the collective memory of their ancestors. The periodicals typically affirmed the need to learn English first, and then concentrated on explaining to their readers why they should continue using Spanish. They advocated that their readers should have pride in their native tongue for "we need to learn the language of our country, and that we are doing; but we don't need to, with such motive, deny our origin, our race, our language."[18] Their ultimate refusal to reject their language is not surprising for, as one Spaniard noted as far back as 1492, "language has always been the companion of empire" and *nativos* did not want to be so colonized.[19]

Furthermore, New Mexican pluralists actively sought to change the minds of those who believed that a common language was central to national identity and unity. They replaced the idea of a universal language with that of a common heritage, one rooted in European ethnicity and a shared conquest of the Americas. Thus, they criticized their Arizona neighbors for passing a suffrage requirement to read and comprehend a section of the U.S. Constitution in English. And unlike Beveridge's Senate committee, which had delighted in the fact that one of New Mexico's educators was unfamiliar with the name of Christopher Columbus, pluralists, led by the talented Larrazolo, spun a tale of a common history that began long before the Pilgrims gazed upon the revered Plymouth Rock.[20]

Larrazolo spoke eloquently and frequently on behalf of his European past. In 1907 he reminded an assembled crowd at the Coronado Commemorative Convention that intrepid Spaniards had crossed the mysterious seas to the New World, willingly burnt their own ships to shore up their determination for conquering the Aztecs, and then Christianized Indians in New Mexico and other parts of Latin America before the English even dreamed of settling at Jamestown. The Spaniards' bold actions led to future conquests in the Americas, and therefore their descendants did not need any tutelage on how to become American; rather, they deserved commendation for making the United States possible. Throughout these speeches Larrazolo sought to build a shared memory and history among people of Mexican descent, connecting them to the romanticized Spanish *conquistadores* of the past. At the same time he linked them to other Europeans, emphasizing how Spaniards had been the first among many European groups to venture to the New World. In this way he established a sense of belonging and community with Anglo Americans as well as a claim to the land and nativity.[21]

Larrazolo was not a lone voice. Benjamin Maurice Read, a prominent attorney, territorial legislator, and native-born New Mexican of Anglo and Mexican descent, also promoted pluralism. Read, whose *nativo* mother had raised him, preferred Spanish over the English language. Troubled by the lack of New Mexican history written in Spanish and the growing control Anglos exercised over political affairs, Read researched and wrote the territory's history from the perspective of *nativos* to provide an alternative to the Anglo narrative of events. In his first book, published in 1910, on the history of the Mexican-American War, Read emphasized the early roots of American expansionism. In his second work, he sought to depict Spanish conquerors more sympathetically than had recent Anglo historians who revived the injurious "black legend." Read's primary aim in writing, since he was not an academic, was to ensure that *nativos* and their culture were not consigned to a secondary place in history and society.[22]

Pluralists further emphasized their European and *conquistador* heritage through a variety of celebrations and speeches. When exclusionists tried to discredit *nuevomexicanos* for their of lack of American roots, pluralists countered by suggesting that perhaps it was the Anglos who failed to understand their country's history and the role Spaniards had played in its conquest and settlement. In 1911, for example, Benjamin Read lauded Don Diego de Vargas's 1693 defeat of the Pueblo Indians, touting it as one of the most important events in the territory's history. George Washington Armijo, the Rough Rider friend of Teddy Roosevelt, concurred—so much so that he dressed as Vargas at the 1911 Santa Fe Fiesta, visually highlighting the role Spaniards and their heritage played in conquering New Mexico.[23]

Some Anglos accepted these arguments and began to emphasize a connection between the history of *nativos* and that of other Americans. In 1909 journalist John Cowan informed his readers that the Spaniard Juan de Oñate had established "European civilization at Santa Fe" before "a Saxon had set foot in New England." Even President Theodore Roosevelt promoted the idea of a shared history, thereby helping to advance the pluralist perspective. In his speech to Governor Otero and other New Mexicans, Roosevelt reminded his audience that "some [Spaniards] had come to New Mexico, as did your ancestors, Governor, at a time when not one English speaking community existed on the Atlantic seaboard" and then further praised these Spanish immigrants for their adventuresome spirit.[24]

But as these accounts attest, there was an exclusionary element to pluralists' representation of their Spanish heritage, for just like "collaborating elites" in others parts of America's empire, pluralists sought to associate themselves with those deemed most American, rather than those on the margins.[25] They enhanced their standing by stressing their role as *conquistadores*, while at the same time remaining silent about the significance of Indians and Africans in their own history. As Phillip B. Gonzales explains, "the very process of remembering requires forgetting," and prominent pluralists such as Read, Armijo, and Larrazolo chose to do just that. They readily remembered Vargas's conquest of New Mexico but conveniently forgot the story of the intrepid Pueblo Indian Popé, who had organized the 1680 Rebellion that expelled Spaniards from the region and prevented their return for thirteen years. Although many people of Mexican descent in the territories were likely the progeny of people of varied backgrounds (Europeans had extensively intermarried with Indians and Africans or others of diverse backgrounds in the region), pluralists never mentioned Aztec or Pueblo leaders, except as conquered peoples.[26]

Although advocates of pluralism did not explicitly discuss the class status of *nativos*, it was clear that the most active pluralists were those of eminent stature who considered themselves at least equal to those of Anglo descent. While they spoke in terms of all *nativos*, it seemed that those with a higher class standing could most easily sell this heritage within and beyond the territories. Historically, class status helped to determine racial status in Mexico and much of Latin America, and those who achieved a high economic standing often attained recognition as a white person. Even some who favored exclusion or marginalization, like the Harvard-educated editor of *World's Work*, Michael Glen Cunniff, were inclined to concede that high-class people of Mexican descent held a pure Spanish heritage, although they would not grant this same racial status to an ordinary worker of Mexican descent.[27] As the statehood debates raged on, pluralists continued to promote and disseminate their strategy for incorporating people of Mexican ancestry into the nation, primarily on the basis of their shared European heritage and history with Anglo Americans. But theirs was not the only strategy to arise from the dispute over the territories.

Marginalization

In 1881 Marcus Aurelius Smith moved from Kentucky to the Arizona territory. Better known as "the octopus," due to his formidable campaign tactics that were seemingly executed in all directions, and the extent of his reach, Smith eventually became Arizona's delegate to Congress and, much later, one of the state's first senators. In the earliest years of the twentieth century, Arizona leaders such as the influential Smith worked closely with New Mexicans to attain separate statehood. An avid supporter of this cause, Smith initially touted assimilation when he argued that the people of Mexican descent within the two territories could learn new ways and become like Anglo Americans. But when legislators rallied around the suggestion to combine Arizona and New Mexico into one mega-state named Montezuma or Lincoln, Smith began to speak differently about New Mexico and its inhabitants. Much as Larrazolo and Otero feared being associated with residents of the newest imperial possessions, Smith wanted to prevent his proposed state from being tarnished as un-American, and so he argued that Arizona was distinct from New Mexico *and* more American, since Anglos dominated its government. Smith further noted that in Arizona the percentage of people of Mexican descent was declining, and that those who remained were safely under the control of their employers.[28] In making this argument, Smith and his allies proffered another strategy for incorporating people of Mexican descent: marginalization.

Those favoring marginalization included many Anglo political and economic leaders in the Arizona territory, while those advocating marginalization in New Mexico were less vocal. Although some of these leaders originally promoted assimilation as a means for attaining statehood, many of them did not believe that people of Mexican descent could or should be entitled to become full Americans. Like exclusionists, they considered them inferior due to their status as lowly workers in the mines, ranches, and agricultural sectors of the territorial economies. Negative views about their class status led to negative views about their race. Because of the jobs people of Mexican descent held, Anglos did not believe these workers to be pure Spaniards and therefore did not consider them as being white.[29] They differed from exclusionists, however, in their ambivalent approach to nonwhites. Although they favored statehood due to the political power it would bring, and believed that territorial residents of Mexican descent would not threaten an Anglo American model of national unity nor overturn its existing class structure, they questioned whether people of Mexican descent could assimilate fully. Once the debate over combined statehood erupted, these marginalizationists staked out a strategy distinct from assimilation and exclusion.

Prior to the 1904 proposal to combine the two territories, a few statehood supporters provide a glimpse of the nascent strategy. In 1902, Smith, then a new delegate to the U.S. Congress for the territory of Arizona, explained that there was no need to fear that people of Mexican descent would challenge the dominant classes because "we never have had any strikes down there, practically speaking . . . they [people of Mexican descent] never bother about that kind of thing." Colonel Ira M. Bond backed him up, testifying that "we have no strikes." Smith noted that while there were some "low and ordinary common laborers" from Mexico, there were only a few, and they "had no appreciable effect whatsoever on an election or on the public spirit of the country." The following year a new Democratic delegate to Congress, John Wilson, explained that while his territory included some Mexican immigrants, only 719 of the territory's registered voters had emigrated from Mexico. He added, "if they come they go back," a statement that presaged future arguments concerning the immigrants' transience in the country. Agreeing with these territorial representatives, a Republican senator from West Virginia, Stephen B. Elkins, jumped into the fray with his version of historical facts, arguing that "Mexicans" were becoming outnumbered. "No race can withstand the Anglo-Saxon. The

Latin races and the mixed Latin races give way before it. That was the case in California; it was the case in Colorado, and it is the case in New Mexico." Not to be outdone by the other party, the Democratic senator from Arkansas, Charles Reid, described how "Mexicans" and "Indians" had disappeared from California and would soon do so as well in Arizona and New Mexico.[30] As these examples demonstrate, those favoring marginalization as a strategy for incorporation emphasized that people of Mexican descent could be brought into the nation via statehood in ways that posed no threat to other Americans: they argued that people of Mexican descent were docile and marginal members of American society who either returned to Mexico or eventually died out.

Once combined statehood became an official bill, Anglo Arizonans promoted their strategy for incorporation more forcefully. Fearing that joint statehood might cause them to lose economic and political authority to the more populous New Mexico, they distinguished themselves even further from New Mexicans, abandoning assimilationist rhetoric in their efforts to persuade Americans outside of the territories just how much they differed from their neighbor. R. E. Morrison, an attorney from Arizona, testified that "we conduct everything in the English language in our schools and in the courts of Arizona. In New Mexico, where they have a large Spanish and Mexican population, an interpreter is present practically all the time in the courts and frequently in the schoolroom." In other words, Arizona was more English-speaking, Anglo, and thus more American.[31] Other Anglo Arizonans referred to the proposed merger of the territories as an "odious union" and explained that New Mexicans differed from them in "race, government, ideas, political ambitions and otherwise."[32]

An editorial cartoon in the *Arizona Republican* (and there were many like this) made these sentiments abundantly clear when it portrayed the Arizona territory as a white woman in a flowing dress and about to be handcuffed to the New Mexico territory, which was depicted as a stereotypical mustachioed Mexican man wearing cowboy regalia and a sombrero. Above the reluctant couple President Teddy Roosevelt wielded a large stick, suggesting that he, with the power of the federal government behind him, would combine the two territories. Titled, "Is This a 'Square Deal'?," the sketch implied that, in fact, it was not. The drawing revealed that while each territory alone might not present a threat to the nation—since neither the feminine and pleading Anglo Arizona nor the cuffed and docile demeanor of Mexican New Mexico were hardly threatening—the real peril lay in the suggestion of interracial union. The picture implied that the Mexican man and Anglo woman would be forced to join together, possibly leading to the production of mixed-race children. As Rosa Linda Fregoso explains, interracial relationships concerned Anglos in the early twentieth century since they believed that a lack of racial purity would lead to degeneracy and the downfall of a nation. People of "mixed blood" were perceived to be worse than those who held a "pure" Indian or African heritage; in fact, many Anglos interpreted the downfall of the Spanish empire as resulting from such interracial liaisons and degenerate offspring. Another message implicit in the cartoon concerned the image of white women as moral, pure, and chaste. To maintain white women's purity, as Fregoso explains it, they had to be protected from men of mixed or nonwhite heritage. In the cartoon, the white woman begged not to be linked to the Mexican man, hinting at the impure relationship and defiling that surely would follow if the two territories combined into one state. Viewers of the era likely understood the artist's point that joining the Anglo woman and Mexican man together would be perilous not only for the territories, in which many interracial relationships would ensue, but also for the nation as a whole.[33]

Arizona marginalizationists further made their case by arguing that the "American white population" in their territory was larger than the census had shown, that it was growing relative to the people of Mexican descent, and that the white population controlled territorial politics. Based on these assertions, they argued that making Arizona a state on its own would not threaten the nation's perceived racial homogeneity.[34] Arizona's governor, Joseph H. Kibbey, explained that most people of Mexican descent did not vote and therefore would not affect the government of the potential state nor the country. His successor, Governor Richard E. Sloan, reiterated that people of Mexican descent had no influence over government affairs. "The Mexican population," he declared, "is not more than fifteen per cent, mostly itinerants, and likewise no important factor in politics, for the American population is increasing while the Spanish-American stands still."[35] Although Sloan in this case used "Mexican" and Spanish American interchangeably, he effectively marginalized the position of people of Mexican descent with his implication that their influence in the proposed state would soon vanish. His words also suggest that the boundaries between the strategies were blurry and that they influenced one another since Sloan, at least at times, used the preferred label of the pluralists.

Some people of Mexican descent indirectly aided the efforts of those who promoted the marginalization strategy. Carlos Ignacio Velasco, an elite intellectual from Sonora, Mexico, immigrated to Arizona for political reasons and eventually decided to stay. In Tucson he published one of the first Spanish-language newspapers in Arizona, *El Fronterizo*, in which he promoted the repatriation of Mexicans to Mexico. His endeavor assisted the fledgling marginalizationists, who were beginning to argue that Mexicans left when they completed their seasonal jobs, such as when Governor Sloan characterized Mexicans as "mostly itinerants." Velasco printed numerous articles promoting repatriation in his effort to make the immigrants as temporary as Governor Sloan had implied. He also recommended that U.S. employers hire and repatriate Mexican laborers rather than contracting for expensive Chinese "coolies" who were difficult to return. Some Mexicans in Mexico agreed with his mission. *La Voz del Estado* (Magdalena, Mexico), for example, called upon its Mexican compatriots to return to Mexico where they would be treated better. The newspaper noted that only those who were "totally Americanized or given to adulation," would be accepted in the United States. Nevertheless, few Mexican nationals engaged in the statehood debates or involved themselves with their compatriots' condition or repatriation, especially given the rumblings of discontent in Mexico on the eve of revolution.[36]

Even in the United States, Velasco's efforts were fairly isolated. One contributor to his paper, Ramón Soto, a native-born cattleman, criticized the emphasis on Mexican issues and called for a concentration on matters in America since many people of Mexican descent were American. Within a few years Soto decided to do just that and founded the organization Alianza Hispano-Americana (AHA), along with Velasco (who had apparently changed his mind), Carlos Jácome (see chapter 1), and other people of Mexican descent. This group sought to help residents with Mexican ancestry living in the United States, but its leaders concentrated primarily on improving workers' moral character as they admonished them to eschew vagrancy, respect work, and to remain in their lowly positions. The AHA's conservative agenda reflected the upper-class status of its members as well as the shaky political climate in which it found itself. If AHA leaders worked too hard to contest the dominant Anglo majority on behalf of the workers, they might threaten their own tenuous political and economic ties within their class community.[37]

In addition, other Arizonans with Mexican ancestry did not help new immigrants much, referring to them in newspaper articles as "peons," and preferred that they remain in Mexico. Although they shared an ethnicity with the recent arrivals, these Arizonans largely believed that they had nothing in common with them.[38] Whereas immigrants before the 1890s had amassed experience working in Mexican mines, newcomers brought skills that were not well rewarded in the workplace. In general, the small

Spanish-language press in Arizona not only did not reach out to support them, but frowned upon any type of class-based organization that might jeopardize their own standing in society.[39]

The growing support for marginalization proved effective, helping to assure the end of the movement for joint statehood.[40] Indeed, these views influenced American legislators, including Representative J. W. Babcock, a Republican from Wisconsin, who concluded that Arizonans represented "sturdy Americanism in its best form" even as he regarded New Mexicans with great suspicion. The marginalization strategy resulted in more legislators supporting the idea of statehood solely for Arizona rather than a combined one with New Mexico. Cunniff, the aforementioned *World's Work* editor, also decided that Arizona was a more American and attractive option for statehood than New Mexico. As he saw it, New Mexico was a place in which "the chief problem lies in the people of the territory" who live with "unlighted streets flanked by squat lines of adobe dwellings" and who constitute a "scene [that] is all Spanish or all Mexican, as you will. It is not American." Only a place and people that fit his definition of being modern and with a modern standard of living could be considered American. Shortly after penning the above words, Cunniff persuaded himself of the merits of Arizona and moved there to improve his failing health from tuberculosis. He quickly entered the political scene and became one of the territory's key delegates to the state constitutional convention. In this role he helped to create the new state's governing documents, which did little to protect the rights of people of Mexican descent.[41]

Charles Moreau Harger of *Outlook* also accepted the arguments of those who advocated for the marginalization strategy, and helped to disseminate them nationwide. He observed how people of Mexican descent were declining in number and influence because "some go back to their native country, others scatter as laborers," adding that "American [Anglo] immigration" had changed the territories such that "to-day, the 'native' [person of Mexican descent] occupies a secondary place." He further explained that people of Mexican descent did not threaten the nation since they neither conducted strikes nor stayed long enough to have any effect on the country. (Harger apparently had conveniently forgotten the strikes in Clifton-Morenci eight years before; it is conceivable that those outside the immediate area had forgotten, too.) Finally, Harger commented that people of Mexican descent could be grouped into two classes—a laboring class and a business one—and quoted a manager of a large ranch as saying that, "'they [*nativos*] do not strike, and, treated well, they remain with you. . . . We must have laborers and this class furnishes them.'"[42] In other words, many of those agreeing to statehood for Arizona favored a limited or marginal incorporation for people of Mexican descent: they wanted them to provide their labor without threatening the status quo and believed, or wanted to believe, that this would be the case.

Unlike exclusionists, however, marginalizationists did not worry much about whether or not the laborers learned English or adapted to Anglo ways. In fact, they perceived people of Mexican descent as permanently working class or transient and thus unlikely to affect territorial, state, or national politics. Moreover, they did their utmost to ensure that this remained the case through legislation that restricted them to marginal positions in society. In 1909 the Arizona legislature succeeded in passing literacy in English as a requirement for voter eligibility, and although this was not directed solely at people of Mexican descent—many in Arizona were concerned about the growing European immigrant population as well—it removed the vote from those who had held that right since 1848.[43] It would be difficult for Spanish-speaking people of Mexican descent to have much political power as long as this new law remained in force.

Success of Pluralism and Marginalization

By 1908, after the jointure bill to combine the territories had failed, most politicians recognized that the two would never agree to be merged. But New Mexico's strategy of pluralism and Arizona's one of marginalization succeeded in persuading sufficient Americans that people of Mexican descent could be incorporated into the union without jeopardizing national unity. Recent elections favoring Republicans, and the fact that New Mexico's new governor George Curry was a close friend of Teddy Roosevelt's, assuaged Republicans' fears that the new states would boost the Democratic Party. Thus, in 1910 the Republicans approved enabling acts for individual statehood for each of the territories.[44]

The stipulations in these enabling acts demonstrated the influence of the various strategies for incorporating "others." People favoring exclusion, such as Senator Beveridge, made a last-ditch effort to delay statehood by requiring that both the U.S. Congress *and* the U.S. president approve the draft constitutions, a dual requirement that had not been imposed upon any other territory. Signs of assimilation, however, were evident in language mandating public schools to teach all primary coursework in English. Pluralists overrode Arizona's 1909 literacy law for the purpose of electing delegates to the constitutional convention and the new state's first elections.

Marginalizationists' major contribution to the enabling acts included the state constitutional requirement that all state officeholders speak, write, read, and understand English well—a specification that limited the opportunities of Spanish-only speakers.[45]

Despite setbacks, pluralists in New Mexico worked hard to maintain *nativo* rights in their state constitution. They had a strong incentive to do so as they well knew how *nuevomexicanos* had been attacked during the statehood debates, and how *nativo* rights had been diminished in Arizona in the years leading up to statehood. Those favoring pluralism succeeded not only because of their class standing and ties across racial lines, but because they had sufficient numbers and political clout to elect thirty-two people of Mexican descent (out of one hundred delegates) to the territory's constitutional convention. Solomon Luna, a wealthy rancher and one of the most respected men of Mexican descent in the territory, was chosen to be the chair of the Committee on Committees, giving a *nativo* substantial say in the composition of the committees that drafted various portions of the constitution.[46]

Those favoring pluralism pressed forward and demanded a number of protections for *nativos* at New Mexico's constitutional convention. The constitution ultimately specified that no person could be disfranchised due to "religion, race, language, or color" or prohibited from serving on juries or holding offices—other than statewide ones that were restricted to English speakers per the enabling acts—because of not knowing how to read, write, or speak either English *or* Spanish. The pluralists required that the proceedings of the convention, ballots, and all public documents be made available in Spanish and English, and they inserted language that granted people facing criminal prosecution the right to have charges and testimony interpreted to them in a language that they knew. They added stipulations preventing the prohibition of wine for religious services, and ensured that "children of Spanish descent" would neither be prevented from attending public schools nor required to enroll in separate ones and would "forever enjoy perfect equality with other children in all public schools and education institutions of the State." The constitution further declared that funding should be provided to train all teachers in Spanish, as well as English, so that they could teach Spanish-speaking students more effectively. Finally, the convention members approved a constitution that made it extremely difficult to alter or amend the sections relating to people of Mexican descent.[47]

Pluralists also incorporated exclusionary elements into the state constitution. An early version of the document allowed school districts to establish separate institutions for people of African descent when two-thirds of the voters desired it, replicating the discrimination and segregation of the Jim Crow South. Only three of the five *nativos* on the Education Subcommittee (and none of the six Anglos) opposed this provision. Although this language was not included in the final constitution, there was no distinct wording protecting people of African descent from being placed in separate schools as had been spelled out for *nativos*. Pluralists also kept silent about Pueblo Indians, creating no special provisions to allow them to vote as they formerly had done under Mexican rule.[48]

In general, pluralists expressed satisfaction with the final draft of the constitution, believing that it helped protect their rights to use Spanish and to continue specific customs. At the close of the convention Nestor Montoya, a Republican delegate and editor of Albuquerque's *La Bandera Americana* (*The American Flag*), presented a gold cane to H. R. Whiting, the sergeant-at-arms of the convention, in gratitude for all the delegates' work in protecting the rights of *nativos*. Montoya explained that "in the name of the Spanish-American members of the Convention, I wish to say, that all delegates here have, as one man, helped to safeguard the rights of the two hundred thousand people of that blood in this Territory." Benjamin Read was equally enthusiastic about the new constitution and its protection of the Spanish language. The newspaper *El Tiempo* (Las Cruces, NM) concurred and lauded the convention results. Even former Governor Otero, now adopting the more popular and pluralist view, stumped around the territory on behalf of the proposed governing document, calling upon "fellow citizens of Spanish-American blood, the same as I am and my ancestors were" to vote for the new constitution. While he acknowledged the limits of the document, specifically its ban against non-English speakers holding state office, he pointed out that New Mexicans did not need to speak English for county- and precinct-level positions and that the current, territory-wide officials all knew English anyway. When it was time for the territorial residents to vote, "in English or in Spanish," for or against the constitution, the residents overwhelmingly approved it. Eventually both the U.S. Congress and President Taft did as well. Finally, in early 1912, New Mexico became the forty-seventh state. As an additional symbol of the pluralists' success, Larrazolo became one of the state's first governors (1916) and in 1928, the first Mexican American in the U.S. Senate. Pluralism in New Mexico persisted, at least in the first years after statehood, as over one-half of the state representatives in 1917 and one-third of its senators were *nativos*. The promotion of Spanish culture also continued with the re-naming of streets in Santa Fe, the glorification of all things adobe, and the celebration of New Mexico's Spanish past.[49]

The pluralists did not fare so well in Arizona. Following heated debates over joint statehood, Arizona marginalizationists persuaded many Americans that their territory was quite different from New Mexico's and more like the rest of the nation. In part this had been achieved through a series of territorial laws or acts limiting the opportunities of people of Mexican descent, including the 1909 literacy law. Anglos also worked to exclude people of Mexican descent from key elected positions. Even in Tucson where people of Mexican descent or *los tucsonenses*—as they called themselves—held the majority, Anglos dominated city politics.[50]

A clear sign of Anglo control was the lack of representation of people of Mexican descent at the state constitutional convention. Only one out of the territory's 52 delegates to the convention was of Mexican descent, Carlos Jácome, despite the fact that *nativos* comprised fully twenty percent of Arizona's population. Jácome, who had resided in Arizona since 1876, had a minimal role at the convention, serving on only two of the 21 subcommittees created to draft portions of the constitution. By contrast, Delegate Cunniff, who had arrived only three years previously, served on four major committees and as convention secretary. Even a delegate of Italian descent, Edward Arthur Tovrea, who moved to Arizona at least a decade after Jácome, served on three substantive committees. Jácome, exiled to the minor subcommittee "Schedule, Mode of Amending, and Miscellaneous" and one for railroads, initiated only one of the 153 propositions presented for inclusion in the constitution and was not recorded as saying anything major in the official minutes and journals of the convention. Nevertheless, Jácome and his fellow members on the Miscellaneous committee grappled with one issue that sparked some debate at the convention. Their five-person committee approved language prohibiting interracial marriage—which they defined as being between whites and "negroes" or whites and people of Chinese descent—in the state constitution. But their fellow delegates thought differently, believing that the subcommittee members had shirked their duties by defining interracial marriage too narrowly. One participant called for the prohibitions to extend at least to Indians and Japanese as well, while another thought it should cover all of the "obnoxious" races. Ultimately, the delegates could not agree on how to define objectionable marriages and thus voted to cast the issue aside, omitting any such prohibitions.[51]

Those favoring marginalization in Arizona instituted a number of other provisions to limit the opportunities of people of Mexican descent: they restricted public works jobs to U.S. citizens and attempted to restrict hazardous but desirable jobs, such as mining, to English speakers only. Some delegates also called for more stringent labor practices, such as prohibiting employers from hiring *any* foreign labor. A representative of the Immigration Restriction League wrote to the chair (and future state governor) of the convention, George P. Hunt, warning that if such a prohibition was not put into place, "it will be New Mexico all over again only a good deal worse." Both of these measures were rejected, primarily because of concern that such bans would result in an insufficient supply of workers. Some marginalizationists also made an effort to codify the 1909 literacy law into the state constitution. They failed in this, however, as sufficient Democratic convention members feared being held responsible (and losing their seats) for disenfranchising Arizonans since the state's enabling acts mandated that no person lacking English-language proficiency be barred from voting for constitutional delegates or in the state's first elections.[52]

Initially some marginalizationists also supported language providing for separate schools for whites and "coloreds," whom they defined as people of African descent. All other children were to be deemed "white" for the purposes of education. But like their New Mexican cohorts, Arizonans eventually avoided including this language and decided to retain the extant laws on segregation. Despite the fact that the state constitution did not prohibit people of Mexican descent from enrolling in white schools, they often attended separate ones and frequently lived in segregated communities as well.[53] Although many of the proposed measures to limit the rights of people of Mexican descent did not become part of the new constitution, those favoring marginalization succeeded in keeping people of Mexican descent on the periphery and prevented them from having much access to political and socioeconomic power. The marginalizationists continued to propose similarly restrictive legislation in the years following statehood.

Perhaps most damaging to the pluralists' agenda in Arizona were purposeful omissions from the state's governing document. Unlike New Mexico's constitution, which specified a variety of protections that helped *nativos* to integrate themselves fully into the nation as Spanish Americans, there were no such provisions in the Arizona constitution. It made no allowance for public documents or ballots to be translated into the Spanish language and offered no protections for monolingual Spanish speakers regarding education, voting, or sitting on juries. These silences were due to the much smaller middle-class population of people of Mexican descent in Arizona, most of whom were concentrated in and around Tucson and Pima County. All five of the Republican representatives from Pima County, including Jácome, eventually voted against the constitution, but they were greatly outnumbered. The constitution passed with 40 in favor (mostly Democrats) and 12 (most Republicans) opposed.[54] The U.S. Congress and President Taft eventually approved it, and on February 14, 1912, Arizona became known as the Valentine State, the 48th state in the Union. Marcus Smith, a key promoter of Arizona's marginalization strategy, became one of the state's first U.S. senators. His voice and those of others like him resonated widely, for marginalization provided Americans with a working narrative for how people of Mexican ancestry could be fit within the nation without altering the dominant understanding of what it meant to be an American.

These two strategies of pluralism and marginalization, exemplified in New Mexico and Arizona respectively, became the primary strategies for determining how to incorporate people of Mexican descent into the nation. Pluralism in New Mexico stood as a symbol for how people without an Anglo background could effectively integrate into the country without jeopardizing U.S. national identity and without having to deny their language and culture. These Spanish Americans, then, could participate as full Americans by voting in local and national elections even while continuing to use Spanish in their daily affairs. In Arizona, however, people of Mexican descent soon discovered that they were welcomed mostly as workers with second-class standing in the community. They were expected to remain in their station as laborers and refrain from any disputes, or return to Mexico. They had no special protections for language rights or cultural traditions, and only limited opportunities to participate in the government. They could be incorporated as Americans—but only the most marginal of ones.

The central difference in the adoption of one strategy or the other had much to do with the demographics and the class standing of the people of Mexican descent in the territories.[55] With few elite people of Mexican descent in Arizona, the Anglo majority dominated the debate and promoted marginalization over pluralism. In New Mexico, *nativos* had wealth, education, substantial landholdings, and political clout and constituted a significant percentage of the population. These factors contributed to their success in persuading Anglos that they possessed the requisite traits—those having a European background and a middle-class standing—to be full Americans on their own terms, which included their continued use of the Spanish language.

Marginalization and pluralism persisted beyond statehood and provided Americans with alternate strategies—besides exclusion and assimilation—for incorporating Mexican immigrants into the polity. As before, the class standing of the entrants had much to do with the decisions made. Future years hinted at the dominance of Arizona's marginalization strategy as Mexican laborers were welcomed into the United States during the First World War and then repatriated in the early 1920s and again in the 1930s. In the first years of the twentieth century, however, it was not inevitable that working-class people of Mexican descent would be regarded, at best, as marginal Americans.

PART TWO

Transformations

The First World War Era, 1917–1922

CHAPTER THREE

Changing Strategies for a New World

Born in Mexico in 1866, Pedro Garcia de la Lama eventually immigrated to the New Mexican territory, becoming an American citizen in 1894. Two years later he moved to the Arizona territory to work as the editor of a Spanish-language newspaper, *El Progreso*. In 1902 he was called before the notorious Beveridge committee to provide testimony about the circulation of his periodical (1,500 subscribers), and whether or not he was born in Arizona. The committee members asked him no other questions, and Garcia likely knew it was futile to interject anything more to defend the merits of his adopted territory. Following statehood, Garcia formed the Liga Protectora Latina, a mutual aid organization designed to help people of Mexican descent to protect their rights and to cover unexpected expenses from illness and death. Unlike most other Mexican mutual aid organizations in Arizona, Garcia's Liga Protectora worked as an advocate for recent immigrants, calling for bilingual education programs, fighting against discrimination in the criminal justice system, and advocating for the right of people of Mexican descent to vote and work, regardless of the language(s) they spoke.

While the Liga Protectora was hardly a revolutionary organization—it shied away from some strikes and unionization—most other local Mexican mutual aid groups operated even more conservatively, planning social functions and encouraging conformity rather than engaging in political activities. Garcia's line of work and organization—with its emphasis on cultural rights in addition to other civil rights—suggests that in the immediate post-statehood years he initially supported pluralism as the best means for incorporating people of Mexican descent into the nation. But in the wake of fierce Americanization campaigns during and immediately following the First World War, the Liga Protectora fell in line with the increasingly conservative environment, urging its members to minimize conflict between capital and labor. Furthermore, it increased membership dues, making it more difficult for working-class people—those most likely to unionize or organize strikes—to remain as members. Within a few years membership plummeted and the organization virtually disappeared. Liga Protectora's then-withered condition reflected the pluralists' declining capacity to persuade Americans of the viability of their strategy for incorporating newcomers.[1]

The achievement of separate statehood in 1912 had represented a triumph for pluralism in New Mexico and marginalization in Arizona, but no sooner had statehood been attained than a surge in Mexican immigration, growing fears about the spread of radicalism, demands for conformity during the First World War, and postwar recession once again made the place of Mexicans in America unclear. The more inclusionary strategies of pluralism, assimilation, and marginalization, however limited, declined under these pressures.

Prior to the First World War, few Americans paid attention to Mexican immigrants, as their numbers were insignificant compared with those entering from European countries. In the half-century following the 1848 Treaty of Guadalupe Hidalgo, Mexican immigration occurred virtually unobserved and unmonitored as immigrants traversed both ways across the newly established border for seasonal work on farms and ranches. When a greater number of Mexicans crossed the border to work in the mines, railroads, and agriculture in the late nineteenth century, Southwestern inspectors made no effort to track the migration and instead concentrated on reducing the number of Asians and Europeans attempting to enter.[2] At the end of the nineteenth century, Americans remained so blasé about the presence of Mexicans that immigration from the south continued with virtually no restrictions: even a newly imposed head tax on immigrants did not pertain to Mexicans.[3] Their immigration was of such minor concern that the commissioner-general of immigration neglected to mention the subject in any of his reports until 1906. Even then the commissioner merely observed that railroad companies were actively recruiting laborers from Mexico—in violation of contract labor laws—and vowed to watch the situation more closely.[4]

When Americans did notice the increasing Mexican population, they directed less animosity toward them than other immigrants. Organized labor, not generally supportive of open borders, agreed with those who favored the marginalization position and considered a Mexican worker to be "something of an American," provided that he performed only the lowest wage jobs and did not compete directly with white laborers for skilled work. In the words of one pro-union editor, these Mexican immigrants had " 'more right to be here than these Japanese and Italians and Greeks.' "[5]

Mexican immigration grew steadily after 1905 due to business expansion in Mexico and the American Southwest. After the Mexican president Porfirio Díaz intensified his efforts to modernize the country by repossessing communal land and selling it to foreign investors, Mexicans who had been pushed off their land left their villages in search of opportunities in urban areas or the nascent mining communities of northern Mexico.[6] This movement, combined with escalating population growth resulting from lower mortality rates, meant there were even more people vying for scarce jobs in Mexican mines and towns. Desperate for opportunities, workers began crossing the border into the United States where prospects in railroads, mining, agriculture, and cattle grazing appeared more promising.[7]

The southwestern United States, outside of New Mexico where few jobs were available, became an increasingly attractive option for Mexican laborers. Jobs proliferated in Arizona's copper industry as well as agricultural work. The expansion of agricultural jobs in this arid region was in part due to the recent implementation of the 1902 Newlands Reclamation Act, which provided incentives for constructing irrigation projects and large-scale farming enterprises. The now arable land, combined with advanced refrigeration techniques in railcars, transformed the area into a major producer and supplier of fruits and vegetables for the nation. Wages were also higher and remained a significant factor for emigrating. In 1910, 90 percent of all Mexicans earned between 20 and 25 cents per day, but by crossing the border they could earn $1.25 per day in fewer hours in the United States, a differential that more than compensated for the higher cost of living. Most who came were unskilled workers.[8]

The Mexican Revolution, which broke out shortly after the exile of Porfirio Díaz in 1911, was also a factor in increasing immigration as Mexicans fled before the various armed factions. Recently, some historians have minimized the revolution's role, arguing instead that Mexico's expanding market economy and interrelationship with the United States had more to do with encouraging immigration than the revolution; in fact, immigration decreased during the most violent years from 1913 to 1916.[9] But historians Linda Hall and Don Coerver record that while unskilled workers were still the predominant group of immigrants during the teens, a larger percentage of those from the middle classes came during the years of peak violence, apparently because they could still afford to do so. Still others did not come as official immigrants and simply fled across the border—often, Hall and Coerver explain, as entire towns—to escape the violence. Regardless of why people came, Mexican immigration during the second decade of the twentieth century represented a dramatic increase over that of the previous ten years.[10]

While separating economic from political motives is difficult, some of the immigrants who came to the United States, especially in the first years of the revolution, were members of the middle- or elite classes who previously had supported President Díaz; later refugees came because they opposed the rule of President Victoriano Huerta. Initially, Mexican and Anglo Americans welcomed the first wave of refugees, especially those who they perceived to be of the same class status as themselves and not a potential burden on the government. But as the revolution continued, historians Hall and Coerver found, some problems resulted from their growing numbers because Americans considered the newest immigrants or refugees to be radicals. As early as 1915, Mexican Americans in the Tucson branch of the Liga Protectora organization advised its members against associating with any particular faction of the revolution and expelled members who did so.[11]

Although exclusionists generally ignored the escalating Mexican immigration, instead concentrating their efforts on limiting Europeans and Asians, their allies in Congress eventually succeeded in passing the Burnett-Johnson Immigration Act in 1917, which affected all entrants.[12] The new legislation stipulated that all immigrants over the age of sixteen be required to read in English or in some other language or dialect.[13] Furthermore, the law increased the head tax for entry to eight dollars and for the first time required that all immigrants pay it, including Mexicans.[14] This act drastically reduced Mexican immigration—even though Mexicans had not been the primary target of the legislation—since the majority of these potential immigrants were illiterate and/or could not afford the tax.

Shortly after these laws were imposed, Congress passed the Selective Service Act, which further decreased Mexican emigration. Although Mexicans were ineligible for the draft due to their foreign status, the legislation required all men living in the United States to register for military service, raising immigrants' fears that they might have to fight. Consequently, Southwestern agriculturalists saw one of their major sources of labor dissipate at the very time that their European pool shrank due to the new literacy requirements, the increased head tax, and perilous wartime seas, which discouraged emigration. The U.S. Army further reduced the number of available workers by conscripting many Americans for the war effort. Still other workers left the rural Southwest for greater opportunities in the war-related industries of the expanding cities.[15]

At the same time, growers' need for laborers rose exponentially. The world war created greater demand for food products abroad as well as for raw materials such as long-staple cotton, which could be used for soldiers' uniforms and for manufactured goods including airplanes, tires, and other military supplies. The boll weevil contributed to the gap between supply and demand by eating the cotton crops in the Sea Islands off South Carolina and Georgia while the pink boll worm and the weevil were inflicting great damage on Egyptian cotton.[16] Anticipating a labor shortfall, farmers pressured U.S. secretary of labor William B. Wilson for waivers from the literacy requirement and requested that he use the hastily inserted language within it, which gave him the authority to admit "otherwise inadmissible aliens" when needed.

Concurring with farmers' assessment of a wartime emergency, Secretary Wilson permitted agricultural workers from Mexico to enter the United States for a short-term period. This edict exempted these agricultural laborers from the literacy test, the head tax, and applicable contract labor laws.[17] It did not, however, mean open access for all Mexican immigrants, but instead required potential employers to follow elaborate procedures. These entailed requesting permission to bring in a specific number of laborers and spelling out the workers' duties, rate of pay, housing conditions, and duration of their stay (not to exceed six months). Employers further had to sign a contract stipulating their agreement to report if their temporary employees chose to work for someone else—necessitating the transfer of that contract to the new employer—or if their new hire deserted or disappeared. The "importing" employer also agreed to arrange for the workers' transportation to the workplace and for their return at contract expiration. In addition, these agreements required extensive documentation, including multiple photographs accompanied by physical descriptions of all contract laborers to ensure that workers could be tracked if they fled from their original employer. These restrictions were meant to guarantee that Mexican immigrants would work *only* in the agricultural sector and remain *only* for the duration of their contracts. Ideally, this would prevent them from competing with American workers or threatening the country's presumed national unity. The Department of Labor further noted that if the immigrants deserted, they would be deported when found.[18] While the initial provisions provided only for a six-month term, this soon was extended—first, for the duration of the war, then until January 1920, and eventually until March 1921 when the emergency rules finally lapsed.[19]

By 1920, the number of Mexicans in the United States had increased significantly. Despite a high return rate to Mexico, estimates indicate that roughly 500,000 Mexicans then lived in the United States, up from approximately 100,000 in 1900.[20] Due to greater numbers and visibility, Anglo and Mexican Americans began to reassess how the newest arrivals might fit within the nation and if the former strategies applied. Could they accept the newcomers as potential Spanish Americans through pluralism, Anglo Americans via assimilation, second-class Americans via marginalization, or should they attempt to exclude them entirely?

Challenges to Pluralism

Pluralism had always been tenuous, especially outside of its power base in New Mexico where people of Mexican descent retained some economic and political authority during the years of the First World War. But by the mid-1920s, pluralism was seriously weakened as a viable strategy for incorporating immigrants as few people, not even those who had favored pluralism, believed that the recent Mexican arrivals possessed the requisite traits to become Spanish Americans.

Pluralism peaked in the immediate years after statehood, especially in New Mexico. There pluralists pointed to high-class Spanish Americans residing in the new state to demonstrate how they could continue to speak Spanish yet still fit within the nation as model citizens who would not imperil national unity. Signs of the pluralists' success appeared in various Anglo-authored articles, which approvingly noted the admirable qualities of people of Spanish descent who the authors regarded as capable of becoming or already being equal to themselves. There were few objections to Spanish customs and traditions. If anything, this culture became more revered since Spain no longer presented a threat to the United States. Thus, Americans could afford to reflect nostalgically upon the past, imagining noble friars who had settled in the Southwest, erecting quaint missions and committing themselves to the admirable goal of civilizing the Indians. Following statehood, Anglos increasingly vacationed in New Mexico, hoping to learn more about the period of Spanish rule and the inhabitants of that era; their interest was enhanced through educational institutions, such as the University of Missouri, which in 1916 offered the country's first course on Spanish American literature. Historians such as Hubert Howe Bancroft, Herbert Eugene Bolton, and Ralph Emerson Twitchell became fascinated with the region's history, writing numerous books on Spanish colonization in the Americas. Intrigued by the association between Spaniards and the New World that pluralists like Benjamin Read and Octaviano Larrazolo had worked so hard to advance, Bolton wrote a book celebrating this connection between Spain and all of North America.[21] In 1918, the *Hispanic American Historical Review* published its first issue to satisfy readers' interest in the subject. Enrollment in Spanish-language university classes also increased significantly, from 5,000 students in 1910 to over 250,000 by 1922.[22] Cecil Robinson has also written of the increase in American literature romanticizing the Spanish influence in the Southwest.[23]

But the growing population of Mexican immigrants in the Southwest presented a new challenge for pluralists. Pluralism flourished when its advocates professed that people of Mexican descent descended from Spaniards, and held or could attain a middle- or upper-class standing in society. Yet most new immigrants from Mexico could not claim such a status because approximately 90 percent of the new arrivals were unskilled workers coming from the lowest strata of Mexican society. Regardless of whether the new arrivals desired to claim a pure Spanish lineage, their socioeconomic standing made it virtually impossible to do so because Americans conflated class and race, rendering the newcomers not Spanish nor European, not white, and therefore not American.[24]

The geographical destination of the immigrants contributed to the decline of pluralism since most of the new arrivals emigrated from Mexico to Arizona and other parts of the nation, rather than to New Mexico, where there were more middle-class people of Mexican descent who held sufficient political and economic clout to help define what being American entailed.[25] During the First World War, Arizona employers alone contracted with 15,576 workers from Mexico, or 31 percent of all Mexicans brought into the United States via Wilson's wartime immigration policies. In the same period, employers in New Mexico arranged for only 411 laborers.[26] By 1920 only 3 percent of all Mexican immigrants in the nation lived in New Mexico; 14 percent lived in Arizona, a less populous state.[27]

Anglo Americans, including some who had previously supported pluralism and the idea that Spanish Americans could be equal to themselves, lacked enthusiasm for recent Mexican arrivals. They questioned if lower-class Mexicans could fit within the nation like the upper-class Spanish descendants who had led the fight for statehood in New Mexico. A journalist for *Harper's Weekly*, a popular magazine of the day, commented on how the Spaniards in New Mexico differed from the newcomers of mixed heritage in Arizona and Texas.[28] Edith Shatto King, a California reformer, remarked: "I remember them [the De Soto kids, whom she described as having an extensive lineage in California] quick and proud, lighter complexioned, with long Spanish faces, in sharp contrast to Carmelita's [described as a recently arrived Mexican girl] round dark face."[29] A Texas banker lamented to a congressional committee hearing in 1920 that no one could determine which of the immigrants were of Spanish or Indian heritage since they were all an amalgam of the two groups.[30] Associating the newcomers with a pure Spanish identity, and respecting them for their Spanish or European culture, had become impossible.

Mexican Americans—whether assimilationist or pluralist—also distanced themselves from the new arrivals, making it more difficult for Mexican immigrants to fit into the nation via those strategies. While middle-class Mexican Americans sympathized with the plight of the recent immigrants and generally supported their presence, if for no other reason than that the newcomers' labor yielded lower food prices, they also stressed the class and cultural divergence between themselves and Mexican nationals. They referred to themselves as *hispano-americanos* and the immigrants as *mexicanos*, keeping the latter at arm's length rather than embracing them as part of their Spanish-speaking community.[31]

While these reasons alone were sufficient to cause pluralism to decline, few recent immigrants relished accommodating themselves to a Spanish American identity. Previous immigrants such as Larrazolo more willingly asserted a European heritage since respect for this ancestry and "whiteness" had been widespread in Mexico, as well as the United States, when he emigrated.[32] Following the overthrow of President Díaz and the ensuing revolution, major cultural changes spread rapidly throughout Mexico. More Mexicans began to question their former president's affiliation and identification with European culture and to learn about their country's indigenous heroes and history; consequently, they began to valorize the underclass in contrast to the elites who had promoted and boosted the value of foreign countries and cultures over that of their own. All of this contributed to Mexicans' growing sense of pride in their heritage. Since there was no concomitant movement to laud the efforts of the poor or indigenous persons in the United States, or to characterize them as the true Americans, Mexicans saw few reasons to change their nationality and incorporate into the nation via pluralism, assimilation, or marginalization.[33]

Despite these problems, pluralist thought continued in three forms. First, while most Anglo and Mexican Americans would not extend a Spanish American identity to the new arrivals from Mexico, they continued to view high-class people of Mexican descent as Spanish or Spanish American. Secondly, pluralism persisted in New Mexico because *nuevomexicanos* continued to have clout in the political arena. Third and finally, pluralists succeeded in marketing their heritage to the American people such that both Mexican and Anglo Americans became increasingly enamored with Spanish colonial history in the United States, but that fascination went only so far and did not extend to the newest immigrants.

Rise and Fall of Assimilation

In the first years after statehood, assimilationists were as willing to extend their strategy to Mexican immigrants as they had been to people of Mexican descent in the territories: they perceived newcomers as Spanish and European, but wanted them to become Americanized in the mold of Anglo Americans. Most middle-class Arizonans of Mexican descent—with the exception of Pedro Garcia de la Lama and fellow members of the Liga Protectora—advocated assimilation over pluralism. Facing rampant discrimination and diminishing rights in the post-statehood years, these assimilationists believed it wiser for the purposes of economic survival to integrate themselves into the dominant and middle-class Anglo American community than to argue for cultural and workers' rights as well.[34] Middle-class organizations like the Alianza Hispano-Americana and the Spanish-language newspaper, *El Tucsonense*, contested labor activism and allied themselves with Anglos of a similar class standing who criticized the strikes and walkouts. These Mexican Americans found the conflict between capital and labor troubling because they feared association with people deemed radical; consequently, they advised conformity whenever possible. Carlos Jácome, the previously mentioned merchant and statehood advocate, was one of these men. He prided himself on his American identity, urged his sons to volunteer for military service, and avoided radical positions.[35] The Alianza continued to stress the work ethic and learning English. Friendly House, a Phoenix organization with substantial Mexican American support, was designed to help immigrants but mostly emphasized teaching immigrants to become domestic workers, learn English, and improve their personal hygiene. Furthermore, it lauded employers' efforts to deport immigrant troublemakers who sought to organize strikes. These assimilationists wanted to Americanize the immigrants (albeit to protect them) as a way of ensuring that the newcomers would be accepted.[36] Yet the boundary between assimilation and pluralism was often blurred as individuals and organizations such as Garcia's Liga Protectora adjusted their stance depending upon the context; still, the general trend during the war years was toward conformity and assimilation.

Other Americans also advocated the assimilation of immigrants during the First World War. In 1918 some residents of Phoenix established an Americanization Committee, which concentrated on teaching immigrants English and civics; a similar group organized in Tucson the same year. The American Legion set up a branch office in Phoenix and intensified its campaigns to teach English to people of Mexican descent, native-born and immigrant alike. One eager Americanizer declared his motto to be "one flag, one language, one country."[37] As limited as these assimilationists may have been in their view of what constituted American identity, they offered a more inclusionary strategy for dealing with immigrants than did marginalizationists or exclusionists since they believed that Mexicans *could* change and become like Anglo Americans. When debating Secretary Wilson's wartime waivers for immigration, Representative Claude B. Hudspeth, a Democrat from Texas, emphasized that some Mexicans were good and patriotic citizens because they had voluntarily served in the military during the recent world war and contributed generously to the government's liberty bond drives. Representative Carlos Bee, another Democrat from Texas, asserted that he knew of "Mexicans from the peon class [who] graduate[d] at the head of their class in high school" when attending integrated (Anglo and Mexican) schools and believed that they assimilated well, acquiring good occupations as clerks and merchants.[38] There was no suggestion—as existed among pluralists—that cultural difference would be an asset to the nation.

While the voices of pluralism diminished during the war, Americanization efforts likewise declined in the postwar years as Americans everywhere concluded that assimilationist reformers had failed to teach immigrants English and change their culture; consequently, the federal government decreased financial and rhetorical support for such programs. Frustrated activists began to believe that Mexican immigrants were indeed either incapable of learning, or stubbornly resistant.[39] Another factor in the demise of Americanization campaigns was the rise of the eugenics movement, whose adherents (some of whom ended up in the halls of congress) argued that Mexicans could not assimilate because they did not belong to the white race and thus were too inferior to become any sort of American. The eugenics movement grew in the postwar era and the 1920s, especially in the West, with members expounding their views that Mexicans were primitive, unassimilable, and inferior, and that the best thing to do was to exclude them from the nation.[40] The pseudoscience they relied upon offered an explanation for why the immigrants were not integrating in the ways in which Americanizers thought that they should, providing a few reformers with a rationale for why they should cease their efforts. Although the voices of assimilation were not completely silenced, they lost momentum and control of the narrative, especially when exclusionists increasingly questioned the potential radicalism of the newest immigrants from the laboring classes of Mexico. Even so, some reformers held on to their belief that assimilation was the best strategy for incorporating people of Mexican descent.

Challenges to Marginalization

During the statehood era, those favoring marginalization did quite well—particularly in Arizona—in limiting the opportunities of people of Mexican descent so that they could not rise from their lowly economic position to compete with Anglo Americans for skilled jobs and political influence. Arizona marginalizationists pursued a variety of laws to assure Anglo control over the immigrant workforce and quickly reinstituted (in 1913) English literacy as a prerequisite for voting.[41] They also succeeded in asserting control over people of Mexican descent by establishing segregated schools, pools, parks, and movie theaters, with some going so far as to relegate Spanish-language religious services to the church basement rather than inside the main chapel. Signs warning "No Mexicans Allowed" proliferated throughout many parts of Arizona. Segregated towns continued to exist immediately adjacent to one another and the dual wage system—lower wages for people of Mexican descent compared with Anglos—persisted.[42]

Despite these victories, those advocating marginalization faced great problems in promoting their agenda. After the Mexican and Russian Revolutions erupted, worrying elites everywhere about employers' ability to keep workers under control and in a second-class position in society, employers had difficulty convincing people that people of Mexican descent would remain contentedly in their lower-class place, or that labor strikes were solely isolated rebellions. Americans read and heard much about those at the bottom rising up to overthrow their leaders in other parts of the world and feared the potential for violence and warfare. The 1915 Plan of San Diego, calling for Mexicans and Mexican Americans to rise up and retake the Southwest from the United States (although there were few signs of any significant following for it), combined with Pancho Villa's surprise invasion of Columbus, New Mexico, the following year, surely did not help matters.[43]

National events intensified these fears as people of Mexican descent participated in the disputes between labor and capital in Ludlow, Colorado (1913), in Ray, Arizona (1915), and then again in Bisbee, Arizona (1917). Such activity caused many Americans to question Mexicans' docility. In Bisbee approximately 1,200 copper miners, over half of whom were of Mexican or Italian descent, agreed to walk out from workplaces controlled by the Phelps Dodge Corporation. The company quickly intervened, not wanting to risk any opportunity to earn great profits during the wartime copper boom, and arranged for the local sheriff, Henry F. Wheeler, to arrest participating strikers. The county official and nearly 2,000 armed men herded the recalcitrant workers onto cattle cars and transported them several hundred miles into the midst of the stifling New Mexican desert. There they were left and told never to return. Initially, much of the region's Spanish- and English-language press supported this deportation. While the townspeople of Bisbee and the Phelps Dodge Corporation later received substantial criticism from President Woodrow Wilson and the national press, ultimately they faced few consequences. The men responsible for the deportation were brought to trial but soon acquitted. In contrast, none of the deported men ever received any compensation for their suffering.[44] What was remembered of these events was the image of the striking Mexicans and how the situation was resolved by transporting the laborers out-of-state. Following these uprisings, the efforts of growers to promote the inclusion of Mexican immigrants into the nation via marginalization, as "docile" and future marginal Americans, seemed increasingly implausible.

The outbreak of the First World War further contributed to the decline in Americans' view of Mexican immigrants as spineless, second-class Americans, especially after the notorious Zimmermann telegram (February 1917) became public. In this communiqué, the German foreign secretary, Arthur Zimmermann, requested Mexico's wartime support in exchange for his country's assistance in recovering the Mexican territory previously lost to the United States. The exposure of this proposal became one of the key factors for America's entry into the war against Germany. While the Mexican government quickly rejected Germany's suggested alliance, the very overture intensified Americans' fears about their southern neighbor, reducing the likelihood that Americans would view Mexicans as benign immigrants.

But even as Americans wondered whether the newcomers could be safely integrated as second-class citizens at the bottom of society, growers and their allies during the First World War continued to assert that these immigrants could become such Americans—marginal Americans—who would not harm the country. When Representative Hudspeth introduced the Hudspeth Resolution to continue Wilson's exemptions from the recent immigration laws, growers and their supporters backed these exceptions by emphasizing Mexicans' docility. As during the statehood era, these marginalizationists stressed that Mexican immigrants disliked politics and would not foment any uprisings. William H. Knox, representative of the 2,000-plus member Arizona Cotton Growers' Association, which, ultimately arranged for nearly 30,000 Mexican workers through the war's temporary worker policy, informed the hearing committee that the Mexican immigrant "is quiet, docile, and peaceable . . . does his work and takes his place."[45]

Most advocates for the extension of Secretary Wilson's temporary worker policy contended that Mexicans came to the United States to sustain themselves and not to disseminate radical beliefs. When Representative Hays White, a Republican from Kansas, queried one supporter during a congressional hearing regarding Mexicans' views on bolshevism, the agriculturalist responded, "He does not know the term; he does not know what it means; he does not care. I never heard of any talking bolshevism in my life."[46] Congressman Carl Hayden, a Democrat from Arizona, explained that most of the laborers were law-abiding people who hailed from farms and small towns in the Mexican state of Sonora, and that the only troublemakers were the few who came from mining communities, areas known to be more fractious in terms of capital-labor conflicts (as was the case with the major strike at Cananea in 1906). Another agriculturalist disputed the charge made by Representative John Box, a Democrat from Texas, that Mexicans actively participated in the infamous Bisbee labor strikes, asserting that the primary responsibility lay with Slavic and Irish activists.[47]

Marginalizationists during the First World War era continued to emphasize that people of Mexican descent would remain second-class citizens under the control of their Anglo employers. They argued that even if some Mexicans, brought in via temporary worker policies, remained in the United States, it would not be a problem because these immigrants knew their place, did not compete with Americans, and remained in the lowest wage sectors. A major grower from Texas, John Davis, informed the House committee members at the Temporary Admission Hearings that Mexicans were the most desirable people "to occupy the place that [they] can occupy," and to perform menial labor, work most Americans refused to do.[48] W. D. Mandeville, a labor agent for the rapidly expanding sugar beet industry in the upper Midwest, agreed and admitted a preference for Mexicans over Japanese workers whom he feared as future competitors. Likewise, Knox, the representative for cotton growers in Arizona, viewed Mexicans as more desirable than the Pima Indians who planted their own crops and competed with Anglos in the marketplace.[49] Representative Hudspeth reinforced the image of Mexicans' permanent, second-class status when he noted how such immigrants had lived on his ranch for fifteen to twenty years and assimilated or Americanized to the extent that they painted their cottages, purchased stoves, and played the latest music, "Trip the Light Fantastic," on their Victrolas.[50] In his view, this was all that they needed to do to become marginal Americans: stay in their place as a steady source of labor, participate in the American consumer culture, and play a little American music. J. A. Happer, spokesperson for the El Paso Chamber of Commerce, clarified for the committee that Mexicans in his city lived and ate separately from Anglos and seldom intermarried with them. He believed, however, that Mexicans could become good citizens, although "not as good as the whites."[51] In other words, Mexicans could become American as long as they remained second-class citizens and lived in segregated communities.

These statements, however, did little to quell Americans' growing anxiety. Many congressmen continued to question the accuracy of Mexicans' docility in view of worldwide revolutionary changes. In the 1920 hearing concerning Hudspeth's proposed legislation, Representative William N. Vaile, a Republican from Colorado, expressed concern that the immigrants might eventually become as radicalized as the peasants in Russia and "like the Mexican mustang, might go wrong, might get 'loco.' "[52] Representative John Raker, a Democrat from California, speculated that the newcomers might be revolutionaries, like the violent Pancho Villa who had invaded New Mexico in 1916, exploring ways to export their ideology to the United States. The chair of the House Committee on Immigration and Naturalization, Albert Johnson, a Republican from Washington, raised concerns about workers on strike in the Mexican cotton mills of Veracruz, and the latest news that some labor leaders were settling around San Antonio, Texas; he felt an uprising would be imminent if immigration continued unabated.[53] The continued criticism of unrestricted immigration caused those who favored marginalization to alter their rhetoric and strategy in order to maintain open borders.

Exclusionists Regroup

Although exclusionists had failed to prevent people of Mexican descent from entering the nation-state via statehood in 1912, most of them did not immediately work to stem Mexican immigration. Outside of the Southwest they concentrated on the more pressing concern of European and Asian immigrants, barely pausing to notice the increasing stream of Mexican immigrants.[54] Within Arizona, however, dormant exclusionists—who had allied previously with marginalizationists and pluralists in their mutual quest for statehood—now began to make their voices heard. In 1914, exclusionists in the Arizona legislature succeeded in passing legislation, which stipulated that companies with more than five workers had to certify that 80 percent or more of their employees were U.S. citizens, or had filed first declarations to become so. The following year, after the U.S. District Court in San Francisco decided that the state's new law had overstepped its bounds and violated the Fourteenth Amendment to the U.S. Constitution, exclusionists countered with the Claypool-Kinney bill mandating that only English speakers be hired for hazardous jobs such as mining. Although this bill also failed, due to the twin efforts of corporations who feared too extensive a loss of employees and the Liga Protectora Latina's strong protest against it, the exclusionists' setback was only temporary.[55]

By 1920 exclusionists—within and outside of Arizona—regained strength and successfully lobbied against the extension of Secretary Wilson's wartime immigration policy. Their victory had much to do with the fact that their efforts coincided with the beginning of a national recession and because the marginalization strategy had lost some of its initial appeal due to an increased number of labor disputes. Such activity caused Americans to become skeptical of Mexicans' willingness to accept a subordinate status.

World events, then, undermined the marginalization strategy. No longer did U.S. legislators accept the arguments that people of Mexican descent were docile, controllable workers with no desire to impact American society. At the same time that the plausibility of marginalization declined, the voices of exclusion became stronger, convincing Americans of the serious threat that continued immigration posed: thus, those favoring marginalization needed a new way to persuade Americans that Mexican immigrants could enter the country without threatening national identity. Instead of emphasizing immigrants' second-class place in American society, they began to describe and promote the idea of Mexicans as only temporary workers with no permanent status in the country. The emergence of this idea—drawn from earlier academic writings that referred to Mexicans' migratory patterns, as well as previous arguments made during the statehood debates about the short-term presence of Mexicans in Arizona—grew and spread during the postwar years.

CHAPTER FOUR

Marginalization Evolves

Image of a Temporary Worker

Carl Trumbull Hayden, born in an adobe home in the Arizona territory in 1877, was reportedly the first Anglo child born in what would become the town of Tempe. He grew up to become one of the longest-serving legislators of the new state of Arizona. Elected as a Democrat in the first year of statehood, Hayden became Arizona's sole representative to the U.S. House of Representatives and then a senator in 1927, serving until age ninety-one. A shy sort and considered a "workhorse" in the halls of Congress, Hayden actively supported his constituents, especially farmers. He supported them long before he ever ran for office when he lobbied on their behalf concerning various irrigation projects. He later came to the aid of corporations such as the Goodyear Tire and Rubber Company, which ran the first large-scale farm of the state's soon to be famous Pima cotton.

To help his agricultural constituents and appease the growing fans of immigration restriction, Hayden promoted temporary legislation designed to permit Mexican laborers to enter the nation on an interim basis: the idea was that they would provide their labor for a brief stint and then return home. While Hayden likely was not threatened by the potential cultural impact of these immigrants—having gone to school with "Mexicans" and speaking "schoolboy Spanish" as a child—he believed that keeping the door to Mexico open would lower the American standard of living. Even so, because he—and the Arizona State Federation of Labor at the time—believed that no Americans in the Southwest would ever pick cotton, he did not favor outright exclusion, instead supporting a position that permitted Mexican workers to enter the country and labor in the fields, at least temporarily.[1] Mexicans could enter the country for work, but were not expected to remain permanently.

For much of Western history people have scorned those who migrate from place to place and job to job. In fact, Europeans believed that "gypsies," or Romani people traveling in their midst, possessed evil spirits. In the late nineteenth century, Arizona settlers, too, viewed nomadic Apache Indians as barbarians, in part because they lacked a fixed domicile. Prior to statehood, one of the arguments against Arizona joining the union was that it was full of itinerant men who, as such, were presumed to be poor workers, wild, and without morals. Americans viewed these itinerants as best left on the fringes of civilization. Words associated with impermanence—such as *temporary, rootless,* and *transience*—suggested a lack of belonging, and those who embodied such terms found themselves repeatedly excluded from civil society.[2]

During the final years before Arizona and New Mexico achieved statehood, those favoring marginalization had begun to view people of Mexican descent as easily marginalized from mainstream American society and under the control of their Anglo employers. After the 1910s, this sort of thinking fell out of favor due to world revolutions and associated fears of having a permanent and growing underclass, which might spark such an uprising at home. As a result, Americans began to side with exclusionists who argued that existing restriction laws should remain in place without exception, and opposed the extension of wartime immigration exemptions. Growers, however, desired more fluid borders so that they could retain a steady supply of workers, maintain low wages, and maximize profits. When their former arguments emphasizing Mexicans' second-class citizenship no longer proved persuasive, they stressed immigrants' temporary stay and lack of belonging in America. While such language occasionally surfaced during the prior struggles over statehood, the words did not resonate since comparatively few Mexicans emigrated during those years. But as Mexican immigration increased, growers and their allies found highlighting the immigrants' temporary prospects an increasingly effective way to persuade other Americans that Mexicans would not stick around long enough to harm America or to change it in any way. Many historians have noted how growers labeled Mexicans as temporary and "birds of passage" in their efforts to retain a ready supply of workers, but this chapter and the following ones emphasize how the linkage between Mexicans and a temporary status developed, grew, and spread over time. While previous historians have emphasized how growers promoted the workers' temporary status for expediency, the subsequent chapters show how Mexican and Anglo Americans, including growers and their political allies, journalists and academics, the Mexican and U.S. governments, and the immigrants themselves, contributed to the developing notion that Mexicans were in the country only temporarily.[3]

Origins of the Temporary Worker Image

The association of Mexicans with a temporary status began with the historical pattern of Mexicans' cross-border travel to shear sheep and perform other seasonal tasks in the years following the Mexican War. Few people in the nineteenth century studied or even commented upon the back-and-forth nature of this movement.[4] Some Arizonans mentioned circular migration during the statehood debates, but it was not something that was widely remarked upon or thought very important. In 1908 the labor economist Victor S. Clark published the first official study on Mexican immigration, in which he referred to Mexicans' cyclical pattern of travel. Mostly, however, Clark discussed how these immigrants fit into the nation in accordance with the dominant strategies of the day: marginalization (as then defined), pluralism, and assimilation. Clark's writing described the new immigrants as docile and approvingly noted their "willingness to work for a low wage" and to accept a primitive standard of living, and their lack of radical thoughts. Clark believed that these immigrants could safely enter the nation at the bottom of society without threatening national homogeneity and unity. To a much lesser degree, Clark also accepted that a few of these immigrants might integrate into the nation via pluralism or assimilation and become like Spanish or Anglo Americans. He identified some traces of European heritage among the new arrivals, observing that, "these laborers have acquired a certain vivacity of expression and demeanor . . . this Spanish manner varies in degree . . . and with the immigrants as a body is less in evidence." His writings suggest that while he was willing to acknowledge partial European ancestry, he viewed most Mexicans as not having a pure heritage and hesitated to consider many of them as Spanish Americans or as having the biological wherewithal to change and assimilate. He perceived these immigrants' class status, and thus their racial background, to be very different from that of the higher-class people of Mexican descent within the southwestern territories.[5]

While Clark was aware of the ongoing debate over whether or not to incorporate people of Mexican descent via statehood, his writings hint at a new way of viewing Mexicans. His work began transforming marginalization from a strategy aimed at turning Mexicans into second-class Americans into one stressing immigrants' temporary stay in the United States. Building on Delegate John Wilson's casual comments about immigrants' temporary status during the statehood debates (see chapter 2), Clark highlighted the significance of Mexicans' cyclical migration by noting that between 66 and 75 percent of them returned home. In contrast to European immigrants, Clark contended that Mexicans did not become members of the community and failed to "acquire land or establish themselves in little cabin homesteads." Neither, he argued, was their situation "analogous to that of the Negro in the South," which he did not explain but presumably meant something akin to second-class citizenship. Instead he asserted that Mexicans "remain[ed] . . . outside of American civilization," and observed that their willingness to travel from place to place to pick cotton and other crops fit well with their "half-subdued nomadic instinct." Clark's interpretation suggests that he discerned something genetic, natural, and un-American about these itinerant practices. He then concluded that the primary value of Mexican immigrants was in their status as "temporary workers," rather than as potential Americans.[6]

A few years after Clark's 1908 report, language regarding Mexicans' temporary status appeared in other writings. In 1911, the commissioner-general of immigration, Daniel Keefe, reported that the "Mexican peon laborer" worked in the United States, "return[ing] to Mexico for a period of rest, and later reenter[ing], and so on indefinitely." In this way he reiterated and bolstered the pattern first noted by Clark.[7] The author Wallace Kirkpatrick concentrated on laborers rather than immigrants but made connections between Mexicans and physical movement, commenting that a Mexican peasant was "by instinct, a rover" with "a fever to wander."[8] His words suggest that he attributed this behavioral pattern to something inherent in Mexican workers. The following year, Samuel Bryan of Stanford University extended this theme of peasants and migration to Mexicans when he criticized them for moving around too much.[9]

In 1911, the Dillingham Commission, chartered by the U.S. Congress to investigate all immigrant groups, published a report using language similar to Clark's, although few pages were devoted to Mexicans. The commission instead concentrated on securing sufficient evidence to limit or exclude southern and eastern Europeans, much as Congress had done to Asians in previous years.[10] When the voluminous report mentioned Mexican immigrants, it did so mostly in accordance with the extant version of the marginalization strategy along with some of the new perspective provided by Clark. Highlighting the previously developed notion of people of Mexican descent as harmless and controllable workers, the commission members described how Mexicans lacked ambition, did not try to acquire their own property or compete with other Americans, and instead worked primarily as unskilled laborers in mines, canneries, laundries, and factories.[11] Despite this docility, the Dillingham Commission detected some disturbing traits or practices among the recent immigrants. Specifically, the commission reported that Mexicans did not fit well—not even as second-class Americans—because of their lack of literacy, English-language skills, and disinclination to obtain an education. The Commission further noted immigrants' propensity toward crime and public relief if they lived in one community for an extended period of time. As a result, the Commission's authors concluded that, "it is evident that in the case of the Mexican he is less desirable as a citizen than as a laborer," foreshadowing the later promotion of Mexicans as only temporary workers rather than as potential Americans.[12] Like Clark, however, Commission members believed Americans had nothing to fear from the new arrivals as they expected that few Mexicans would stay in the United States due to their itinerant lifestyle.[13]

Agribusiness leaders also promoted Mexicans' pattern of returning to Mexico as a way to address exclusionists and other Americans' concerns about unrestricted borders. Because if the immigrants did not remain in the country, Americans would not need to worry about how to include them, or to fear that they would subvert national identity. At the beginning of the First World War, these growers lobbied the U.S. secretary of labor William B. Wilson for exemptions from the existing immigration rules, specifically from the 1917 literacy act, which mandated literacy and the payment of specific taxes and fees for entry. Secretary Wilson's decision to grant waivers from these requirements codified the immigrants' "temporary" stay in the United States, making the practice seem more common, real, and even natural through its very formalization. This decision had enormous ramifications since it allowed those favoring marginalization to accept the immigrants' labor without having to worry about the consequences of permanent settlement.

The above argument relies on the concept of "policy feedbacks," coined by political scientist Theda Skocpol. As Skocpol argues, policies are important for they both expand the reach of the state and affect social groups and identities, which in turn may then impact the state, resulting in additional policy changes. Wilson's decision to grant exemptions is an example of this in that his policy led to more Mexican immigration as well as a clearly stated way in which Americans could view Mexicans, and they could view themselves. This set of occurrences then resulted in a new set of policies, one of which eventually included repatriation.[14]

The rhetoric of people who debated Wilson's policy, the resulting articles in the Spanish- and English-language press, and the actions of the immigrants themselves all reinforced the growing notion of Mexicans as only temporary workers. After granting several emergency extensions for his ad hoc temporary worker policy, Secretary Wilson determined that once the Great War ended he could no longer justify exemptions from the literacy act without legislation to support it. As a result, Wilson and the agriculturalists turned to Congress for assistance.[15] In the first months of 1920, Congress members debated the continued importation of otherwise inadmissible Mexican agricultural workers for one more year.[16] The discussion over what was known as the Hudspeth Resolution centered on whether or not the immigrants would actually be temporary. If they were, then questions of incorporation or exclusion would not have to be considered. But if they did remain in the country, the familiar and sensitive questions over whether and to what extent to admit the foreigners would arise once again. Because many who favored marginalization wanted to avoid this type of debate, one that would undoubtedly lead to a greater restriction of Mexicans, they attempted to persuade their adversaries that the original exemptions under Wilson succeeded both in supplying growers with valuable labor *and* in getting the immigrants to return to Mexico.

As mentioned previously, Representative Hayden took the lead in promoting Mexicans' interim status. Familiar with the rhetoric from the statehood era, in which people argued that people of Mexican descent could become good second-class Americans under the control of their Anglo employers, it was not a major shift in outlook for Hayden and the growers he represented to modify the marginalization strategy slightly; changing it from one emphasizing a second-class American status to that of a temporary worker in the United States.

Hayden worked assiduously to convince his fellow congressmen that the aforementioned Hudspeth Resolution was itself only a temporary measure to address the immediate agricultural emergency. He further explained that Mexicans wanted to emigrate only until their country's political situation stabilized, and that after that occurred they would return to develop their homeland. Hayden used words like "temporary," "return," and "emergency," repeatedly during his testimony in front of the Committee on Immigration and Naturalization to emphasize why Mexicans had no long-term interests or rights in the United States. To reassure nervous politicians that the short-term immigrants would not stray from their initial employers, Hayden added that the growers in his state meticulously tracked the workers who entered under Wilson's initial exemption policy, and would continue to do so after passing the new resolution. To politicians concerned about extensive monitoring, bureaucracy, and the immigrants' lack of freedom, Hayden argued that the immigrants retained the choice not to come to the United States in the first place and added that, "as an alien . . . he had no right to do anything here other than that which he agreed to do," which was to work in a prescribed place, for a specific employer, and for a finite period of time.[17]

Other Arizonans followed Hayden's lead and promoted the image of Mexicans as only temporary workers. William H. Knox, the head of the Arizona Cotton Growers' Association, explicitly stated that he and fellow association members wanted the immigrants' labor only to help develop the Southwest and provide "homes for thousands of white people." He and his members were "not asking for the Mexican to come in here as a permanent resident. . . . We are asking only for him to come in here as a temporary resident."[18] These assertions, however powerfully made, were somewhat suspect given that a number of Arizona employers had been accused of pressuring immigrants to naturalize in order to circumvent the state's constitution, which stipulated that only citizens labor on public works contracts. Still, the growers' insistence upon the immigrants' temporary duration likely assuaged some legislators' concerns.

Regardless of whether these new marginalizationists believed their own language about the short-term status of the newcomers, their repetition of certain themes and arguments in the congressional debate fueled the rise of a mental image of Mexican immigrants as only temporary workers.[19] Representative Carlos Bee, a Democrat from Texas, who at times argued that he thought Mexicans could become good Americans (see chapter 3), believed that Mexicans preferred warmer temperatures and would rather leave Texas for far southern climes when the weather cooled.[20] Texas cotton growers also tended to support the proposed legislation, reassuring cautious legislators of how temporary the immigrants' residence would be. John Davis, an agriculturalist, informed committee members that passing the Hudspeth Resolution would not only aid American farmers, but also help to improve circumstances for Mexicans who "come over here with sandals on their feet," and return "with their shoes on." In saying this he also promoted the idea of Americans as modern and Mexicans as not.[21] Congressmen Claude Hudspeth and John Nance Garner, both Democrats from Texas, reported—although they supplied no hard evidence—that between 80 and 90 percent of the immigrants returned to Mexico after the harvest was in. Garner added that of the few Mexicans who remained, only 2 percent moved outside Texas, suggesting that the immigrants who stayed permanently would remain safely within the confines of one state rather than spread throughout the United States to compete with American workers for skilled jobs, or to endanger national identity.[22]

Various Spanish- and English-language periodicals reported regularly on these congressional debates and, in doing so, helped to feed and sustain the growing image of Mexicans as temporary. *El Tucsonense* (Tucson, AZ), a middle-class and conservative Spanish-language newspaper, remarked upon Wilson's exemption policy frequently enough to bolster the nascent link between the new immigrants and their temporary status. In a seemingly unrelated story, a prominent Mexican American called upon club members of his civic association to work with those Mexicans who were "simply passing through . . . enjoying the hospitality of the American nation."[23] Servando Esquivel, a writer for *Outlook* magazine and a member of the Mexican Frontier Committee of the YMCA, stressed Mexicans' temporary prospects in the states even as he requested that more be done for them while in the country. He argued that the workers should obtain some benefit in exchange for their hard labor, and called upon the United States to provide funds for an educational center so that Mexicans returning to Mexico could go back with more than just the "*padrone*" idea as a model for citizenship.[24] A national journal, *Literary Digest*, emphasized the immigrants' migratory tendencies by reporting how many Mexicans returned home after the harvest season to "spend their wealth in easy living in Mexico."[25] A columnist for *Survey*, another popular magazine, emphatically asserted "Mexicans have no intentions of coming to the United States to reside."[26] The titles of the articles themselves often reiterated the notion that Mexicans were only temporarily in the United States, "Back and Forth to Mexico" being just one of an increasing number of colorful stories about Mexicans' circular migration.[27]

The immigrants' own actions further deepened the image of them as temporary residents. As several historians have shown, however long Mexicans may have resided in the United States, most of them planned or at least dreamed of returning to Mexico one day, waiting only until they had saved sufficient resources.[28] Few made any effort to become citizens due to the abusive treatment they experienced in the United States and the spirit of nationalism growing in their native land.[29] As historian Gabriela Arredondo shows, Mexicans lacked interest in becoming citizens of a state that segregated them, discriminated against them, and viewed them only as "Mexican" and never American. In response, Mexican immigrants in Chicago embraced a Mexican identify to unify their diverse community (in terms of class, color, and language as well as heritage) against the various "barriers of prejudice."[30] Efforts to coerce Mexicans to Americanize during the Great War backfired, further reducing their interest in becoming permanent residents. But even before the wartime pressure, the Dillingham Commission reported that of the 978 Mexican immigrants who had been eligible for U.S. citizenship during the period of study, only sixteen had naturalized and seventeen others started the process. The commission further noted Mexicans' especially slow progress in learning English relative to other immigrant groups.[31] Their citizenship decisions suggest that Mexicans separated where they worked from what they considered to be their home. As Eric Meeks finds on the border, it seems that Mexicans were making decisions about work and not necessarily ones about national identity.[32] The ongoing trend of low naturalization—with less than 5 percent of Mexican immigrants naturalized in 1920—only solidified the idea of them as temporarily in the United States because, initially, they had hoped to be short-timers as well.[33]

The immigrants' lodging in the United States likely reinforced their temporary status in their own minds as well as in those of the general public. Some of the first Mexicans, who immigrated to work on the railroads, moved frequently and in a serial fashion as they transferred from one boxcar home, supplied by a railroad company, to another, and still another, so as to be closer to their jobs when they moved down the line. By the early 1920s, enormous boxcar communities had been constructed for rail employees, with the largest two outside of Kansas City (housing nearly 10,000) and Gary, Indiana. During the war years, so many Mexicans entered the United States, either through the Wilson exemptions or otherwise, that the workers found housing wherever they could, including within deplorable tent camps in Arizona, among the railroads' boxcar communities, in ramshackle hotels and basement units, or within the cramped rooms of rundown boarding homes. The even more desperate and resourceful slept in cars or local parks. These overcrowded communities bred germs and disease, including the dreaded tuberculosis that preyed upon those in close and dirty quarters. Employers justified the poor housing quality by noting that there was no better available lodging and that sanitation was not as dire as critics alleged. Regardless, the massive boxcar communities, as well as the tent camps in Arizona, announced to everyone that Mexicans would not and should not be in the country for long. More permanent structures would not be necessary if the immigrants lived in the United States for only a season: to harvest crops, earn some money, and return home.[34]

The growing emphasis on Mexicans' temporary status had some basis in reality. Employers ended up returning nearly half of the immigrants they brought in—as stipulated by their contracts—via Wilson's exemptions. In March 1921 the Department of Labor instructed its participating employers to return "all such aliens then in their employ." By June of that same year the process was well underway, and the commissioner-general of immigration reported that 34,922, or nearly 50 percent of the 72,862 Mexicans who contracted for temporary work, had been sent back to Mexico.[35]

The statistics of their return, along with the writings and actions previously mentioned, all contributed to the public understanding of Mexicans as only temporarily present in the United States. As Anglo Americans continued to see and hear about Mexicans who lived and worked in the United States for only a short while—and who moved from job to job and town to town—they began to view them as naturally restless and rootless. The belief spread that any people who tolerated such an unorganized and unnatural lifestyle must be primitive beings and thus incapable of becoming Americans.[36] No longer were Mexican immigrants granted a marginal but permanent status in the United States. Once the rhetoric of transience took hold, Americans tolerated the physical presence and hard work of Mexican immigrants on only a temporary basis.

Was the Temporary Worker Fictional?

Even as the image of the temporary Mexican spread throughout the nation, there were signs that this notion was often more strategic than factual.[37] While many immigrants *did* indeed return to Mexico, a significant portion remained or later came back again and again, causing some Americans to question just how ephemeral the immigrants' status was. Representative John Box, the exclusionist Democrat representing East Texas and an opponent of Secretary Wilson's exemption policy, asserted that since Mexicans remained permanently in the United States: "The swinging door is seen to swing in only one direction."[38] Furthermore, although almost half of the imported workers had been sent back by June 1921, the Department of Labor reported that another 21,400 (29 percent) of those entering via the exemptions deserted for unknown locations. The growing Mexican *colonias* or neighborhoods in various cities made it clear that significant numbers of immigrants were establishing roots and staying longer than anyone originally envisioned.[39]

In part, this more permanent status was a consequence of the immigrants' own decisions. Even though few expressed any real interest in citizenship, they remained in the United States for better-paying jobs, more opportunities, and political stability. Their actions confirmed this as many of the imported workers deserted their initial short-term contracts in favor of more lucrative jobs outside of the agricultural sector. Although it was possible for an initial employer to transfer an immigrant's exemption contract to another company for the remainder of his term, more frequently the immigrants left without any notice. Desertion freed them to remain in the country as long as they liked, or at least as long as their presence went unobserved. Exclusionists opposed to the Hudspeth Resolution, which permitted the ongoing admission of otherwise inadmissible Mexicans, assembled an impressive array of statistics demonstrating how the immigrants, lured by the "bright lights of the city," often violated their initial agreements by remaining longer in the country than their contractual terms specified.[40]

Railroad corporations and other employers contributed to immigrant dispersal by moving them outside the American Southwest. This dissemination provided Mexicans with greater access to cities and jobs distant from the Rio Grande, but made it more difficult for them to return to Mexico. Often the distance and cost of leaving were prohibitive since the imported workers were sent to pick sugar beets in faraway Idaho and Michigan, or to maintain railways in distant Pennsylvania and various parts of the Northeast. When immigrants broke their contracts to work for another employer, their new boss felt no obligation to pay for their return as the original employer had been mandated to do. In most cases, so far as the current employer knew, the new hire was a legally admissible immigrant who did not have a limited term and requirement to go back to Mexico. Undetected, immigrants who skipped out on their contracts could remain long past the expiration of their temporary agreements, even permanently.[41]

The problems inherent in this temporary worker policy became even more apparent in the postwar years. By 1921, the U.S. economy had sunk deeper into depression. Job-hungry Americans returned from the European theater of war at the very same time as the federal government cancelled war-related contracts and the price of cotton and other agricultural products plummeted. Amidst this crisis, Mexicans were among the first to lose their jobs, often becoming destitute and dependent upon available charity.[42] Wilson's exemption policy had required that the contracting companies return their temporary employees to the border within six months, or whenever the extended contract expired, but employers frequently failed to do so because their immigrant employees fled before fulfilling their contractual obligations. Although some Mexicans may have desired to return to Mexico during the economic downturn, few had sufficient resources to do so. Instead they congregated in cities throughout the United States, hoping to secure jobs. The federal government had never committed to pay the immigrants' return passage and neither the original employers—who lost the workers' labor when they deserted—nor any subsequent ones felt any obligation to do so.[43]

Some immigrants wanted to remain in the United States regardless of their dire condition and the rhetoric surrounding temporary workers. Knox, the chief lobbyist for Arizona's cotton interests, explained that while in the process of transporting contract workers to the border, several Mexicans "deserted" from the truck. Clearly, some immigrants had a strong desire to remain in the United States despite their impoverished circumstances.[44] An immigration inspector in Denver found that the unemployed immigrants knew just what to say when picked up in local police raids. A typical response to interrogation involved denying that they had entered via Wilson's exemption policy and affirming their duration in the country for more than five years, thus avoiding deportation as a public charge. That inspector believed that Mexicans' interest in staying in the United States was so strong that it was futile to round them up and deport them because they would only attempt to return at their earliest convenience.[45] As a discerning Arizona inspector observed, all anyone needed to do to enter the country was "to simply walk across the line at either Morley Avenue or at the railroad crossing in Nogales, Ariz., without baggage."[46]

Some of these inspectors themselves contributed to keeping the imported workers in the United States. One such immigration official argued that it was expensive to send workers back to Mexico, costing about $120 per immigrant, not including the expense of a sleeping car fare, an attendant, and the time and effort to find the fugitive.[47] Other bureaucrats attempted to legalize literate contract workers by having them return to an immigration station with the appropriate head tax once they could afford to pay. In this way some immigrants legitimately became free to stay and work for whomever they chose. Savvy border inspectors understood that some immigrants had no desire to enter the United States temporarily and used the waiver policy only as a ploy to evade the literacy and head tax requirements.[48] A few of these officials took decision-making into their own hands and permitted even illiterate Mexicans to enter if they believed that they would make good Americans due to having respectable families or holding jobs. Although the majority of immigrants were men traveling alone, a significant number emigrated with their families, likely contributing to their interest in remaining in the United States as well as providing them with a greater appearance of stability, which Katherine Benton-Cohen has shown to be important for acquiring jobs. Despite the isolated decisions of a few bureaucrats, the commissioner-general of immigration reiterated the federal policy of admitting inadmissible Mexicans on only a temporary basis and within the framework of a limited-term contract.[49]

Employers, too, often worked around the official provisions of Wilson's waiver. According to the Department of Labor, managers easily dodged contract labor prohibitions by recruiting literate laborers in Mexico, bringing them in via Wilson's exemptions, and then returning them to the immigration office the following day to pay the requisite head tax, which made them legal to remain permanently. In this way the company owners evaded the applicable contract labor laws, which prohibited direct recruiting in Mexico, and gained access to a pool of legitimate immigrant workers who could remain as long as they liked. This ploy also saved employers from the hassle of tracking and returning Mexicans when they quit.[50] Employers frequently complained that they did not want to bear the cost of returning imported workers—some of whom deserted immediately upon arrival—when they had not benefited sufficiently from their labor. Often employers did not have any idea where their imported workers went, recording only "skipped" or "deserted" in their voluminous ledgers. Few bosses had the time or inclination to watch their workers at all hours while others worried about the practicality and legality of doing so. A spokesperson for the California-based Spreckels Sugar Company wrote immigration officials about the possibility of hiring guards to ensure that no immigrants slipped away in the night to seek more lucrative employment.[51]

While those favoring marginalization hailed the effectiveness of the wartime temporary worker policy in providing a supply of workers who did not remain in the country, there was much evidence to suggest that Wilson's exemption had actually increased the number of immigrants who stayed permanently in the United States. Ultimately this information helped exclusionists to table the Hudspeth Resolution, which would have extended Wilson's exemption policy for another year. Mark Reisler finds that in 1921, after the depression intensified and agribusiness took a financial beating due to a steep drop in prices, few growers had any interest in lobbying for additional laborers or waivers from restriction laws.[52]

Enforcing the Temporary Worker Image

Despite the increasing reality of many imported workers' de facto permanent status, the wartime temporary worker policy helped to create an image of *all* Mexicans as transient and only temporarily living in the United States. Consequently, during the postwar depression, Mexicans and Americans debated only *how* to enforce the immigrants' temporary status and return them to Mexico, rather than considering whether they should have the right to remain. There was no discussion that the local or federal government should take responsibility for providing for these workers in their current locations throughout the country. There was no question of assisting them in becoming U.S. citizens. Instead, policy debates centered solely on the immigrants' temporary stay and lack of belonging in the United States. Even many Mexicans who had every right to remain permanently—because they had entered the country legally, paying the full head tax and meeting the applicable literacy requirement—became linked to this image.

By 1921 Mexicans experienced increased pressure to leave regardless of whether they entered the country officially, came in under the special waiver provisions, or crossed the border illegally. Upon losing their jobs, these immigrants commonly found themselves dependent upon the largesse of charitable institutions, former employers, or local governments for their daily survival: they lived in makeshift housing in crowded tent communities or slept in the basements of churches. Some of these immigrants then turned to Mexican consulates for relief, bombarding them with requests to return to Mexico where they thought they might fare better or at least be among a more sympathetic population. The consuls generally agreed with their petitions and worked to assist their constituents in moving back to Mexico.[53] The Mexican government covered the cost of transporting its citizens from the U.S.-Mexican border to the immigrants' hometowns. In a few cases it funded the entire repatriation from the United States, such as when one Mexican consul arranged for 110 Mexicans stranded in New York to return to Mexico via the *Antonio Lopez*, a Spanish ship.[54] Under pressure, the Mexican government also established a repatriation commission that, until the organization ceased in 1923, disbursed more than $250,000 to bring its residents home.[55] Some estimates indicate that as many as 100,000 Mexicans returned in the years 1921 and 1922. If this is accurate, more immigrants returned to Mexico than had legally arrived (72,000) via Wilson's waiver.[56]

When funds from the Mexican government proved insufficient to the task of repatriating destitute immigrants, Mexican consuls lobbied U.S.

and local government officials to fund the transit of Mexicans to the border.[57] Such entreaties were generally rebuffed. In one case the Mexican consul in Chicago, Francisco Pereda, appealed to Mayor William Hale Thompson for repatriation assistance, but city officials denied the request because they did not believe they bore any responsibility for immigrants they had not imported.[58] Other local governments and charitable organizations came to the immigrants' aid, but in the process reinforced the notion that all Mexicans were temporary. While these agencies sympathized with the immigrants' plight—organizing bread lines, bean lines, and finding places for the immigrants to sleep—they stressed that they could not continue to do so and that, moreover, the federal government needed to take responsibility for the results of its policies and return the immigrants to Mexico.[59] In Texas, the head of the Fort Worth Welfare Association reported that there were over 10,000 Mexicans without work and homes in his city. He recommended that immigration officials "arrest" the idle immigrants and immediately deport them.[60] The St. Vincent de Paul Society in Detroit gave up waiting for the government to do its part and relied upon its own resources to finance the return of approximately 400 people to Laredo, Texas, near the boundary with Mexico.[61] The City and County of Saginaw, Michigan, pooled their funds to send 200 Mexicans to the border in the hope that the Mexican government would pick up the cost and administration from there.[62] Mexicans in large cities, such as Los Angeles, faced repatriation too, although the drives to remove them did not rival later ones in the 1930s.[63]

During the early 1920s, the American press continued to report on the poor condition of the imported workers, emphasizing their lack of belonging and need to return home to Mexico. They noted that the immigrants' circumstances in Denver were especially dire in 1922, with over 3,000 unemployed Mexicans living in the city.[64] The Great Western Sugar Company in Denver took charge of housing about 125 to 150 of its former employees in basements, and the Denver Sunshine Mission administered to many others in a variety of ways.[65] Once the work vanished, newspapers portrayed immigrants as a serious encumbrance and recommended that they be returned to their former homes and lives in Mexico.[66] The situation in Denver had deteriorated to such an extent that the local district attorney suggested filling a train with destitute Mexicans and sending it to the border.[67] Although the conservative Alianza Hispano-Americana in Arizona was one of the few voices calling for Mexicans to remain in the United States, its reporting on the great exodus actually confirmed the growing notion of Mexicans as belonging only temporarily in the United States.[68]

Deportation, police raids, violence, and the threat of all three led many Mexicans to cross the U.S.-Mexican border. Government officials in Denver called upon the municipal police chief to address the problem of Mexicans, whom they considered responsible for increased crime in their communities. As a result, the Denver police chief raided pool halls and other establishments where he suspected he would find destitute Mexicans who had overstayed both their temporary contracts and their welcome in the United States. In one such raid in November 1921 he arrested three hundred people of Mexican descent, only thirty-five of whom admitted to having entered through the exemption policy and therefore subject to deportation.[69] Fear of these raids, and the lack of jobs, influenced immigrants' decisions to leave on their own terms rather than being forced out in accordance with someone else's schedule and without any of their possessions. One railroad agent in Colorado reported increased ticket sales to the border city of El Paso after stories of stepped-up enforcement spread rapidly throughout Denver's immigrant community.[70] In Texas, impoverished Anglos, frustrated with their own plight, attacked Mexican workers, warning them to leave the following day.[71] Such actions were widespread and made it clear that the immigrants' sojourn in the United States had ended, at least for the present. The swinging door had swung back toward Mexico.

By the time Secretary Wilson's exemptions from the immigration act expired in March 1921, the previously identified strategies for including people of Mexican descent—pluralism and assimilation—had lost credibility with most Americans (see chapter 3). Pluralism and assimilation no longer effectively helped people to imagine how the newcomers might fit within American society. Even the marginalization strategy with its more limited form of incorporation—of Mexicans as marginal Americans, permanently consigned to the most menial of jobs—no longer prevailed. Instead, those favoring marginalization learned that a more effective way to retain an open border with Mexico was to emphasize Mexicans' temporary status. Although exclusionists prevailed in tabling immigration waivers, those favoring marginalization avoided more heated and emotional battles over how and if Mexicans could assimilate by simply arguing that it was irrelevant because they would not stay in the country. When calls for Mexican restriction intensified in the middle to late 1920s, this altered strategy became the dominant way in which those favoring open borders justified the immigrants' continued presence in the United States. Rather than lauding Mexicans as docile yet solid second-class citizens, marginalizationists consigned them to a still more marginal place in American society as only temporary workers. Despite the fact that many Mexicans had entered without regard to the temporary provisions and settled permanently in the nation, Americans began to accept this newly articulated strategy—and the resulting mental image of Mexicans as temporary workers—as a way to sidestep seemingly irreconcilable conflicts over immigration.

The notion of Mexicans as transients or only temporarily in the United States—as constructed by growers, the state, the press, the Mexican consulates, other Mexican and Anglo Americans, and the immigrants themselves—brought serious consequences to all people of Mexican descent in the United States. Among the basic assumptions embedded within this temporary worker image were that Mexicans did not belong and were forever foreign. As Representative Benjamin Welty, a Democrat from Ohio, had so bluntly and critically stated in 1920, the immigrants would be deported "at the end of a bayonet" when their presence was no longer desired.[72] His prescient voice foretold the repatriation drives that commenced the next year.

By the early 1920s, then, a discernible shift had taken place from the days following statehood. Americans, tired of the former battles to ensure national homogeneity and unity, avoided revisiting them by emphasizing that Mexicans who immigrated to the United States would not stay for long. The idea was that Americans could reap the benefits of Mexican labor without having to consider inconvenient questions about how their presence might influence the country. By the time Wilson's exemption policies ceased, and even after it had become increasingly obvious that over half of the previously admitted immigrants remained far longer than anyone had presumed, the linkage between "Mexican" and "temporary" was well established and resistant to any evidence to the contrary.

While some Americans, especially reformers associated with religious organizations, continued their belief in assimilation throughout the 1920s, the primary narrative shifted from those calling for assimilation to the dominant culture or a pluralist incorporation, to that of a swinging door in which many agreed that Mexicans should be allowed to enter, but expected to leave after a short while, and especially during an economic downturn.[73] It was not that no one believed that Mexicans could become American, but that in the face of the increasingly unwelcome political climate—due to the growth of the eugenics movement and an economic recession—reformers who had supported Mexicans' greater incorporation into the nation now bought into the language of the marginalizationists and accepted or resigned themselves to providing relief and assistance for the immigrants' eventual return. Increasingly, the image of Mexicans became linked to one of temporary status in the United States.

PART THREE

Immigration Restriction Debates, 1926–1930

CHAPTER FIVE

Closing the Door?

By the mid-1920s, Americans and Mexicans well understood how a swinging door for entering and exiting America could work. In 1917 the door swung inward to the United States—allowing Mexicans to enter due to exemptions from contract labor laws and the new literacy and head tax requirements. During the 1921 depression, the door swung outward as many immigrants returned to Mexico as required by contract, via their own volition, or through a combination of financial assistance and pressure from Americans or the Mexican government. These immigrants had provided needed labor at a low cost, acted as a safety valve for the Mexican state whose leaders feared economic uprisings, and in many cases eventually returned to Mexico as desired by both the Mexican and American governments. Mexicans' brief or even continuous presence had not endangered American national identity since few became naturalized citizens and many had not remained in the country. Still, marginalizationists—those growers and their allies who argued that Mexicans posed no threat to national unity—had not persuaded everyone, and alternative strategies for ensuring national unity and addressing Mexican immigration persisted. Throughout the late 1920s increasingly powerful exclusionists, revived assimilationists, and a dwindling group of pluralists continued to promote their strategies for how to deal with immigrants while protecting national identity and unity.[1]

Exclusion

Exclusionists had every reason to feel confident that they could close the Mexican border since they had recently achieved many of their other objectives. In 1917 they succeeded in excluding virtually all Asian immigrants, imposing literacy requirements, and in implementing an increased head tax on all potential immigrants, which effectively reduced the total number of eligible legal entrants. A few years later exclusionists convinced Americans that the continued influx of European immigrants was still too high. In both 1921 and 1924 they passed additional restriction bills that reduced immigration to a trickle, especially from the southern and eastern parts of Europe, and that banned South and East Asian immigration entirely. Exclusionists achieved some success in restricting Mexicans as well by denying the continuation of the temporary worker policy, which had flourished during and immediately after the First World War. With their increased political muscle they then directed their efforts at Mexicans, whose presence was rendered ever more visible due to the decreased inflow of Europeans and Asians. The Democratic senator from Georgia, William F. Harris, had attempted to add the Western Hemisphere to the 1924 restriction bill, but his proposal failed 60–12 because few senators then worried as much about Mexicans as Europeans, and since exclusionists likely knew that they needed Western senators' support, who generally favored open borders for Mexicans, to pass European restriction. For the time being they were willing to compromise on Mexican immigration.[2]

Perhaps not surprising, exclusionists' success in decreasing immigration from Europe and Asia resulted in the unintended consequence of contributing to greater emigration from the Western Hemisphere, and especially Mexico. Continuing to face few employment options at home, Mexicans traveled in greater numbers to *el norte* to fill jobs left vacant by the declining pool of Europeans and Asians. In addition, during the late 1920s, refugees fled the outbreak of the Cristero War in central Mexico in which the Catholic Church and its followers protested the government's crackdown on religion and enforced secularization. These immigrants provided the labor to expand the production of cotton and also food crops, including sugar beets, persimmons, avocados, lettuce, and cantaloupes, throughout the American Southwest and Midwest. They also moved into the industrial cities of Chicago, Detroit, and Bethlehem, Pennsylvania, for better-paying factory jobs and settled into growing *colonias* or neighborhoods. There they put down roots by dedicating churches such as Our Lady of Guadalupe in Detroit (1923), founding labor organizations similar to Los Obreros de San José in Indiana (1925), and establishing Spanish-language newspapers like *El Amigo del Hogar* in the Midwest. Although these new entities regularly grappled with finances due to the transience of their patrons, their very existence suggests that Mexicans remained in the United States for more than a season.[3] And more were coming. Mexicans had represented only 3.8 percent of all immigrants coming to the United States during the decade from 1911 to 1920, but that percentage grew nearly fourfold by 1924—when 87,648 Mexicans represented 12.4 percent of all immigrants entering the United States—and continued to grow once European restriction laws went into full effect.[4]

As their numbers and visibility increased, exclusionists redefined Mexican immigrants as the newest and most serious threat to American national identity. One early observer compared the increase in Mexican immigration to a rising temperature on a thermometer, a dangerous foreboding of a virus embedding itself in an unwary host.[5] Taking note of such symptoms, exclusionists regrouped to protect the nation from this Mexican "menace" and to "close the back door."[6] Heads of patriotic and eugenicist organizations, labor leaders, and other exclusionists now advocated that the restriction laws applied to Europe and the Eastern Hemisphere in 1924 be extended to the Western Hemisphere as well, or at least to Mexico, which opponents argued was their primary intention.[7] Exclusionists successfully lobbied politicians to propose various restriction bills that the U.S. Congress debated extensively from 1926 to 1930.[8] These bills, introduced by members of both parties—sponsors included Congressmen Albert Johnson (Republican) and John Box (Democrat), as well as Senator Harris—all provided for quotas which would restrict Mexican immigration to approximately 1,500 to 2,200 entrants per year, depending on the particular proposal.[9] These numbers contrasted dramatically with the approximately 60,000 Mexicans who immigrated annually from 1926 to 1929.[10]

In working to pass this legislation, exclusionists adopted a twofold strategy. First, they defined Mexicans as not Spanish, not European, and not white, arguing that this made them even more dangerous and unassimilable than the recently restricted Europeans. Second, they then contested the marginalizationists' new claim that the immigrants remained only temporarily in the United States. They provided support for the first part of their argument by emphasizing the immigrants' mixed blood and Indian heritage, which exclusionists believed was antithetical to an American identity, and distinguished them from those they recognized as Spanish. The exclusionist editor of the California *Holtville Tribune,* Russell Bennett, asserted that the immigrants did not have more than a "dash of Spanish blood" and were, in fact, "Amerinds" rather than "Mexicans of Spanish descent."[11] William C. Hushing, a representative of the American Federation of Labor, testified to a congressional committee reviewing immigration that Mexican immigrants were "Indians" and not "of Spanish stock" while Robert F. Foerster, a Princeton University economist, reported that Latin American immigrants had 90 percent Indian blood. Consequently, Harry Laughlin, the eugenicist from the Eugenics Record Office in Long Island, called for only those Mexicans who had a pure Castilian (Spanish) ethnicity to be admitted into America.[12] These exclusionists worked hard to make distinctions between the recent Mexican immigrants and those they considered to be Spanish American, viewing the former as being of mixed race or Indian heritage and having a "peon" status, and the latter as white, European, and of a higher class standing. In doing so they demonstrated the lingering influence and success of pluralist efforts to assert the equality of Spanish and Anglo Americans during the statehood era.[13]

In fact, a growing number of Americans argued that the recent immigrants held a mixed or Indian heritage that was different from the Spanish Americans in New Mexico and other parts of the Southwest. In the magazine *Foreign Affairs*, Glenn Hoover summed up the distinctions between people of Mexican descent in New Mexico and recent Mexican immigrants, explaining that the latter were "almost all of the Indian type, and to this extent differ somewhat from the Spanish-speaking population in New Mexico, descendants for the most part of white settlers with but little admixture."[14] Policy makers in the Labor Department agreed with these assessments, noting that Mexicans were not of pure Spanish or Indian descent and instead held a mixed heritage.[15] The *New York Times* added weight to the argument by cautiously reporting that "it is commonly asserted that this older stock is almost pure Spanish, whereas the newer working element that has drifted across the border . . . is largely Indian in blood."[16] Because many Americans increasingly believed that the newcomers had a diverse or more Indian background, they became more receptive to exclusionists' proposals to close the border.

Advocates of exclusion also sought support for restriction by conflating class and race, suggesting that only Indian "serfs" would accept such migratory working conditions and miserable pay; according to them, no self-respecting white man of any class in the United States would do it. Norman Blaney of the California Farm Bureau explained that "a white man of any value at all, demands steady work to maintain their [*sic*] rightful standard of living."[17] Chester Rowell of *Survey* magazine found it astounding that while Europeans had been restricted primarily for "political and economic grounds" and Asians due to "reason of race," Mexicans, "to whom all of these objections apply," continued to be admitted. He added "the Mexican peon is racially as alien as the Chinese coolie" and less assimilable in his view than "the Balkan peasant." To clarify, Rowell explained that the "Mexican peon is not a 'white' man. He is an Indian." But Rowell differentiated between the recent Mexican immigrants and those of "Latin American culture" in Mexico City, whom he viewed as better than the peons at the bottom of Mexican society. Rowell's considerable emphasis on the class status of all the immigrant groups, as evidenced by his use of pejorative terms such as *peon*, *peasant*, and *coolie*, makes it abundantly clear that there was no room in his American society for this kind of an underclass or lower caste. Americans, in his view, were not only white and of European descent, they were also independent workers of a higher class standing.[18]

Other exclusionists agreed that class mattered in preserving American identity. The head of the congressional committee on immigration restriction, Representative Johnson, noted that "it is the peon type" as opposed to Mexicans from a higher class "that has been sucked into the United States in large numbers since 1917," and on that basis Johnson supported the restriction of immigrants from Mexico.[19] A Republican representative from Maine, Wallace White, opposed restricting immigrants from Canada on class grounds because Canadian immigrants, who immigrated in equal numbers to Mexicans, soon naturalized and became "an integral part of our body politic." He noted that in contrast to Mexican immigrants, Canadians "are doctors, lawyers, merchants, skilled mechanics—they are men of industry, sobriety, and are a worth-while addition to the population of the New England States."[20] In other words, because he believed that they provided skilled or professional labor, they should not be limited from entry. Class standing also infused the objections of a *Washington Post* article, which called for the restriction of the "Mexican peon" who the author believed possessed "poor material" for citizenship.[21]

The significance of immigrants' class status mattered even to such ardent exclusionists as the newspaper editor Russell Bennett, who unwittingly argued that assimilation was possible for Mexicans with a higher class standing. While disparaging the publisher of the *Beverly Hills Citizen* for opposing Mexican restriction, Bennett noted that the newspaperman lacked familiarity with Mexican field workers and instead "rub[bed] elbows with such Mexican cheap labor as Lupe Velez," the popular Mexican movie star in Hollywood.[22] Bennett's sarcastic language implied that he himself would not mind if Vélez, an attractive and presumably wealthy starlet, remained permanently in the United States. His objections were to the low-wage Mexican workers who, Bennett alleged, the publisher of the *Beverly Hills Citizen* knew nothing about. Although historian Rosa Linda Fregoso points out that there was some concern about the presence of Mexican actors during the Great Depression, it did not appear to faze Bennett.[23]

Other exclusionists believed that the immigrants' class status had harmed their own culture and would thus infect America as well. August Fast, a private citizen, supported restriction because he believed that Mexicans suffered from a culture of inertia, "Mexicans prefer to remain industrial slaves, they have no ambition."[24] Another exclusionist thought that Mexicans should be restricted because of their migratory habits, deeming them too "transient" to become American. A newspaper publisher agreed, arguing that it was impossible to assimilate the "mostly nomadic" Mexicans.[25] Labor leader William Hushing also perceived the Mexican immigrants as lacking in the drive for upward mobility. He saw them as nothing more than "a roving class," incapable of establishing permanent homes. These exclusionists felt that Mexicans' lower-class standing would prevent them from becoming American because they lacked stability, were not independent workers, and did not have the goal to become so.[26]

A few exclusionists did not care about the race, class, or culture of the immigrants and opposed their entry simply because of their nationality and the opportunistic policies of the Mexican government. Romano Herrera, a representative for Mexican American day laborers, submitted letters written in Spanish and translated into English to the commissioner of immigration to protest the presence of Mexican immigrants in Laredo, Texas. These letters decried the American government's decision to allow Mexican immigrants to work in the United States, thereby lowering Americans' wages, while the Mexican government refused to reciprocate and permit Americans to work in Mexico. Herrera's complaints were not based on how the newcomers would integrate into American society—after all, they shared the same language, ethnic heritage, and class status—but rather on the injustice of granting only Mexican nationals the opportunity to work in both countries.[27]

Even some Mexican officials held exclusionist views, contributing to the growing movement for restriction. These bureaucrats wanted to keep their constituents in Mexico, if for no other reason than to demonstrate that their revolutionary experiment was working. A number of Mexican officials feared that they were losing their best workers to the United States and that these immigrants would never return. Alfonso Fabila, a Mexican government secretary, lamented how Mexican immigrants pined for their return to Mexico, but became so entranced with their new opportunities for consumption that they racked up too much debt to leave.[28] At the same time as these Mexicans emigrated, some Mexicans expressed concern that foreigners from Syria, Turkey, Palestine, Lebanon, and China were arriving in Mexico with the potential to upset Mexico's own fragile national identity.[29]

In the United States, support for exclusion grew as Americans continued to worry about how unrestricted immigration would affect the country. While the leadership of the American Federation of Labor (AFL) initially avoided supporting restrictionist proposals, preferring to work informally with Mexican labor organizations to stem emigration, they joined the exclusionists' ranks in 1928 after other methods had failed to prevent Mexican laborers from emigrating. In addition, the governor of Arizona and the state legislatures of California, Arizona, and Oregon all went on record opposing Mexican immigration.[30] *Literacy Digest*, a national magazine, reported that the majority of its readers favored Mexican restriction; the *Saturday Evening Post*, another popular magazine with a circulation of nearly three million readers, regularly published articles urging greater restriction.[31] Furthermore, a nationwide survey conducted in 1930 demonstrated that the majority of its respondents feared the "Mexican invasion" and believed that "these people [Mexicans] can never be assimilated with white Americans."[32]

To bolster their case for closing the door, exclusionists contested the claims that Mexicans moved to the United States only temporarily, pointing to the growing "Mexicanization" evident in expanded *colonias* or "Little Mexicos" throughout the United States.[33] George Lorimer, editor of the *Saturday Evening Post*, observed that Mexicans were "pushing farther North" and "crowding in the slums" rather than departing as other Americans claimed.[34] Exclusionists denied that Mexicans returned to Mexico after a harvest season, and railed against employers who turned "Mr. Mexican loose to shift for himself," giving Mexicans the opportunity to take American jobs—apparently referring here to more permanent and lucrative factory work—or simply to subsist on local charity.[35] Another exclusionist warned how "CALIfornia [*sic*]" would soon become "MEXIfornia [*sic*]," and alleged that dramatic—albeit impressionistic—changes had occurred in his area's school population, which was "once 100 percent white, now over 80 percent Mexican peon."[36] The eugenicist Laughlin anticipated that Mexico eventually would reconquer and repopulate the American Southwest due to his claim about the increasing number of female

Mexican immigrants and their higher birth rate relative to Anglo women.[37] Still others such as Charles M. Goethe raised the specter of interracial liaisons and their impure offspring with his reference to "Guadalupe and Patrick, hybrids from an Amerind stock with a menacingly prolific birth rate."[38] Finally, Representative Johnson explained that while he heard much testimony regarding how the workers returned to Mexico, he had yet to see any documentation supporting this. Moreover, he noted that the AFL's recent decision to support immigration restriction suggested that Mexicans had remained in the country and now posed a threat to American workers.[39]

Through their various writings and congressional testimony against Mexican immigrants, exclusionists simultaneously increased Americans' awareness of the level of Mexican immigration and successfully promoted their views that Mexicans of lower class standing were incapable of becoming American. Many Anglo and Mexican Americans agreed with this assessment, and believed that being American meant having a pure or primarily European heritage, being an independent worker, and having a decent standard of living: criteria that they saw the newest immigrants as failing to meet.

Assimilation

Americans advocating that Mexicans could assimilate were harder to discern in the immediate postwar era. Hardly any testified in the temporary waiver or restriction debates, especially when compared to how active assimilationists had been during the discussions over statehood. The failed Americanization campaigns of the Progressive Era had taken their toll. Yet while assimilationists played less visible roles in the congressional debates, they continued to contest the exclusionists' vision that only northern Europeans could be assimilated. Via religious, academic, and reform organizations, they promoted assimilation as the best way to incorporate immigrants of Mexican descent and ensure national unity. Primarily they concentrated on changing and educating those Mexicans already in the United States rather than engaging directly in the battle between exclusionists and marginalizationists over whether to close the door to America. In doing so they inadvertently strengthened exclusionists' arguments that the immigrants were *not* temporary, for if there were Mexicans who were in need of assimilation, they could hardly be temporary. Moreover, assimilationists broadly agreed that Mexican immigrants who did not transform into Anglo Americans posed a danger to the country. Like exclusionists, they believed that effective integration depended upon having a European heritage—although they felt a southern or eastern European heritage sufficient—and either emphasized Mexicans' white or Spanish ancestry or expressed ambivalence about whether those who held a mixed heritage could fit within the nation. However, unlike exclusionists, they did not think that class status was permanent or foreordained, or that the immigrants were incapable of changing their culture; instead, they believed that immigrants—at least those who were not at the very bottom of the economic ladder—*could* improve their class standing and learn American ways.

Some assimilationists were Mexican Americans who worked to integrate newcomers into the nation by emphasizing Anglo American culture rather than a Spanish or Mexican one. The League of United Latin American Citizens (LULAC), a national organization initially established in Texas in 1928, was central to this effort. Ben Garza, president of LULAC, stressed the immigrants' potential American qualities and noted that many who had lived in the United States for decades believed that they were citizens even if they had never been naturalized; they thought it happened automatically, alongside cultural change. There was some historical logic to such thinking. Although Garza did not make this argument, the first people of Mexican descent who were annexed to the nation in 1848 *did* obtain citizenship automatically. Regardless of their *de jure* status as noncitizens, LULAC argued that the critical issue was that the immigrants considered themselves to be fully American. Garza agreed with exclusionists that Mexican immigrants were not in the country temporarily, but he saw strong possibilities for their participation in the country as U.S. citizens. He added that his organization educated immigrants on citizenship, patriotism, and the English language, and encouraged them to acquire additional education so that they "not only make a better living but they may make a more substantial contribution to the citizenship of our country."[40] Garza believed that these immigrants should not be condemned to remain on the margins of society, and encouraged them to modify their culture, become educated, and improve their class standing. He thought this possible because he viewed them as members of the white race and believed that, as such, they were reasonably entitled to an American status. Garza made his views on immigrants' racial background evident when he informed a congressional committee that it should not restrict Mexican immigrants because their labor was needed and "no other white race can stand it [the type of work]."[41] Two other representatives of LULAC, attorneys J. C. Canales and Alonzo Perales, also rejected restriction, arguing that Mexicans could become good Americans once they learned English.[42]

Apparently, however, not all LULAC members agreed with their leadership. The honorary president and general vice president of the league, C. N. Idar and M. C. Gonzales, complained that Garza, Canales, and Perales had not properly represented LULAC's position. They asserted that "immigration from Mexico is foreign to the general purposes and aims of the league, which is an organization exclusively based upon principles of Americanism." These members agreed with exclusionists that the border's door should be closed, but, like other assimilationists, felt that Mexicans already within the United States could be assimilated.[43]

The boundaries between the four strategies were fluid and LULAC members sometimes promoted them all. While some individuals stressed the difference between citizens and aliens, and conveyed an anti-immigrant or exclusionist tone, at other times writers suggested that all current residents could and should be assimilated and learn English and the dominant Anglo American culture. In still other situations, some LULAC members glorified their ancestors in a pluralist vein, making a positive distinction between themselves and Anglo Americans and recent immigrants. One such member warned readers that "the greatest care should be exercised to distinguish between the character of the citizen and the alien of latin-extraction," adding that at least with regard to Texas, "the real, true-blue 'Americans' are native citizens of this State of Latin extraction." The author further suggested a pluralist incorporation for long-term residents by stressing, as had New Mexicans during the statehood debates, that the "Latin-American" was the "first white race to inhabit this vast empire of ours." Still, it was clear that the author was not extending this august past to the recent immigrant.[44] Regardless of how various LULAC members perceived the new immigrants and restriction, it is clear that most agreed upon an Americanism rooted in whiteness and the English language—rather than one promoting a mixed heritage, the Spanish language, and a Spanish American or Mexican American identity—as the best way to achieve equality in America.[45]

Missionaries and social workers accepted the exclusionists' claim that the people of the United States needed to consider how Mexicans would fit within the nation because they were clearly not as temporary as the marginalizationists had alleged; but only very few became exclusionists. Protestant religious leaders generally preferred open borders as a way to evangelize and extend the reach of the church to more people, at home and abroad.[46] The prominent Presbyterian minister, Robert McLean, called for a greater effort to Americanize immigrants, contesting congressional testimony that depicted Mexicans as "rovers," and as a people who returned to Mexico. In his review of over one thousand interviews with Mexican nationals in San Antonio and Los Angeles, McLean found that only a few went back—and generally then only for the holidays.[47]

Reformers in religious or Americanization-type organizations generally agreed on the importance of Americanizing the immigrants who remained. But their advocacy of assimilation often conveyed some ambivalence or doubts about their eventual success; at times their views bordered on that of the exclusionists as some perceived the newcomers as not white and/or of a lower-class standing than previous immigrants. Don Lescohier, presenting at the 1927 National Conference of Social Work, worried that Mexican nationals possessed too much Amerindian blood, which he feared would make them incapable of assimilating. At the same conference in the following year, Charles Thomson also expressed concern about the "Indian blood" of the recent arrivals and how this heritage affected their intelligence, yet he seemed to believe that they could be assimilated if they were not so concentrated in one place. Still, in a separate publication, he called for restriction to prevent future racial problems.[48]

Even more than Thomson, other reformers such as Helen Walker also had concerns about the dominant U.S. population, wondering if they would ever learn to accept Mexican immigrants, with mixed blood or otherwise, as equals. If not, she felt that restriction might be better than admitting people who would be forced to remain in a second-class status.[49] Like Walker, the scholar James Batten lamented that many Americans opposed naturalizing Mexicans and at a conference on the status of Mexican immigrants warned that "90 percent of our citizens . . . consider him [a Mexican immigrant] merely as a 'labor commodity' and a temporary necessity."[50] At a time when few considered the immigrants as potential Americans, assimilationists faced an uphill battle to garner resources and support for their efforts.[51]

Few of the testifiers in the immigration restriction debates of the late 1920s shared the desire of the reformers in wanting Mexican immigrants to become fully assimilated Americans. One who stated that he did, E. K. Cummings, lived in Nogales, Arizona, a city that literally straddles the political border between Mexico and the United States. Cummings, as head of the local chamber of commerce, likely had an economic motive for his pro-assimilationist and anti-exclusionary views because open borders would make economic exchange across national boundaries much easier. Thus, Cummings asserted that "the better class of Mexican is a mighty fine citizen. I wish we had a lot of the better class of Mexicans in the State of Arizona." He further added that the Mexicans of Arizona were different from the migrants otherwise discussed in the hearings and testified that most of the Mexicans he referred to had a substantial European heritage with only "some Indian blood in him." When asked by Representative Johnson if Mexicans intermarried with "Americans," he affirmed that they did but again stressed that it was the "better class of Mexicans" that did so. He added that "their mode of living is equally as good as that of the average American family; their homes include every convenience."[52] Evidently, Mexicans with some financial standing, modern trappings, and the proper cultural inclination could buy their way into a greater European heritage and thus American citizenry or social acceptance.

Although reformers, some members of LULAC, and a few in the business community believed that the recent Mexican immigrants could integrate fully into the United States, their voices were in the minority. The aforementioned surveys demonstrate that most Americans did not want Mexicans to enter the United States permanently and become full members of the country. Subscribing to the exclusionists' ideas that the new immigrants were racially different from the Spanish Americans in New Mexico and higher class Mexicans, or posed a threat to the American standard of living, Americans no longer believed that Mexican immigrants could integrate smoothly into the national fabric and become like Anglo Americans.

Pluralism

While the Spanish American identity of people of Mexican descent was a key factor in the statehood debates, it rarely came up during debates over restriction. By the late 1920s, few pluralists attempted to extend their strategy of incorporation to recent Mexican immigrants. In fact, in some ways, exclusionists and pluralists joined together to define the new arrivals as outside of American national identity because of their perceived lack of European heritage and lower-class standing. Oddly, this convergence occurred around the same time that Americans became increasingly intrigued with their country's Spanish heritage.[53]

This "vogue" for all things Spanish proliferated as various authors glorified Spanish *padres* and their extensive mission work.[54] In 1926, Cleve Hallenbeck explained in his history of Spanish missions that the priests who had settled the American Southwest belonged to the Franciscan rather than the Jesuit order. This mattered, he explained, because the Franciscans did not follow or enforce the Spanish Inquisition's requirement to exile or otherwise harm infidels, and were more tolerant than their Jesuit brethren in the rest of Latin America. Consequently, Hallenbeck believed that these Spanish *padres* should be celebrated as the bearers of white civilization who taught and improved the indigenous people of the Southwest. Ironically, the same U.S. Congress that was working to restrict Mexican immigration approved funds for the commemoration of Spanish fathers who landed at the port of Long Beach, California. The purpose was to recognize and praise the "first white settlers" in the area, who had "introduced civilization to the Indians."[55]

Other authors, such as Sarah Bixby-Smith, also promoted a romantic version of the Spanish past in American history. In her memoir, Bixby-Smith waxed nostalgic as she recalled the lyrical Spanish names of the California towns of her youth, and the beautiful flowers planted in distant years by the long-absent Castilian *padres*. In contrast she remembered the living Mexicans as hot-headed, exotic, and migratory—people who materialized to perform the arduous task of sheepshearing and then disappeared when the work was done. She did not connect the Mexican laborers of her past with Spanish missionaries or any type of European ancestry.[56]

During the restriction debates, a few Mexican Americans attempted to forge an association between current Mexican immigrants and a Spanish heritage to minimize or erase any link to an indigenous past. Frank J. Palomares, manager of the Agricultural Labor Bureau for the San Joaquin Valley, argued that Mexicans could become like himself, a good American "of Spanish ancestry," since his relatives too had been "citizens of Mexico."[57] While Palomares considered his status to be above that of Mexican workers because of his elite family background and marriage with an Anglo woman, he made an effort to improve immigrants' lives and likely recognized that racism directed toward them might some day be directed at him as well. But he was one of only very few Americans to extend the pluralist strategy to newcomers. Even so, his practice of recruiting Mexicans to work in low-wage picking jobs and to live in company camps suggests something more akin to his employers' marginalizationist leanings.[58] Other people of Mexican descent, like those belonging to Club Latino in Arizona, were sympathetic to the suffering and condition of new arrivals but made clear distinctions between themselves, the long-term *hispano americanos*, and *mexicano* newcomers.[59]

Despite their increased attraction to Spanish culture and history, Anglo Americans were less willing to associate Mexican immigrants with this ancestry than they had been during the years preceding statehood. This was primarily because most of the newcomers came from a lower-class standing, while the *nativos* living in prestatehood New Mexico, and to a lesser extent Arizona, had been comparatively better off and more established. Conflating class and race, Anglo Americans perceived the recent Mexican immigrants as *mestizos*, or Indians, rather than as the descendants of dashing *conquistadores* and virtuous missionaries. They made racial distinctions between Spanish Americans, whom they accepted as racially white, and the recent immigrants, whom they saw as dark skinned and presumed to be the progeny of Indians or mixed parentage. Some Anglos reported that people with a Spanish heritage had been better able to fit within the nation because of their white race. One Anglo woman explained her understanding of the variation between the groups to the economist Paul S. Taylor: "The Spanish are a higher type than the Mexicans, use better language, and are better dressed."[60] An Anglo cattleman from Texas sympathized with the upper-class people of Mexican descent who were denied service at hotels, for "they are really Spanish and white, but the laborers are Indians."[61] A track foreman also understood the difference, explaining that Mexicans could remain in the United States but would have to live and be educated separately from Anglos, whereas he found that "the Spanish are all right; they are our equals. But we would not mix with the Mexican Indians."[62] Hushing, the aforementioned AFL representative, testified clearly that Mexican immigrants were "not the same type as the Spanish Americans who have testified here recently."[63] Hushing was referring to several LULAC members mentioned previously who, as attorneys and businessmen, held a middle-class status.

Despite the benefits that might ensue, the newest immigrants also did not claim a Spanish identity or assert that they were racially white. While one immigrant acknowledged, "I used to say that I was Spanish," others recognized the benefits in the late 1920s of allying closely with Mexico and its local consulates, even to the extent of wearing buttons proudly asserting themselves as *Ciudadanos de Mexico* ("citizens of Mexico"). These recent immigrants embraced the discourse of the Mexican Revolution and perceived themselves as Mexican—a people who prided themselves on their mixed European and indigenous heritage—rather than as a people with pure Spanish lineage.[64] Indeed, the economist Taylor discovered that some upper-class Mexicans and immigrants were offended at being described as Spanish. To them, this label highlighted the heritage of imperialism and conquest and the prerevolutionary emphasis on a European identity rather than a *mestizo* or Mexican one, which they then preferred.[65]

Pluralists had not expanded their vision for incorporation much beyond what existed when New Mexico and Arizona became states in 1912 and was virtually absent from the national debates over immigration restriction. While some of their ideas still lingered, few articulated this vision as a possibility for the newly arriving Mexican immigrants. Since most Mexican immigrants in the 1920s came from the lower classes, few Anglos were willing to regard them in the same way that they thought of the educated, upper-class Spanish Americans they knew from New Mexico and a few other pockets of the Southwest. While a few Mexicans claimed a Spanish heritage to improve their opportunities in the United State, most recognized this action as futile, or had little interest in claiming such an ethnicity. Likewise, those pluralists who claimed a Spanish American identity for themselves made few efforts to share this identity with newcomers. Thus, the pluralist strategy of belonging, which had opened and retained a space for some long-term residents of Mexican descent in the American nation, could not be practically extended to the masses of Mexican immigrants in the 1920s.

Despite the growing success of the marginalization strategy, specifically with regard to immigrants' temporary duration in the United States, Mexican and Anglo Americans continued to debate alternate strategies of exclusion, assimilation, and pluralism as they sought to deal with new arrivals and ensure national unity. To most of these Americans, being American necessitated a European or white heritage and an accommodation to the dominant Anglo American culture. Increasingly, important topics in the debates were an awareness of the new arrivals' working-class background, and the argument that being American entailed having a certain standard of living. Few Americans believed that Mexicans, willing to do the least desirable jobs for low pay, possessed the necessary drive to advance beyond a menial existence. In addition, the growing image of Mexicans as a people forever trapped in regular movement—from place to place and job to job—made the immigrants appear even less capable of becoming American. Consequently Anglo and even some Mexican Americans began to associate the newcomers pejoratively with poverty, movement, and transience. This discourse merged well with the strategy espoused by marginalizationists—that Mexicans would not threaten the meaning of

American identity because they would not remain long enough to do so. By 1930 exclusionists and assimilationists had succeeded in bringing national attention to the related issues of Mexican immigration and assimilation, but even as they did so marginalizationists continued to influence the contours of the debate such that the door to America remained open and swinging, back and forth, to admit and eject Mexicans as needed.

CHAPTER SIX

Promotion of the Temporary Worker

By the mid-1920s, advocates for closing America's borders to those from outside northwestern Europe succeeded in drastically reducing the admission of Asians and many Europeans into the United States. In the process they amassed substantial national influence, overwhelming the voices of assimilationists who claimed that new immigrant groups could integrate seamlessly into American society. Following this success, exclusionists worked to persuade Americans that Mexican immigrants, like those from Asia or outside of northwestern Europe, lacked the requisite traits to become full Americans because they were of mixed racial heritage, belonged permanently to the lowest economic class, and adhered to a primitive culture. For all these reasons, exclusionists believed that Mexicans could not be assimilated and should be excluded much as other immigrant groups had been; thus, they proposed that the new European quota laws be extended to Mexico, thereby decreasing Mexican immigration by more than 95 percent.[1]

Despite exclusionists' success in portraying Mexicans as un-American, they failed to define them as a permanent threat to the nation. Growers, or marginalizationists who advocated for an open border, borrowed the exclusionists' language, denigrating Mexicans' migratory culture, to make the case that Mexicans would do no harm since they would not remain long enough to inflict any damage to the country. Ultimately, Congress rejected all of the exclusionists' restriction bills during the years 1926 to 1930.

Robert Divine explains these failures as being due to nascent pan-American relations and fears of offending Mexico, an important trading partner; more recently, Mae Ngai has added that the Great Depression and increased enforcement of existing immigration laws—including the head tax, literacy test, and contract labor prohibitions—effectively reduced Mexican immigration, rendering the passage of restriction laws moot.[2] Yet these factors alone do not fully explain the failure to restrict Mexicans from entering into the United States. The growing dominance of those who promoted marginalization as the best strategy for incorporation—and its appeal for Americans who desired to balance concerns about Mexicans' cultural influence and the American standard of living, against that of the benefits of Mexican labor—also factored into keeping America's door swinging open.

Those who favored marginalization, including growers, industrial employers, and their political allies, generally agreed with exclusionists that Mexicans could not become full Americans: they perceived Mexicans as being of mixed heritage, dependent, lacking in aspiration, and overall a people with an inferior culture. But unlike exclusionists, they did not care or think it mattered. Instead, they asserted that these immigrants would live in the nation only temporarily—to provide needed labor—and then return to Mexico. Moreover, if a few did remain, they would not subvert U.S. national homogeneity and identity or affect other industries because they would remain safely under the control of their American employers, staying marginalized from the rest of society. Created during the statehood era and growing rapidly during and after the First World War, this marginalization strategy became the dominant way for explaining how new immigrants would fit within American society: they would not. Instead, they would be encouraged to enter and work in the lowliest jobs and then expected to keep to themselves or leave.

Promoting the Temporary Worker

Many historians have noted Mexicans' temporary status within the United States and how Americans promoted it, but they have not fully developed how this idea gained credence, discussed the varied groups who participated in its creation, or the growing pervasiveness of this strategy.[3] By the late 1920s, Americans largely accepted arguments in favor of Mexican immigration due to the shortage of laborers available for migratory, agricultural, and unskilled jobs at the current wages, and their belief that Mexicans would remain in the country only temporarily. As crop production in the U.S. Southwest expanded, growers increasingly experienced difficulty in finding sufficient pickers. Immigration quota laws, imposed against Europe and the Eastern Hemisphere in 1921 and 1924, further reduced the supply of workers. In 1929 the California Farm Bureau Federation reported that every year it faced more serious labor shortages.[4] In that same year, the U.S. Chamber of Commerce published a study concluding that economic development—including agriculture, railroads, mining, and factories—in the American Southwest, West, and Midwest would be severely hampered without Mexican immigrants. By 1930, the United States dedicated far more land to agriculture than thirty years before, but workers on this land were less than in 1900.[5]

This labor shortfall occurred, in part, because Americans preferred to do other kinds of work for higher wages. Between 1920 and 1930, 6 million Americans moved from rural areas to urban ones, eschewing agricultural jobs in favor of the steadier and more lucrative employment in towns and cities.[6] Employers advertised extensively for migratory laborers, only to find that few Americans responded, and even fewer took the jobs. Representatives for the Phelps-Dodge Corporation explained that of the Americans who had applied for mining jobs, most rejected the low-skilled positions, accepting only specialized or advanced ones. Fred Cummings of the Great Western Sugar Company in Colorado received petitions from over 3,700 farmers requesting more employees and concluded that this gap existed because educated white workers felt that they were above picking beets.[7] The president of the Utah State Agricultural College realized that the "American farm boy" aspired to be a manager and that the "average American does not want his own children or relatives to become exclusively or predominantly menial workers."[8] Similarly, J. T. Whitehead, the manager of a reclamation project in Colorado, explained that it was necessary to have a class of people performing the lowliest jobs that few Americans would do in order to "preserve Americanism." Presumably he meant that no American would, or should, accept less than middle-class standing in society.[9]

Other Americans agreed with these views and called upon Mexican laborers, frequently recruited in family groups, to perform the jobs increasingly defined as unsuitable for U.S. citizens.[10] Even as late as 1927, when Mexican immigrants gravitated toward temporary, agricultural, and unskilled work, the national American Federation of Labor (AFL) did not complain about Mexicans entering the country to perform jobs that few Americans saw as providing a decent standard of living and the kind of respect and autonomy they expected as citizens. The AFL was far more concerned about those immigrants who did not remain on farms, venturing to cities for better-paying employment and competing with Americans for more advanced positions. In 1928, when the AFL perceived more immigrants as staying and competing with American workers for jobs, the union changed its stance and opposed ongoing immigration.[11] This prejudice then provided a rationale for why Mexicans could not become American: real Americans never would have accepted such poor wages and working conditions. Real Americans did not hold—and would not accept—such a low-class standing and standard of living.

Gradually, Americans began to see a migratory lifestyle and temporary farm work as defining characteristics intrinsic to Mexicans as a group.[12] National newspapers picked up on the language and arguments used in congressional debates and academic studies and began to incorporate these words and ideas into their articles. A writer for the *New York Times* referred to the "transient laborers" who "drifted across the border" and explained "for the most part they [Mexican immigrants] return to their old homes as soon as they have laid by a few hundred dollars."[13] In an extended essay to the *Los Angeles Times* in 1928, another journalist reported that, "regardless of America's need for them," the immigrants were going home to accept jobs on agricultural projects in Mexico. Still another writer summarized that a Mexican "can and does, for the most part, vanish back over the border again when he is no longer required."[14] The *Los Angeles Times* continued the growing trend when it suggested the development of a more equitable system for the Mexican laborer "when he is here," implying that he would not be so for long.[15] Likely even the growing proliferation of Mexicans traveling in automobiles assisted the association between Mexicans and a temporary status because the car enabled them to move quickly between one seasonal job and another, and presumably back to Mexico as well.[16]

In contrast to these transient Mexicans, Anglo and Mexican Americans then considered themselves to be white Americans who were independent and upwardly mobile members of fixed and stable communities. Increasingly, they regarded the recent immigrants as racially distinct from themselves, permanently of the lower classes, and as a migratory people who moved from job to job and place to place, with no real stability or belonging in the American nation or, perhaps, anyplace. As Mexicans left one location for a job in another, their nomadic practices made them seem perfectly equipped for the requirements of agricultural labor with its seasonal tasks. R. G. Risser of the California Vegetable Union explained that a Mexican immigrant was most appropriate for agricultural work because his "migratory character makes him fit into the needs of each locality for transient and mobile labor."[17] In short, itinerant work became something that Mexicans did and Americans did not.

Those favoring marginalization found Mexicans more desirable than Puerto Rican, Filipino, or black laborers because of the ease with which they could be sent away. These other groups either faced greater distances to travel to return home, and/or held more rights as Americans. These groups' permanence in the nation helped those advocating marginalization to strengthen their arguments for hiring the presumably temporary—and therefore more desirable—Mexican immigrants. Ralph Taylor of the Agricultural Legislative Committee of California argued that if Mexicans could no longer enter the country, the "vacuum" might be filled by the "Porto Rican negro [*sic*]," people he saw as a greater threat to the nation than temporary Mexicans.[18] E. J. Walker of the Central Chamber of Agriculture and Commerce summed up the stance of many growers with his assessment of the problem when he noted that the "Porto Rico negro" was an American citizen who "becomes a fixture," whereas "an alien is returnable to his own country."[19] Walker and other employer representatives conceded some rights and claim of belonging to Puerto Ricans but extended no such courtesy to the Mexicans they hired.[20]

Initially, growers in the Southwest hoped that Puerto Rican migration would ease their labor shortage and arranged in 1926 for 1,100 workers to be transported from the island. This experiment ended disastrously as the Arizona Cotton Growers' Association found their new employees too demanding—the association's representative complained that Puerto Ricans expected to be taken care of, and then insisted upon being returned to their native isle when certain wages and conditions failed to materialize.[21] Reporting on this incident, the *Pittsburgh Courier* noted that "a horde of unfortunate black men, women, and children" were promised free transit from Puerto Rico to Arizona, as well as decent wages and living conditions; instead, the growers' association charged them $66.50 for their transportation, an additional amount for meals, and then tried to pay them less than the prevailing wages from the preceding year. Because Puerto Ricans refused to work under such unjust terms, the growers' association moved the migrants into the state fair grounds in Phoenix "without proper food or shelter in an attempt to force them into submission."[22]

Eventually these unfortunate Puerto Ricans made it to Texas, where they appealed for assistance. There, Mary Wood of the United Charities of Galveston requested financial help from the U.S. House of Representatives' Committee on Immigration and Naturalization for the destitute petitioners from Arizona. According to Wood, the migrants did not have jobs, did not speak English, and needed money for the cost of a steamer back to the island. The committee refused to cover these expenses by explaining that the Puerto Ricans, as American citizens, could not be deported and therefore the government bore no responsibility to pay for their return.[23] While the Arizona press expressed sympathy for the Puerto Ricans' plight, it was clear that the editors did not want any more of them to enter the state when they argued "any further entry of these people should be prevented."[24] Local growers agreed and began touting the merits of Mexican laborers who held no rights of citizenship, and who generally left at their own expense.

Filipinos, as colonial subjects or "nationals," might have filled the void, but few growers relished the idea of Filipinos taking the available agricultural jobs. Like Puerto Ricans, Filipinos lived too far away for most to afford to leave on their own, and they could not readily be sent away because their colonial status granted them the right to remain permanently and move freely throughout the United States and its territories.[25] In part because of these rights, as well as the colonial connection, Filipinos reportedly learned English quickly, intermarried with white or black Americans, organized strikes against unfair pay and working conditions, and moved on to more lucrative jobs and positions whenever they could. Contemporary congressional testimony shows that Americans feared Filipinos' ability to displace them from good jobs and businesses and did not want to encourage more of them to migrate across the Pacific. Outside of Congress, newspapers also played to fears regarding interracial liaisons and the specter of racial mixing with such salacious stories as "Mercenary Women Influence Brown Man's Ego" regarding Filipino males and white taxi dance hall girls who proffered dances for a fee. According to several of these articles, Mexicans provided the preferred menial labor since "the Mexican when finished serving the agriculturist or orchardists, returns to Mexico to await the next seasonal work" as compared to the Filipino, a "continual glut in the market."[26]

Southwestern and midwestern employers also avoided hiring black Americans from other parts of the country. As with Puerto Ricans and Filipinos, African Americans could not be so easily removed from an area. Their employment posed other problems since agriculturalists worried that they would be "pirating [workers] between sections [of the U.S.] and industries" and that the "negroes would create a much larger social problem and school problem than do Mexicans since the latter are not American citizens and a very large percentage of them return annually to Mexico."[27] Employers feared that after the seasonal work had ended, African Americans would remain in the community and become dependent upon local charity. Again, it was the very permanence of black Americans that made them less desirable than Mexicans.

Agriculturalists and their political allies preferred Mexican laborers precisely because they lacked rights and protection under the law. Growers perceived Mexicans as short-timers with little interest in competing with Americans or remaining within the United States. The president of the *Los Angeles Times*, Harry Chandler, testified that Mexicans were "not enterprising like other races, but are more desirable from our standpoint."[28] Fred Hart of the California Farm Bureau agreed, explaining that Mexicans did not compete with Americans as other groups did since "you don't find the Mexican buying land and settling down and doing those things."[29] Chandler added that few Mexicans interacted with other Americans—in terms of where they chose to live or whom they chose to marry—or attempted to naturalize. "Mexicans do not come here to live, they do not come here to mix . . . They keep to themselves."[30] George Clements of the Los Angeles Chamber of Commerce went even further, asserting that even if Mexicans did remain, there was an easy solution for "in any event, he is an alien, which offers the possibility of relief should we desire it through deportation" as had occurred previously during the early 1920s.[31] Clements understood that Mexican laborers remained only at the whim of the American people; they did not belong in the nation and could be removed whenever so desired.

By the mid-1920s, marginalizationists recognized the advantages in promoting Mexicans as temporary inhabitants rather than as potential second-class or subordinate Americans. Still, observing that some Mexicans did not return to Mexico, a few marginalizationists continued to stress that immigrants who remained would not threaten the nation since these newcomers would be satisfied to stay on the bottom rung of society's ladder. One Arizona farmer testified at a congressional hearing that although he was not sure whether Mexicans made good citizens or not, he believed that they made "passable" ones.[32] A sugar beet grower informed legislators that Mexicans generally "drift[ed] back," but that if they stayed they were only "worker[s] and never will be anything else."[33] A Texas farmer argued that the immigrants generally returned but when they did not he noted that "I think Texans [meaning Anglo Americans] . . . feel satisfied that they are fully capable of maintaining their superiority over the Mexican."[34] A representative of the El Paso Chamber of Commerce agreed, explaining that while half of the city's residents were Mexican (presumably of Mexican descent), "the Mexican is not in any way controlling the institutions or retarding the Americanization of the city of El Paso."[35] In other words, Mexicans would not slow America's progress.

Marginalizationists strengthened the nascent idea of Mexicans as only temporarily living within the United States by bombarding Americans with anecdotes and statistics regarding the immigrants' interim status. Chandler testified that "a large number of them [Mexicans] come in automobiles and then they drive home."[36] In close questioning by skeptical legislators, employers asserted that when Mexicans left they returned to Mexico rather than taking jobs in other parts of the country. Representative John Garner (Democrat) of Texas assured fellow legislators that "80 percent of the Mexicans that come over for temporary work go back" since "all they want is a month's labor in the United States, and that is enough to support them in Mexico for six months."[37] The Central Chamber of Agriculture and Commerce in El Paso reported that 80–90 percent of Mexicans returned.[38] A resolution submitted by the Anaheim, California, Union Water Company informed Congress that Mexicans were "temporarily resident in the United States," with "most of the laborers returning home at the close of the harvest season."[39] Many others concurred, repeating these or even larger percentages of the number of Mexicans who had left. Few provided any hard data. Statistics were slippery and reliable data difficult to find. While the U.S. immigration commissioner reported few cases of immigrants returning to Mexico in his annual reports, Mexican officials cited a much higher number.[40] In any case, the incessant repetition of the claim that the immigrants were leaving reinforced the idea of Mexicans as only temporarily present in the United States, making it easier for marginalizationists to keep the door to America swinging open.

Writing the Temporary Worker into Law

Few marginalizationists were as active as Congressman Carl Hayden in defining Mexicans as temporary. Hayden did not merely promote this idea but also called for the codification of the existing back and forth practice into an official temporary worker program. Although serious problems existed with a similar policy during the First World War, which left destitute Mexicans stranded far from the border without food or work, Hayden believed it could be improved and that a German program offered an attractive model to follow. According to Hayden, the German state successfully imported Polish workers for seasonal work and then returned them before they jeopardized Germany's racial character or endangered "the

German standard of living or way of thinking." Hayden further emphasized "their temporary admission had no effect upon either the Government or the people of Germany."[41] He made no mention of how the Poles or the Polish state regarded this program.

Even an ardent exclusionist like Washington congressman Albert Johnson, who led restrictionists' efforts against southern and eastern Europeans in the early 1920s, seemed intrigued with the possibility of creating a temporary pool of workers. Politically astute, he recognized that this was a potential way to balance the labor demands of agribusiness against the concerns of those like himself who feared the changes the newcomers would engender in the nation and their impact on the job market. In debates over restriction bills, Johnson questioned witnesses on both sides of the issue as to what they thought about a temporary worker program; generally responses were positive. One factor that prevented Johnson and his followers from embracing this idea was their uncertainty over how to ensure that the temporary status would apply to the entire Mexican family without violating federal laws.

Johnson understood that the birthright citizenship clause in the Fourteenth Amendment to the U.S. Constitution, as interpreted and upheld in the 1898 Supreme Court case *U.S. v. Wong Kim Ark*, clearly conferred citizenship to children born in the United States regardless of the status of their parents. This decision posed a problem for him as he weighed the merits of a temporary worker program: immigrants could be sent back to Mexico per the terms of the contract, but their citizen children had the right to remain. Another exclusionist who sponsored restrictionist bills, Representative John Box from Texas, also demanded to know just "how is Uncle Sam going to force them into Mexico—those children born into the United States?"[42] Johnson wondered the same as he grilled program supporters in committee hearings about potential problems if they needed to remove children. He also queried them about the possible relationships that Mexicans might form with Anglos, and if there should be any prohibitions on interracial marriage lest such relationships tempt immigrants to remain longer than intended. Further troubling Johnson was how migrating families might impact temporary status as he pondered whether those who emigrated in family units would be more or less likely to return to Mexico.[43] This was a practical concern because, compared with most other immigrant groups, more Mexicans emigrated as families.[44] Clearly, the problems in devising such a program were in how to work around certain principles and details: how long the season would last, who would bear the cost and responsibility for workers' return, and how much could Congress restrict the immigrants' freedom in terms of movement and marriage. Ultimately, the difficulties overwhelmed Johnson and his fellow exclusionists who did not support or approve any formal, temporary worker program.

Despite the failure to establish such a program, the mere subject and discussion of it contributed to the growing discourse of Mexicans as temporary. Throughout this and other debates regarding Mexican immigration, agribusiness representatives, legislators, and other participants providing testimony frequently used language that referred to Mexican immigrants as *sojourners*, *homers*, and *rovers*, or *migratory* and *seasonal*, as well as *temporary* and *transient*.[45] Often those testifying did not actually know where the Mexicans went, or for their own purposes in retaining open borders may have preferred that the answer remain muddled and merged. In the final analysis, the success of marginalization as a policy strategy did not rest on whether some migratory workers stayed in the United States. What mattered was the marginalizationists' ability to depict *all* Mexicans as mobile and restless so that other Americans would not recognize the immigrants' growing permanence or the impact that their extended presence might have on America's presumed homogeneity. Although people questioned the accuracy of the marginalizationists' claims—that the immigrants remained only temporarily—the critics' use of the same language emphasizing Mexicans' constant movement and migration (in their efforts to disparage the immigrants and close the open door), only served to enhance the growing mental image of Mexicans as temporary residents.[46]

Although Americans, too, had a migratory history, they viewed themselves as settled, stable, and permanent while perceiving others who moved about—generally newcomers or people deemed foreign—as barbaric, unstable, and wild. This image was clear during the earlier struggles over statehood when legislators opposed to Arizona's admission railed against the territory because of its significant population of single, transient men. These mobile men, they had argued, lacked morals and the general attributes of civilization. Those who favored statehood emphasized that the people of Mexican descent who lived within the territories were exceptionally stable and thus imminently American. This former debate language made it less likely that Anglo or Mexican Americans would consider recent Mexican immigrants as potential or even second-class members of the United States. Their regular migration suggested that they did not belong anywhere at all.

But the simple truth was that *colonias* in the Southwest, Midwest, and even parts of the eastern United States *were* growing, demonstrating that the immigrants did remain and establish permanent communities.[47] By 1930, the Mexican population in Chicago surged to over 21,000, up from 1,141 residents ten years before. The sociologist Emory Bogardus reported that many Mexicans in California had become homeowners, suggesting that former immigrants settled permanently. The number of Mexican children on California school rosters likewise increased dramatically.[48] But the length of the immigrants' stay in any particular place and the precise meaning of "temporary" was rarely discussed or defined. While policy makers presumed it was of a seasonal duration, lasting three to eighteen months, immigrants understood their temporary status in very different terms, relating it to certain events or occurrences rather than rigid time frames: they spoke of returning to Mexico only for the holidays, or dreamt of returning permanently when violence in Mexico ceased or the economy improved. These amorphous plans for their return made it easier for marginalizationists to fight against various restrictive measures, for no one needed to explain exactly when the immigrants would leave, just that they would eventually do so.

Even American authors and scholars, who noticed the immigrants' growing presence, unwittingly promoted the marginalizationists' agenda. As they learned of Mexicans' ambivalence toward the United States due to the discrimination, segregation, and ostracism they experienced within it, they incorporated these findings into their studies and disseminated them throughout the nation. The scholar James Batten concluded that Mexicans "cross[ed] the border physically" into the United States but remained within Mexico "racially and nationally."[49] Sociologist Helen Walker reported that Mexicans were disinterested in becoming citizens and held "no desire to become a part of our body politic." She added that even those who held citizenship status were generally "peons" who avoided voting because they believed that they were "not part of the real America."[50] Even an English-language teacher, in a profession generally linked to Americanization campaigns, thought she was contributing to "international goodwill" by teaching English since she fully expected that her Mexican students would eventually return to Mexico.[51] In making such statements, these researchers and educators further developed the image of the immigrants as only temporarily in the United States.

But U.S. agricultural interests, their legislative allies, and a handful of American scholars did not alone convince Americans of the merits of the idea of Mexicans as only temporary workers: they received help from Mexicans as well. With so many Americans extolling their temporary status, Mexicans saw few reasons to think otherwise and pursue permanent residency or citizenship.

Mexico Promotes the Temporary Worker

The Mexican government and its officials did much to reinforce the image of Mexicans as only temporary sojourners to the United States. Though frequently embarrassed by the number of Mexicans fleeing the country—at a time when the authorities were trying to promote the nascent revolutionary state and prove that it could provide for its citizenry—government officials also regarded emigration as an effective safety valve: the immigrants' absence served to defuse growing economic tensions until the new leaders could resolve the state's economic problems. Immigrants also provided valuable remittances, an important source of income for the faltering Mexican economy.[52] Despite the recognizable benefits from their short-term absence, the Mexican government preferred that the immigrants remain connected to their homeland so that they would continue to send money and eventually return to rebuild the war-torn society when Mexico was ready to absorb them. Voluntary repatriation, at some undetermined date, was the ultimate goal.[53]

To increase the likelihood of the immigrants' continued allegiance and eventual homecoming, Mexican officials established *comisiones honoríficas*, or honorary commissions, to extend the reach of the Mexican consulates deep into the United States. In the early 1920s, as Jaime Aguila has described, fewer than sixty official consulates existed to serve 2 million Mexicans residing in the United States. Consequently, Mexican president Alvaro Obregón (1920–1924) encouraged the creation of honorary organizations—with the first one established in Texas in 1921—to help Mexicans to remember and think fondly of their native country. Under the official sanction of the Mexican consulates, these commissions offered various kinds of assistance to Mexicans immigrants, such as helping them to contest mistreatment by the police or their employers and to fight against incidents of discrimination. The commissions also sponsored nationalistic activities to maintain ties with the immigrants abroad, registering them with the consulate and offering classes in literacy, Mexican history, and the Spanish language.[54] They also established libraries which included maps, history, and literature, all emphasizing the greatness of the Mexican nation. In part these organizations provided such activities to counteract the Americanization efforts of similar groups, such as the Friendly House in Phoenix, which taught immigrants literacy and the English language. In the late 1920s a few consulates established private schools to further combat assimilationist efforts, as F. Arturo Rosales has shown, with some consuls going so far as to visit various *colonias* to urge parents not to permit their children to Americanize. By the end of the decade many honorary commissions had sprung up throughout the United States, extending the influence of the Mexican government well into *el norte*.[55]

Rosales further explains how, in addition to these honorary commissions, Obregón encouraged the creation of Brigadas de la Cruz Azul Mexican (the Blue Cross) to raise money for Mexican immigrants: Blue Cross members fed and clothed the impoverished and visited the immigrants hospitalized or incarcerated in the United States.[56] Although George Sánchez believes immigrants and their offspring held ambivalent attitudes toward the Mexican government, and that the consulates were not as effective as others have asserted, such efforts served to reinforce a family's connection with Mexico, and the notion that their time in the United States was only temporary.[57] The existence of the Blue Cross, honorary commissions, and Mexican consulates reminded Americans that Mexican immigrants belonged in Mexico and that they had little interest in becoming connected to the United States.

At the same time that the Mexican government sanctioned emigration, it also professed itself eager and willing to welcome the return of its citizens from the United States, and actually provided funds to recruit those with experience in the United States to establish farming colonies in Mexico. The colonization plans involved assisting returning immigrants with their transit home and grants of land and resources. Repatriates were expected to use their recently acquired knowledge to establish efficient and successful farms; these schemes, however, usually failed. The land proffered was usually of poor quality, the projects underfunded, and the immigrants provided with inadequate equipment and machinery to make the farms a success. The immigrants themselves, as former crop pickers in the United States, generally owned few resources and lacked experience in developing a farm.[58]

Various Mexican scholars and writers also enhanced the image of Mexicans as only temporarily in the United States with their position that all persons of Mexican descent, whether seasonal migrants, Mexican citizens in the United States for a longer duration, or even American citizens of Mexican origin, belonged to an "imagined community" affiliated with the Mexican nation.[59] According to Lore Diana Kuehnert, these writers desired and encouraged many of these *hijos de México* (children of Mexico), to return to Mexico, bringing what they had learned of modern agriculture, industry, work habits, and technology back to their mother country.[60]

Manuel Gamio, a prominent Mexican anthropologist, argued in this vein and recommended that Mexicans travel to the United States for experience but then return to develop their homeland. He further argued that such "transitory migration" would be beneficial to both countries, noting that, in fact, it was already occurring as his interpretation of migratory data suggested that few Mexicans remained in the United States.[61] Kuehnert argues that many Mexicans in the mid-1920s shared Gamio's viewpoint and optimistically regarded the returning Mexicans as "super-Mexicans," who had "undergone socioeconomic mestizaje [mixture]." These repatriates were expected to improve the Mexican nation by training their countrymen in the methods they had learned abroad. Such writings emphasized the idea that the *hijos*, no matter the length of their absence, were really a part of Mexico and would be welcomed whenever they returned. Some Mexican authors extended this argument to include even those who had never lived in Mexico but had been in the territory taken by the United States via the Treaty of Guadalupe Hidalgo. Despite this welcoming propaganda, the Mexican government did not have much success in getting immigrants to return.[62] Still, the discussion and encouragement helped to cement the mental image that Mexicans belonged in Mexico and lived and worked in the United States only on a temporary basis: they would always be Mexicans.

By the late 1920s more Mexicans were returning to Mexico, either because of financial hardship or because the U.S. government deported them. At this point the Mexican government openly discouraged their constituents from leaving Mexico because they did not want to finance their return.[63] They supported the efforts of the Mexican labor union, Confederación Regional Obrera Mexicana, to stem emigration, and required immigration officials to warn the would-be immigrants of the perils they stood to face in the United States. They also began enforcing a 1926 Mexican law, which stipulated that immigrants provide evidence of a U.S. work contract before receiving a travel visa.[64] In 1928, Enrique Santibañez, the Mexican consul in San Antonio, tried to do his part to discourage emigration by informing Mexicans of the lack of opportunities in the United States. He emphasized that Americans would not accept them as potential citizens, and consequently, Mexicans would experience discrimination and financial hardship. Santibañez argued against further emigration since he discovered that even when immigrants lost their jobs, they did *not* return to Mexico. Instead, they became like *nómadas* (nomads), looking for work wherever they could find it with no home or sense of belonging in either the United States or Mexico.[65]

With all their efforts to stem emigration proving fruitless, the Mexican government began to favor and promote an official temporary worker program, one mandating the immigrants' short-term belonging in the United States.[66] Bureaucrats believed that while the Mexican government was doing all it could feasibly do to stem the movement to *el norte*, it needed to make even greater efforts to discourage *nuestras compatriotas* (our compatriots) from establishing permanent roots in the United States. The editor of *El Heraldo Mexicano* called upon the Mexican government to establish a temporary work program in which American employers would be required to send workers back to Mexico; in this way Mexico would retain a pool of laborers to rebuild the country when it was in a position to do so.[67] Consul Santibañez concurred and argued that the best solution was for Mexicans to emigrate in accordance with a fixed contract-labor program, in which American employers would be financially responsible for returning the laborers to Mexico in a few months' time.[68]

Mexicans also helped to promote the image of the immigrants as only temporarily living in America by emphasizing that Mexico, rather than the United States, was responsible for the immigrants' welfare. *El Diario*, a Mexican newspaper, criticized its government and consulates for not helping immigrants with their poor living conditions, forcing them to rely upon private organizations or *mutualistas* to resolve serious problems. While one Mexican journalist called upon other local organizations in the United States—such as independent schools and job placement organizations—to help the indigent, he did not make similar demands upon any level of American government: he believed that the emigrants did not belong in the United States for the long term, and that Mexico was primarily responsible for their welfare.[69] When the Mexican government attempted to get *mutualistas* and charities in the United States to pay for the immigrants' return, many Mexican citizens berated their government for not doing more to help the impoverished repatriates who flooded their border communities.[70] Important elements of Mexican society strengthened the marginalizationists' argument that Mexican immigrants moved to the United States only temporarily and that the nation to which they belonged was Mexico.

Mexican Immigrants Sustain the Image of a Temporary Worker

Some Mexican immigrants in the 1920s, as shown by F. Arturo Rosales and Eric Meeks, regarded their sojourn to America as temporary and expressed no interest in assimilation.[71] Whether or not they ended up leaving, these immigrants spoke openly and frequently of returning to their *patria* or homeland. One septuagenarian explained that he recently immigrated to the United States but intended to stay only until he could afford to purchase a barbershop back in Mexico.[72] A seasonal railroad worker reported that he considered Mexico his "home and final resting place."[73] Mexicans as far distant from their homeland as Chicago made various references to their eventual return once they saved sufficient money, the political situation in Mexico improved, or more opportunities for advancement developed in their *patria*.[74] Certainly some immigrants recognized that their duration in America would be lengthy—others not—but virtually all shared the *desire* to make their time in the United States brief, regardless of how likely that might be.

This desire grew not only from nostalgia or yearning for some aspect of a remembered homeland, but also from the efforts of the Mexican government and their consuls in the United States to keep Mexico alive in the hearts and minds of the immigrants. These officials hoped to generate a sense of community amongst Mexican citizens abroad and at home, especially in the wake of the tumultuous Mexican Revolution. As the scholar Rosales has found, this so-called *México lindo* ("beautiful Mexico") movement, or campaign for the immigrants' devotion, included all kinds of elaborate celebrations and pageantry. Festivals in the United States memorialized various political events such as Cinco de Mayo—commemorating Mexicans' success over the French in the 1862 battle at Puebla—and *Dieciseis de Septiembre*, which celebrated September 16, 1810, the beginning of Mexico's efforts to obtain independence from Spain. Likely influenced by such efforts, most Mexicans in the United States prominently displayed some symbols of Mexico in their homes, including portraits of the revered indigenous president, Benito Juárez, and the Virgin of Guadalupe, an important religious icon in Mexico.[75]

Despite the distance from their homeland and their emphasis on daily survival, immigrants were well aware of and attracted to the dramatic changes and increased nationalism pulsing throughout Mexico. In the Midwest, Mexicans organized to sponsor art exhibits of the latest works of David Alfaro Siquieros, one of the foremost artists associated with the incipient Mexican nationalism. In 1928 hundreds of Mexicans showed up in Chicago to hear José Vasconcelos, a well-known Mexican official, lecture on a similar topic. Vasconcelos spoke eloquently of *la raza cósmica* ("the cosmic race"), a slogan he coined to express the Mexican nation's more expansive view of Mexican identity as being rooted in the melding of an indigenous and European heritage (he did not emphasize African heritage).[76] Such revolutionary changes in Mexican identity kept expatriate Mexicans connected to their native country, and gave many a stronger sense of belonging there; few pursued naturalization in the United States.[77]

At the same time that immigrants became engrossed with this new version of Mexican nationalism, they faced greater hostility from Americans, who were more aware of their growing presence. Increasingly Mexicans recognized that Americans perceived them as second-class Americans, if they viewed them as any kind of American at all. The immigrants' exclusion from permanent status in the United States, and their own disinterest in naturalization, fed upon each other and compounded both. Although Mexicans received some favorable attention from missionaries or social workers, other reformers daily impressed upon Mexicans just how they would have to change—in terms of dress, religion, food, language, and housing—in order to become successful in American society. This kind of pressure irked the new arrivals who resisted this intrusion into their personal lives. Felipe Hale, an immigrant, proudly explained how he continued to cook his meals in an *estilo mexicano* ("Mexican style") rather than adopt American foods and preparations. He further recounted how he had decided to send his daughter to be schooled in Mexico, rather than in Arizona, where he believed flag worship outweighed respect for education.[78]

Mexican immigrants faced a difficult situation: They were working in a country whose citizens did not want them to become members of the nation, and being wooed by the country they had left but that could not provide them with jobs. They managed this conundrum by asserting their undying allegiance to Mexico even as they continued to work and live in the United States.[79] To remain connected to Mexico and apart from Americans who discriminated against them, a few immigrants pointedly refused to learn English.[80] Others dreamt of their return and wrote *corridos* (ballads narrating history or injustice) expressing this sentiment, "I go sad and heavy-hearted to suffer and endure; my Mother Guadalupe, grant my safe return."[81] The writers for *El Correo Mexicano*, a Spanish-language newspaper in Chicago, expected that most immigrants—including themselves—would eventually return to Mexico, and lauded those Mexicans who organized themselves into associations closely affiliated with their homeland. According to these Spanish-language papers, the Mexican nation would reward these immigrants for their loyalty when they finally returned to their *patria*.[82] Although George Sánchez argues that immigrants held mixed feelings toward Mexico and that Mexico could not control the developing and changing culture of immigrants and their offspring, some first-generation immigrants continued to remain culturally and psychologically

Mexican or, as Gabriela Arredondo asserts, "became Mexican" in the face of increased prejudice in Chicago.[83]

Success of Marginalization

Although exclusionists successfully portrayed Mexicans as un-American due to their race, class, and cultural background, those favoring marginalization persuaded or at least influenced a sufficient number of Americans into believing that the immigrants would provide their labor and then leave. Growers' efforts in promoting the idea of Mexicans as only temporarily present in the United States, combined with those of American authors and scholars, Mexican officials, and immigrants themselves, contributed substantially to the marginalization strategy's success in preventing the European quota laws from being applied to Mexico. It had also become the dominant way in which Americans regarded Mexican immigrants—as temporary workers rather than as potential Americans.

Five times during the latter part of the 1920s legislators in the U.S. Congress debated whether to restrict Mexican immigration, and in each of these five times they opted against doing so, instead favoring the status quo of open borders and unlimited Mexican entrants. By 1930, however, Americans recognized that the debate over restriction had dissipated since fewer Mexicans were emigrating from Mexico due to the deepening depression and the greater enforcement of existing legislation on literacy and fees. The ardent marginalizationist Senator Hayden enthusiastically declared "the Mexican quota problem has been solved."[84] In Arizona alone, the number of Mexican immigrants entering the nation had decreased from a high of 9,041 in fiscal year 1926 to 749 in 1930.[85] As this decline paralleled that of the nation's overall, the more pressing concern then became what to do with the thousands of Mexicans whose continued presence during the growing economic crisis was a glaring reminder of how fictional the image of the temporary worker had been.

Some Mexicans *were* temporary workers who followed a regular and circular path of migration, but many others remained to settle in the growing *colonias* of America.[86] But the success of the temporary worker image overwhelmed this distinction: to many Americans in the late 1920s, *all* Mexicans were in the United States only temporarily, conveniently providing their labor and then quietly returning home. The disconnect between those immigrants who put down roots and those Americans who believed them to be in the United States only temporarily would prove problematic, especially when the U.S. economy declined in the 1930s and Americans belatedly recognized that the immigrants *had* established families, communities, and deep roots in American society. It would prove even more troublesome for those immigrants who, regarded as temporary and without an official voice in the United States, would have trouble protecting themselves from cries for their removal.

PART FOUR

Repatriation, 1930–1935

CHAPTER SEVEN

"To Keep America American"

The Door Swings Outward

Born in Mexico circa 1907, Santiago Lopez grew up near Tucson, Arizona. At some point he returned to Mexico, but in 1925 he crossed the border again. Two years later the U.S. Border Patrol arrested Lopez, ordering him to leave the country. He did so, but within two hours walked back into the United States by entering a few miles west of Nogales, Arizona. Seven years later Lopez was working on a ranch owned by the Southern Arizona Bank and Trust Company when immigration authorities nabbed him again; this time they initiated formal deportation proceedings. Hearing of Lopez's troubles, Hubert H. D'Autremont, then vice president of the Tucson Bank and formerly the director of the copper mining Calumet & Arizona Company, wrote to his congressional representative, Lewis W. Douglas, requesting his intercession in the case. D'Autremont vouched for his employee by recounting Lopez's extensive history in the country and explaining that his presence would do "no harm to the United States."[1] By this time Lopez had lived continuously within the United States—except two hours—for nine years. Additionally, he had spent some period growing up in Arizona and was only about twenty-five years old. To which country did he belong?

In the nineteenth century Lopez might have continued his transnational travels, hardly noticing his journey across invisible boundaries. If he had reached adulthood in the first decade of the century, he might have apprenticed himself much as Carlos Jácome (see chapter 1) had done in Tucson, rising economically to become a member of the middle class and accepted as an assimilated American or Spanish American. But by the mid-1920s his initial encounter with border agents had convinced him to stay put, remaining in the United States rather than risking a trip outside the country.[2] If asked, Lopez likely would have said his preferred home was in the United States; clearly his efforts to fight deportation suggest that he wanted to live there.

By 1930, however, growers, the U.S. and Mexican governments, and some academics, journalists, and immigrants had succeeded in defining Mexicans' presence in the United States as only temporary. Perceived as short-timers, these immigrants purportedly would not affect Americans in any way, except to benefit them through the sweat of their labor. The growing prevalence of this image of a temporary worker would upend the lives of people like Santiago Lopez who had committed to a life in Arizona. The immigration bureau, unimpressed by Representative Douglas's intervention, ruled that Lopez had violated the 1924 immigration law for crossing without a visa, as well as the 1917 Immigration Act for entering the United States in violation of the literacy law. Having been granted permission to depart in 1927 on his own recognizance and in lieu of a formal hearing, Lopez had unlawfully returned to the United States within a few hours. Because he violated this agreement, Lopez could not then apply for admission despite his employer's offer to cover his fees and teach him English. Despite his time in the United States, American bureaucrats quickly determined that he did not belong there. The conviction that Mexicans should remain in the country only temporarily surely facilitated the ease with which immigration officials deported Lopez.[3]

The Lopez case shows the success of the marginalization strategy in retaining relatively open borders as well as the perils for Mexican immigrants in the United States. Although the marginalization strategy, which Mexican immigrants had unwittingly contributed to as well, touted either their temporary status in the United States or their permanent second-class standing by filling jobs that no Americans wanted. This rhetoric soon collided with the Great Depression and the realities that many Mexican immigrants *had* settled permanently, especially in the Southwest and Midwest, and that low-skill work was now something that Americans *did* want to do. The underside of this strategy was that if Mexican immigrants remained, or if the economy changed, they could be removed. This chapter shows how the growing image of the immigrants as temporary contributed to their voluntary and involuntary exodus during the Depression years, as well as why, initially, so many Americans and Mexicans thought this the appropriate resolution: they were never to have been there so long in the first place.

Background on Repatriation

During the cotton boom of the 1920s, growers successfully persuaded many Americans that their strategy for dealing with Mexicans was the best one. These growers and their allies had argued that Mexicans should be admitted into the United States because they either would become subordinate Americans—destined to remain in dead-end jobs—or be only temporary residents. In either case, the results would be the same: Mexicans who came to the United States would not threaten national identity or unity, nor would they harm Americans' livelihoods since they would stay in their lowly jobs under their employers' control, or return to Mexico. Cotton growers' profits would remain high since the continued supply of Mexican workers allowed them to pay low wages, and at rates less than most Americans would accept.[4]

The growing consensus over marginalization depended on a variety of factors: relatively open borders, a good economy, and a continued belief in the immigrants' temporary stay in the United States. This consensus increasingly muted strident exclusionists and the few assimilationists and even fewer pluralists who wondered how and if the most recent Mexican immigrants had the requisite racial heritage or class status to integrate into the nation. It also blinded Americans to the reality that immigrant behavior was contradicting the image of Mexicans as temporary workers.[5] The economist Paul Taylor observed that Americans overestimated the number of temporary workers because they had failed to distinguish between internal and international migration. While some Mexicans traveled between the United States and Mexico, other families migrated along regular circuits from Texas and New Mexico to the beet fields of Colorado, Michigan, and other parts of the Midwest.[6] The sociologist Ernesto Galarza reported that while there had been much "back-and-forth" Mexican immigration in the first years of the twentieth century, this practice had changed to "a more or less permanent settlement in the United States."[7]

Indeed, many Mexican immigrants *had* decided to stay. Despite the growers' assertions to the contrary, Devra Weber shows how some California employers encouraged Mexicans to remain for a longer duration by providing schools for migrant workers' children and keeping migrants indebted to company stores. Gabriela Arredondo provides evidence of midwestern sugar beet growers who proffered financial incentives to encourage their Mexican workers to winter in the city, in the hope that they would return to work the following spring.[8] Some Mexicans brought their extended families with them, bore children, and thereby increased the population in crowded urban *colonias* or *barrios* of the United States. These Mexican *colonias* sprang up across the nation in various cities in the Southwest, in eastern Pennsylvania, and on the outskirts of Detroit, Chicago, and other towns throughout the Midwest. By 1930, the U.S. Census calculated that at least 1,422,533 people of Mexican descent lived in the United States, double their estimated population in 1920.[9] Despite the immigrants' increased numbers, Paul Taylor wrote that most Americans presumed Mexicans would "melt like the snow" when they were no longer needed.[10]

But as the Depression intensified, Americans became aware that the immigrants had not melted away as expected. An editor of *Survey* magazine observed "what we have to reckon with are the fortunes of a permanent Mexican population."[11] By 1931, the Arizona state legislature felt sufficiently concerned to warn the U.S. Congress that "large colonies of Mexican people" inhabited their state. Moreover, Anglo Arizonans worried that Mexican immigrants held "little desire or intention to become American citizens" and were taking jobs from "citizen workers" and lowering their standard of living.[12] Feeling entitled to enforce what they perceived as the immigrants' temporary status, they called for Mexicans' repatriation or removal.

The economic downturn of the early 1920s had evoked a similar response, but the difference was that in the 1930s there were no contracts stipulating the immigrants' date of return. There was no temporary work program or fixed policy, only rhetoric implying Mexicans' temporary status. In fact, there was no requirement at all for legal immigrants to leave; they could live in the United States as long as they liked. Even those who entered the country illegally prior to the 1924 Immigration Act could not be deported for this reason alone, or for becoming a public charge, if they lived in the United States continuously for at least five years and could prove that they had done so.[13] Many Americans, however, did not grasp or accept the difference between those who could and could not be forcibly removed. While the U.S. government had no jurisdiction to conduct wholesale deportations against any immigrant group that had legal claims to be on American soil, some Americans began to argue that all people of Mexican descent—regardless of the technicalities of their birth or citizenship—needed to be removed from the United States to protect American workers. Having accepted the idea that Mexican immigrants would stay in the United States on only a temporary basis, some Americans perceived *all* Mexicans through this lens and believed that it was time for them to go. Just as many Americans and Mexicans in the 1920s had concurred that open borders for Mexicans made good policy, they now agreed that the other element implicit in the marginalization strategy—the right to remove immigrants whose labor was no longer needed—should be enforced as well.

Estimates vary, but the scholarly consensus is that approximately 500,000 people of Mexican descent left the United States in the first half of the 1930s, representing an exodus of about one-third of all people of Mexican descent in the United States. This included people the United States deported, those people who various local governments or organizations helped to return, and those who repatriated themselves.[14] In the 1920s, the federal government actually did not deport very many people from any immigrant group. However, in the 1930s, Mexicans were disproportionately expelled compared with people of other nationalities. Cybelle Fox demonstrates how social reformers targeted Mexicans for expulsion—as opposed to Europeans—deeming them more dependent upon government resources, despite evidence to the contrary.[15] In 1931, 8,335 Mexicans were sent away, compared with 2,276 Canadians and 6,162 others from all parts of Europe.[16] Another 10,000 plus immigrants, from all over the world, left annually as "voluntary departures." These were cases in which immigrants agreed to leave on their own terms, rather than awaiting a decision from a formal hearing that resulted in deportation 95 percent of the time. The vast majority of such voluntary cases were of Mexican descent.[17] The advantage of avoiding deportation was that immigrants could apply for reentry. Once officially deported per the 1929 Deportation Act, immigrants could never apply for re-admission.[18] Unfortunately, many of those who opted for a voluntary departure later discovered that it was next to impossible to return legally because immigration officials considered these visa applicants as "likely to become a public charge," a legitimate category for denial, and rejected their requests for admission. Immigration authorities made determinations based on the immigrants' financial resources, whether they ever received any form of relief while in the United States, or if they had previously left the country at any government's expense. Since most immigrants attempting to cross the border lacked funds, and many previously received rail fare or relief, bureaucrats had ample reasons for denying most applications for entrance visas: in July 1931, immigration officials rejected 78 percent of Mexicans' admission requests.[19]

Still, most immigrants returning to Mexico repatriated themselves. Repatriation was ostensibly voluntary, in the sense that they were not forcibly removed, but they faced various pressures encouraging them to go. The rise in anti-immigrant legislation in many states and municipalities prevented immigrants from working in a variety of public works jobs and professional fields (by limiting licenses to citizens), making it difficult for them to "live where they could not work."[20] Two-thirds of the repatriates interviewed by sociologist James Gilbert identified job loss as their primary motivation for returning to Mexico.[21] Increased incidents of racial discrimination, the omnipresent fear of being arrested and deported, threatened removal from relief rolls, and intimidation or violence all contributed to immigrants' decisions to leave. The persuasive and combined efforts of various Mexican consuls, American government officials, and various charitable and relief organizations further encouraged Mexicans to take advantage of potential new opportunities in Mexico. These included colonizing Mexican land, constructing national highways, or guarding and excavating archaeological ruins such as Monte Alban in Oaxaca and the now famed Teotihuacán outside of Mexico City.[22] The massive return migration, voluntary and involuntary, suggests that those who supported the marginalization strategy achieved some success in imposing a temporary status upon the former immigrants.

Enforcing the Temporary Worker Image

When the panic of 1929 first hit, some Mexicans fled the United States immediately but many others chose to ride out the hard times. Once Americans recognized that immigrants were not leaving in the anticipated numbers, they encouraged or coerced them to depart. The Colorado Fuel and Iron Company fired its Mexican employees, offering to pay for their transit to the border in appreciation of their good service, as well as to remove any obligation of providing for them in the future.[23] Senator Carl Hayden, who previously had promoted immigrants' temporary status, advocated stepped-up deportation drives and increased funding to remove Mexican workers.[24] Initially marginalizationists—employers and their political allies—desired a surplus of Mexican laborers so that they could have their pick of workers at low wages, but by the early 1930s they no longer depended upon only Mexican labor since they could choose from a ready supply of Americans who had become willing to accept formerly distasteful jobs after losing their tenancies or property on the Great Plains.[25] By January 1933 there was a sizable surplus of workers with more than two for every agricultural job in California.[26]

Exclusionists, who had focused on immigrant restriction, now joined unemployed Americans and marginalizationists in calling for Mexicans' deportation. The ardent exclusionist J. C. Brodie, who disliked immigrants and headed up the nativist Committee on Mexican Immigration in Superior, Arizona, demanded that the federal government deport *all* Mexicans, mistakenly believing that the state had done so in an earlier depression. He reminded officials that "the Harding Administration . . . did a splendid thing for the Southwest and America in 1921 when they deported 150,000 Mexican indigents" and called for a repetition of this policy as "a final and complete solution" to what he deemed the "problem" of Mexican immigration.[27]

While immigration officials found Brodie to be a tiresome crank, they took him seriously enough to investigate his myriad complaints. In one case his perseverance caused Margarito Sanchez, a meter reader for Arizona Edison Company, to lose his job for lack of American citizenship, despite the fact that Sanchez had lived in the United States for 15 years, raised three U.S.-citizen children, and formally begun his own path to citizenship by filing the initial paperwork. Other Mexicans found their cases intensely reviewed at the behest of the indefatigable Brodie. His incessant letters eventually brought immigration officials to his town to hunt for immigrants who had not entered the country through the proper channels.[28]

Brodie was not alone in his efforts to deport Mexicans and preserve jobs for Americans, particularly white Americans. R. E. Pasters, a cohort of Brodie's in the Committee on Mexican Immigration, claimed that Anglo and Mexican Americans in his town all agreed that it was "next to impossible for white laborers and mechanics to get employment," and called for officials to deport the city's immigrants. He believed that there were at least 400,000 Mexicans throughout the country who should leave, and demanded a massive deportation campaign.[29] In Texas, W. L. Warren lobbied "to return these people back to Mexico where they belong" so that they would not live off San Antonio's charitable resources.[30] From California, Cora West wondered "if there isn't something that can be done to keep the Mexicans and Phillipinos [*sic*] from getting all the work?"[31] And H. Hanshaw of Port Huron, Michigan, implored President Franklin Delano Roosevelt to allocate the necessary resources and authority to immigration agents so that they could clear her city of Mexicans.[32] Some Americans also threatened violence to ensure that few immigrants would gain employment. In Chicago, Mexicans faced the hostility of Americans and of other immigrant groups who congregated outside the packinghouses where Mexicans worked in order to intimidate them.[33] In Terre Haute, Indiana, violence erupted when American laborers attacked Mexicans working on the railroad, leading the immigrants to quit in fear for their safety.[34] In another case, an enraged crowd forced a California contractor to take refuge in a municipal building because he employed immigrant workers.[35]

Many elected officials shared the belief that Mexicans should go. In the process of removing them, these politicians often disregarded the law as they clumped together all people of Mexican descent regardless of citizenship or legal status. Charles Ryder, the Mayor of Wickenburg, Arizona, declared public works jobs to be off-limits not only to Mexican immigrants but also to Mexican Americans.[36] Americans in many local communities and state legislatures around the country acted similarly to Mayor Ryder, passing various exclusionary and anti-alien measures. By 1933, ten states—generally in the Midwest, West, and Northeast—had laws requiring citizenship for employment on public works contracts; four others gave U.S. citizens preference for such jobs. Although these laws affected *all* immigrants, they hit Mexicans especially hard due to their low naturalization rates as well as greater numbers in migratory jobs.[37] Wyoming required that immigrants must have filed their first papers toward citizenship before being eligible for this type of work. Anti-alien laws also extended to various trades and professions, with three states requiring barbers to be citizens.[38] Some states also passed more stringent residency requirements—of one year or more—for jobs on public works projects, making it particularly hard for people of Mexican descent, immigrant or otherwise, to qualify since many regularly migrated within several-month cycles to different states and jobs.[39]

As described by Amy Davis, Governor Edwin C. Johnson of Colorado called for the expulsion of all aliens, by whom he meant primarily Mexicans, from his state. When immigration officials ignored Johnson's wishes, declining to deport the Mexicans who were legally present in the country, Johnson responded by announcing his own plans to round up Mexicans and hold them in an internment camp in the town of Golden, near Denver, until the necessary arrangements could be made for their permanent removal to Mexico. Although Johnson's pet project never materialized—and it is possible that he never expected it would—he hoped his announcement would cause Mexicans to fear being removed and so depart on their own.[40]

Shortly after Johnson's proclamation, Davis further narrates, a group of people of Mexican descent requested gas money from a charitable organization so that they could return to jobs they had held previously in Greeley, Colorado. Instead of assisting, relief workers turned them over to the local sheriff, who detained forty of the travelers and ordered them out of the state. Although half the exiled workers were American citizens, Johnson denied this, declaring that those expelled were "mostly aliens without passports."[41] His words and actions suggest that, to his way of thinking, a person of Mexican descent could never be American.

Johnson was not alone in his thinking. The New Mexico and Texas governors wired their support, hoping to adopt similar practices within their own states. The Mexican Consul in Colorado also backed Johnson because he knew that there were no jobs for Mexicans in the Colorado beet fields and thought it better to help workers to leave the country. Other Mexicans raised few complaints, believing that the governor and Americans held the right to protect their citizens first. Unfortunately, they did not recognize how American many of the Mexican nationals felt that they had become in their long absence from Mexico.[42]

As Davis explains, Governor Johnson finally overstepped his bounds when he declared martial law and established checkpoints on the southern border of his state to scrutinize entries. Johnson alleged this was necessary to preserve jobs for American workers. Within only a few days, Colorado officials denied entry to over 422 people. The New Mexico governor, Clyde Tingley, who previously supported Johnson's actions, turned against these draconian sweeps and searches when he learned that many of those detained were Mexican Americans whose families had lived in New Mexico long before it became part of the Union. Eventually, Johnson backed down.[43]

In addition to exclusionists such as Johnson, some assimilationists joined the growing consensus for Mexicans' departure. Primarily middle-class religious and secular reformers of Anglo and Mexican descent, assimilationists had declined in numbers and fervor since the First World War. The economic downturn and widespread appeals to preserve all available jobs and relief for American citizens inclined many assimilationists to support making Mexicans as temporary as the marginalization strategy had purported them to be. These former assimilationists justified their support for repatriation drives in humanitarian terms. Rather than permitting Mexicans to starve in their midst, they argued, the best way to advocate on their behalf would be to encourage and assist them to depart for Mexico where they might find more sympathy and opportunities. Placida Garcia Smith, a Mexican American from Colorado and director of the Friendly House, an Americanization agency in Phoenix, made repatriation a part of her mission. In July 1933, she reported helping 130 families to the border since the previous spring.[44] A similar organization, the Neighborhood House in St. Paul, Minnesota, no longer considered Mexicans legitimate neighbors and worked in conjunction with the Ramsey County welfare office and the Catholic Church to repatriate 15 percent of St. Paul's Mexican *colonia*.[45] In 1932, one member of the middle-class Americanization organization, the League of United Latin American Citizens (LULAC), expressed anger at being associated with immigrants whom he regarded as "cotton picking 'drifters,'" suggesting that he had nothing in common with such people and would do nothing to help them integrate into the nation.[46] In 1931, the Pueblo, Colorado, Family Service Society explained that it had always helped Mexican immigrants and was doing so again by assisting two hundred people to leave.[47] A social worker in Detroit rationalized his efforts by observing that a Mexican worker and his family "would be happier in their own country."[48] Even Chicago's famed Hull House helped some immigrants return to Mexico.[49] Remsen Crawford, a writer for *Current History* magazine, applauded this anti-assimilationist trend, noting approvingly how efforts to avoid "alienizing Americans" had replaced flagging campaigns to Americanize immigrants.[50] A few years later, in 1933, the journalist Carey McWilliams agreed with this assessment, although not the sentiment that underlaid it, noting that assimilationists who had been so eager to transform Mexicans in the 1920s then remained silent or went so far as to promote and facilitate repatriation.[51] Regardless of the motives of the (former) assimilationists who assisted Mexicans with repatriation, since many likely believed the immigrants would be better off in Mexico and wanted only to help them, the result was the same: a reinforcement of the idea that Mexicans were only temporary residents of the United States.

One member of the assimilationist organization LULAC, however, did not embrace repatriation so readily and provided a more nuanced view of the situation. While he observed that Mexican immigrants seemed happy to repatriate, he wondered how smoothly their readjustment would be, especially that of the children who primarily knew the United States. He also commented upon the quandary of those legal residents, and those who had not yet been questioned, who were fearful of remaining but also worried that all would not go well when they returned. Noting poor conditions in the Mexican border towns, the author seemed skeptical, too. He questioned if repatriates would receive sufficient resources from the Mexican government and pondered what would occur when Americans again desired Mexican labor.[52]

Like assimilationists, pluralists—people who favored viewing people of Mexican descent as Spanish Americans—had dwindled considerably in numbers and authority since their heyday during the first years of statehood. Mostly located in New Mexico and a few pockets of Arizona, pluralists did not generally regard recent Mexican immigrants as potential Spanish Americans; instead, they viewed the newest arrivals as of a different class and racial background than themselves and, as such, did not criticize repatriation and deportation policies. In a few cases, they actively supported them. Mr. Delao, an Arizona businessman of Mexican heritage who referred to himself as Spanish American, urged the U.S. government to deport Mexicans who had not become citizens or made any effort to do so.[53] Journalists for *El Tucsonense*, a Spanish-language newspaper, cautioned that officials exercise more discretion—but not cease—their efforts to repatriate and deport immigrants. They recommended that Mexicans without documents be sent away first, then recent immigrants, and finally, if necessary, long-term Mexican residents.[54]

The few times in which people like Mr. Delao openly criticized repatriation were when Anglo Americans extended discrimination and repatriation to all persons of Mexican descent, regardless of their nationality or class status. One such situation that roused them to activism was Governor Johnson's expulsion of Mexican Americans from Colorado.[55] But mostly they, like assimilationists, either assisted with repatriation or ignored it.

Growing Support for the Consensus

Throughout the 1920s, some Mexican government officials, journalists, and other prominent Mexicans encouraged immigrants to remain connected to their homeland and to consider repatriation at some indeterminate point in the future. Therefore during the early years of the Great Depression, when the immigrants' labor was no longer in demand, these same Mexicans felt an obligation to assist fellow citizens with their return to Mexico.

Mexicans' interest in helping their expatriate countrymen stemmed from humanitarian and nationalistic impulses. They wanted to help their compatriots, as well as to use them to fulfill nationalist agendas of settling and improving land that officials considered to be underutilized. In 1931, a journalist for the Mexico City *Excelsior* urged repatriation "not only for the sake of patriotism and national dignity but for that of humanitarianism" because of the poor treatment the immigrants experienced in the United States.[56] Other writers for the same periodical complained that while it was important to "repatriate the nationals," they believed that U.S. investigators did not review individual circumstances sufficiently, often expelling the heads of families, leaving dependents without a source of income. Despite this mild criticism, the paper supported the overall objective of sending Mexicans back to Mexico.[57]

Initially, Mexican officials expressed delight at the immigrants' return and considered how to do even more to encourage it.[58] In 1930, the Mexican secretary of exterior relations promoted legislation, which never became law, calling for the removal of citizenship status from those Mexicans absent for ten years or more since he believed it would entice more Mexicans to return.[59] The following year, Governor Andrés Ortíz of the state of Chihuahua approvingly observed that several hundred repatriated families had settled around Villa Ahumada, building adobe homes and farming land that had not been tilled since the first years of the Mexican Revolution. He demonstrated his eagerness to have more such repatriates or *repatriados* for he believed that "they are experienced farmers with a knowledge of the American system of cultivating."[60]

While various colonization schemes had long been proposed to settle and secure the northern territory of Mexico, with varying degrees of success, the Mexican government expanded its investment in such ventures in the early 1930s. This time government officials anticipated greater results since they believed that the returning nationals would bring new skills and knowledge, thereby improving the land along with the Mexican economy.[61] They also hoped to divert the *repatriados* from moving to communities already overburdened with unemployed workers. To facilitate such colonization, Mexican officials promised long-term loans as well as land, seed, food, and tools. In the end they committed to more than they could deliver, incorrectly anticipating that the repatriates would bring more of their own supplies. These resettlement projects mostly failed.

One of the most famous and spectacular failures was that of *Pinotepa Nacional*, a tropical swampland in the state of Oaxaca. Sociologist James Gilbert tells the story of how Mexico's National Repatriation Committee initially planned for over five thousand settlers to clear the land of trees and brush, establish productive farms, and grow a variety of market crops including pineapples, mangoes, and watermelon alongside the usual subsistence crops of corn, beans, and vegetables. Instead, only seven hundred or so repatriates arrived during the winter of 1932–33. As Gilbert describes it, the *repatriados* thought that they would have more control over their settlement, but soon became frustrated with the dictatorial attitude of the organizing officials. In truth this was the least of their difficulties, for although the colonizers succeeded in clearing some land for housing and recreation, they also became sick. Gilbert further explains that the region's native peoples had warned them that no outsiders ever grew old there, and apparently they were right. Shortly after these dire pronouncements, two to three people died each day. The newcomers had no immunity against the various disease-infested mosquitoes, *nihua* bugs, which burrowed under fingernails, *jejens* or black flies, and the *pinolillo* insect that made people itch. Eventually, the *repatriados* fled the ill-fated community. One small group evacuated after only a month, walking eight days through dense tropical forests and high mountains to reach the city of Oaxaca. Several months later the remaining repatriates, withered from disease, hunger, and malnutrition, marched twenty-three days en masse toward the sea and Acapulco. There they encountered the campaigning Lázaro Cárdenas, the future president of Mexico, who ensured that they received provisions and transit to Mexico City, where they might find jobs. By the spring of 1934, Gilbert reports that the *Pinotepa Nacional* project had collapsed. Although other such ventures did not suffer this ignominious of an end, none lasted very long.[62]

Since only 5 percent or so of the former immigrants went to these colonization projects, the Mexican government attempted to assist other *repatriados* as well.[63] The government lacked sufficient resources to transport them from interior locations in the United States, but did pay the transit costs from border cities to inland Mexican communities. For the first leg of the journey, consuls and other prominent Mexicans worked closely with local governments and charitable organizations in the United States to fund rail fare to the border. Ignacio L. Batiza, the Mexican consul in Detroit, was especially active in this process, believing it was his responsibility to help his compatriots since the Michigan *colonias* had been hit especially hard by the Depression. In this effort he allied not only with members of community organizations, but also with the Mexican artist, Diego Rivera, who happened to be in the United States in 1932, working on a mural at the Detroit Institute of Arts. Rivera was reportedly so distressed upon observing long lines of Mexican nationals awaiting handouts that he used the opportunity to organize them into a socialist-style agrarian community near Zihuatenejo in the Mexican state of Guerrero. To drum up support, Rivera established the League of Mexican Workers and Peasants, donated 700 pesos for agricultural tools, and, along with Batiza, made promotional speeches to encourage participation in his colony. Within two weeks, 850 workers signed up.[64]

While Batiza, Rivera, and others in Michigan helped approximately 1,300 Mexicans to return, many remained skeptical that their fortunes would improve in Mexico and instead opted to ride out the Depression in the United States. Batiza and Rivera's activism, however, reinforced the temporary worker image in the minds of many Americans as they saw that even Mexican officials and prominent Mexicans believed that the immigrants belonged in Mexico. Later both Batiza and Rivera would reverse their views—once they discovered that the Mexican government had failed to provide sufficient support or opportunities for the repatriates—but by then many Mexicans had already left so that the image of the temporary worker was further enhanced in the minds of many Americans.[65]

Despite the defection of Batiza and Rivera, some Mexicans in Mexico continued to support the temporary worker image. In 1932, the Mexican state decided that it would no longer collect statistics for emigrants since they did not regard any citizen as having left the country permanently.[66] Mexican officials also helped *repatriados* by lifting the onerous *franquicia* tax that had been imposed on their goods when they returned to Mexico; this tax forced them to sell their property for less than its value in the United States or to spend their last resources to cover the prohibitive fees. This policy reversal helped the returning Mexicans to preserve their funds and assets, and gave them a better chance of re-establishing themselves in their once and future homes. Some used the cars they drove and the tools they carried with them to offer taxi services or to work as mechanics. More than one brought their barbershop chairs so that they could set up the businesses they had lost due to shrinking Mexican *colonias* in the United States or other consequences of the Depression.[67] The Mexican government also assisted repatriates by passing restrictive immigration laws preventing most foreigners, except wealthy tourists, from entering Mexico. This decision ensured that all available jobs would be preserved for Mexican nationals.[68]

While the Mexican state and most of its constituents supported repatriation, other Mexicans expressed frustration with their compatriots' "habit of emigrating." They wondered why they had left in the first place since people in the United States mistreated them and they were "thrown out time and time again." One journalist so objected to this emigration that he called for measures to restrict Mexicans from leaving.[69] Others complained about the *repatriados* who had returned, called them *gringos*, a derogatory term for Americans, and discriminated against them.[70] Regardless, sociologist James Gilbert found that over 80 percent of the repatriates he interviewed believed that they had not been abused, and that most Mexicans treated them as fellow citizens who merely had fallen upon hard times.[71]

Government Support for the Temporary Worker Image

As in Mexico, prominent Americans and government officials supported the idea that Mexican workers did not belong in the United States and developed various schemes to encourage them to leave. The impetus for this, as noted by historian George Sánchez, came from the top when President Herbert Hoover declared Mexicans to be the primary cause of unemployment since he believed that they took jobs from Americans.[72] As described by Abraham Hoffman, William N. Doak, Hoover's secretary of labor, immediately acted upon the president's words and took it upon himself to ensure that immigrants be removed from the United States. In February 1931 he issued an order to all 35 immigration district offices, calling upon them to work with local charitable agencies to rid the country of as many aliens as they could. To do so, he relied upon a provision of the 1917 Immigration Act that permitted the federal government to pay for the removal of immigrants who had been in the United States for less than three years, faced serious economic problems after entering, *and* wanted to return. He anticipated that many would apply for this generous grant of transit and was disappointed to learn that only 159 Mexicans left under this provision, although several hundred immigrants from other countries took up the offer.[73]

Secretary Doak's next step was to work with various local officials in Los Angeles to encourage Mexican immigrants to return to their native country. Charles P. Visel, head of the Los Angeles Citizens' Committee on Coordination of Unemployment Relief, eagerly complied with the new agenda, masterminding a plan to create an atmosphere of anxiety that would induce immigrants to flee in advance of deportation or other reprisals. Those involved in this campaign believed that such policies would result in more jobs for Americans and/or reduced relief expenditures. Although Doak was criticized for his aggressive tactics in ordering immigration officials to conduct raids, many of which turned up few deportable immigrants, he succeeded in his objective to persuade or force many immigrants, legal or otherwise, to leave.[74]

While accelerating the repatriation of Mexican immigrants from Los Angeles, the U.S. Department of Labor also investigated various complaints against Mexicans in other communities. Often the bureaucrats determined that the immigrants were legal and not eligible for deportation. A welfare worker for Associated Charities in Superior, Arizona, W. W. Simon, explained that most Mexicans on her relief rolls had lived in her town "for years and years." Visiting immigration officials confirmed the accuracy of her statements and noted that none of the people on her list could be deported. Still, there were immigrants who did not have the proper documentation; these Mexicans either hid until the officials traveled to the next community or decided to repatriate themselves before being deported.[75] In this way the federal government assisted the out-migration of Mexican immigrants who had remained longer than Americans wanted.

The federal government also sanctioned and facilitated repatriation initiatives already underway. When John Zurbrick, the U.S. district director of immigration in Detroit, learned that Mexican trains failed to arrive at the border as scheduled and that repatriates had been forced to wait inside enclosed trains "without light or heat" for many hours, he solicited funds from his boss, the U.S. commissioner-general of immigration, Harry E. Hull, to improve the quality of the trips. Zurbrick believed that if these campaigns went smoothly the news would encourage others to leave, freeing up more jobs or relief funds for American citizens.[76] Approving Zurbrick's request, Commissioner Hull expressed his pleasure "that so many citizens of Mexico and their children, who were entirely or partly destitute, have been started to their home country."[77] Other federal employees agreed. Congressman Douglas noted that Mexicans in Arizona would be more comfortable in Mexico since it was "their own country and they will be happier there as well as more healthful."[78] John S. Littell, the American vice consul in Mexico City, found other reasons to commend repatriation, observing that the returned residents would boost the Mexican economy since it had lost "most able-bodied and enterprising citizens" in the preceding three decades.[79] There was little sense among U.S. government officials—even those stationed in Mexico—that repatriation could create problems for individual families or for Mexico itself.

American journalists and writers began echoing the words of government officials regarding Mexicans' preference for residing in their homeland and the temporary nature of Mexican migration. They titled their articles, "Back to the Homeland," "Guitars Strum as 400 Mexicans Start Home," "Jobless Latins to Be Sent to Homes," and "Send Them Home."[80] Edna Ewing Kelley, the author of another similarly headlined story, "The Mexican Goes Home," reveals how much she had absorbed of the marginalizationists' rhetoric when she wrote, "It was not difficult to entice them back, for they had only been sojourning in this country." She further depicted Mexicans' departure as a merry occasion, reminiscent of a "fiesta," observing how even a friendly dog trotted "happily" at the side of a retreating caravan. Oddly, she matter-of-factly mentioned how "one man died and six babies were born while the party was en route," as if this were merely to be expected in such a long journey.[81] Kelley clearly never considered that any of these immigrants belonged in the United States on a permanent basis (or that the six babies born en route would likely be U.S. citizens) or that they might have established deep roots and regretted having to leave.

Contesting the Temporary Worker Image

Some immigrants did agree to return to Mexico as most Americans and Mexicans had thought and hoped they would. They went back hoping for better circumstances across the border in their native land, or because they were frustrated due to the lack of opportunities in the United States, increased anti-alien laws, discrimination, and incessant pressure to leave. One man in his seventies indicated that since he had been gone for five years it was time go home. Others longed for and were intrigued with the various possibilities promoted by the Mexican consuls for their own plot of land and a new start, and signed up for incipient colonization projects.[82]

But many more immigrants demonstrated that they preferred to remain within the United States since they now considered it their home. Paul Taylor discovered in his field research among Mexican immigrants that "bonds to the mother country have become tenuous."[83] While U.S. welfare officials and Mexican consuls initially expected the immigrants to register in droves for free transit back to their Mexican homeland, they were surprised when few did. Instead, the bureaucrats had to rely upon persuasion, coupled with the coercive power of anti-alien laws and threats to remove individuals from relief rolls, to get immigrants to agree to depart. In Detroit, relief workers used special techniques to encourage Mexicans to leave, referring any person of Mexican descent who applied for welfare to their "Mexican Bureau." This bureau worked to persuade applicants to return to Mexico, rather than to process their welfare applications. Mexicans who expressed a reluctance to leave found that they could receive their monthly food allotment only in a public cafeteria, rather than enjoying meals in privacy like other recipients. Even so, many accepted this indignity over the alternative of repatriation.[84]

Others patiently explained to frustrated bureau workers, year after year, why they had no interest in moving to Mexico. One such Mexican national repeatedly informed welfare workers that he had lived in the United

States for over twelve years, that he had American-born children, and that he had no relatives in Mexico. In one of the most egregious cases, fifteen-year-old Mary Lou enlightened her persistent interviewer that she did not wish to move because she was an American citizen and had never been to Mexico. Moreover, she had little interest in ever going there for she had heard only negative things about it.[85]

Some Mexicans tried to remain in the United States but found themselves caught in the complicated web of U.S. immigration laws, which made little or no allowance for family relationships or the length of time immigrants lived in the States. One such case involved a Mexican woman who settled with her father in Cudahy, Minnesota, in 1924. A few years later she bore a child there and in 1930 briefly returned to Mexico to visit her ailing grandmother, leaving her two-year-old baby behind. When she attempted to return a few months later, the government denied her entry because of the belief that she would fall into the category of "likely to become a public charge," a legal reason for denial. Yet rejection on this basis made no sense given that her father owned two houses, retained a stable position at Burlington company—a job that he had held for ten years—and earned $90 per month, sufficient to support his daughter and her child.[86]

Another case involved that of Celia Vasquez, who had the misfortune of growing up in a household so large that when her family immigrated to the United States her parents could not afford to pay the entrance fees for all its members. Thus, Celia and her siblings, Belen and Alfredo, entered illegally through Nogales. Years later, Celia married an American citizen. Having been reported as delinquent by her estranged brother Alfredo, who faced a deportation charge of his own, Celia showed up for a similar hearing the day after her wedding. Her new husband moved quickly and successfully to have her take advantage of the bureau's voluntary departure policies, which allowed her to leave on her own recognizance and then immediately apply for readmission. On October 17, 1932, Celia left the United States and applied for reentry the following day. Although she succeeded in obtaining a visa, the authorities denied her entrance in December. The records do not show why Celia was rejected or if she was ever readmitted. What is clear is that her home was in the United States. Her parents, most of her sisters and brothers, and her husband with whom she had been together for many years prior to marriage, all lived in Arizona; she was in Mexico alone.[87]

Celia's case was not unusual. An anonymous man, born in the Yucatán peninsula of Mexico, emigrated as a young teen after both his parents had died in 1915. Other than a few visits to Mexico, he lived permanently in

New Orleans, where he married and then raised two children. Despite his life in the United States, he was deported when immigration officials found that he did not have the proper paperwork. Distressed with his exile, he plaintively wrote to President Hoover, hoping for restitution. He justified his case by explaining that after fifteen years in New Orleans he thought he was an American citizen and begged for the opportunity to become officially so, adding, "I feel as I were one." With his family in New Orleans, he declared that there was nothing for him in Mexico. He then stated simply, "I like to get back home." But it was too late; extant laws did not permit his return. He then became what he had alleged at the beginning of his letter, "a man without a country."[88] Some scholars refer to this understanding of belonging as "cultural citizenship," in that the man felt that he was an American because of the length of time he had lived and worked in the United States. But this understanding of his place and belonging in the United States was at odds with that of the growing consensus concerning the temporary status of Mexican immigrants and the desire to enforce it.[89]

Tiburcio Navarro, a thirty-eight-year-old legal Mexican immigrant and musician who resided in the United States for most of his life, also faced increased scrutiny during the hypercharged anti-immigrant years of the Great Depression. Navarro's legal status came under question in this atmosphere, despite the fact that he, his wife, and their children (four of whom were born in the United States) had lived in Arizona for eleven years, from 1919 to 1930, and that his parents lived and worked there as well. When J. C. Brodie, an Arizona activist opposed to Mexican immigration, called upon immigration inspectors to investigate Navarro, the bureaucrats readily complied. The records showed that Navarro's wife and U.S.-citizen children had returned to Mexico in 1930, possibly due to social and economic pressures to repatriate, while Tiburcio remained in the United States to work at a variety of jobs to bring them back, including a position at the Humbug Gold Mine, roadwork, copper smelting, teaching music, and playing in dance halls throughout the Phoenix area. In 1933, Navarro filed his first papers for citizenship so that he could begin the process of bringing his wife and children back into the United States. His 1934 report to the immigration inspector indicated his clear preference for raising his children in Arizona rather than in Mexico. Although immigration officials ultimately upheld Navarro's right to remain, the more numerous voices of marginalization had succeeded in persuading sufficient Americans to presume that families like the Navarros were likely temporary, and thus could be questioned and have their unification imperiled despite their long history in the United States. It is unclear if his family was ever approved to rejoin him.[90]

Unlike these cases in which Mexicans tried to remain in or get back to the United States, others agreed to return to Mexico, but often only because they had no other choice. Mrs. Antonio Frías, awaiting a train south to the border, pointed to her crying children and noted how they would miss their schools and friends. In another case, Mrs. José Perez stated that she and her husband did not want to leave because they "loved it here," but since her husband could not find work in America, they were going to seek it elsewhere.[91] Others boarded the southbound train, as if intending to repatriate, but either had a different agenda—that of getting to another region of the United States where jobs or family might be more plentiful—or changed their minds en route; twelve people asked to disembark in San Antonio. Informed that the railroad officials would not permit them to leave, these passengers were then forced to ride to the Mexican side of the border; clearly, the trip south had become less than voluntary for them. Recognizing their limited options, a few intrepid souls jumped through the train windows at Laredo, hoping to hide in the rail yard and remain in the United States. The following morning the authorities rounded up the wayward repatriates and put them back on the train to Mexico.[92]

Once Mexicans in the United States heard of other repatriates' travails, and the failures of colonization, they became even less inclined to follow their compatriots south. Repatriates shared with researchers that while they initially had been pleased to reunite with former friends and family, they yearned to return to the United States as soon as possible. A forty-four-year-old barber who had lived in the United States for twenty-four years complained that he and his wife did not wish to be in Mexico and were extremely unhappy. James Gilbert discovered that many of the younger repatriates desperately wanted to return and pestered him incessantly about job opportunities in America and assistance in getting there. Eventually, many of the repatriates found employment in Mexico, working as taxi drivers or as agricultural workers, but they were often dissatisfied with their circumstances.[93]

Children and young adults, born in or mostly raised in the United States, experienced a harsh adjustment because Mexico had never been home to them. They complained of cultural differences, the lack of things to do, the absence of economic opportunities and consumer goods, and in general missed their schools and friends in America. One repatriate expressed deep frustration with his situation, explaining that "even if I can't get work there right away. I'd rather be there. There is nothing here. I'm just wasting my time." An eleven-year-old repatriate disliked the new environment in arid Mexico with its stark landscape and lack of daily comforts such as hot water and a soft bed. She had trouble in school, too, having to repeat several years because she did not understand Spanish well enough to move forward with her studies. Gilbert concluded that 70 percent of the children or young adults he interviewed had become "cultural misfits," people who did not belong in Mexico.[94]

The few extant statistics available on repatriates' attitudes indicate that many yearned to be in the United States and likely considered it their home. The scholar Osgood Hardy reported that all of the repatriates he interviewed wished to go back to the United States. Gilbert found that of the 101 he interviewed, 73 wanted to settle permanently in America, while the remaining 28 were either unsure or planned to visit at least temporarily.[95] The Mexican anthropologist Manuel Gamio found Mexican repatriates divided about whether they wanted to stay permanently in Mexico.[96] Regardless of the exact numbers, it seems that just a few years after the major repatriation movements, at least half of repatriates indicated that they had not really wanted to leave the United States and intended to return as soon as they could. At one border entrance immigration officials estimated that 90 percent of the people detained for illegal entry were former repatriates.[97] Some repatriates succeeded in recrossing the border within a short period of time. In 1933, H. M. Brown complained that "dozens of those who were sent to Mexico by the Red Cross have returned" to Arizona.[98] William A. Carlson, a member of the county commission of Greeley, Colorado, notified immigration officials that Mexicans who had previously been repatriated with county funds were already coming back, "unsolicited, uninvited and unwanted" and called for their deportation.[99]

The many unhappy repatriates had little recourse to change their situations. Growers and their supporters allied with powerful U.S. legislators, various officials in the U.S. and Mexican governments, Mexican and American journalists, and ordinary Americans to promote the image of Mexicans as temporary workers. Mexican immigrants, constrained by their circumstances in the 1920s, initially contributed to this developing notion as well, but by the early 1930s many of them changed their minds and decided that the United States had become home.[100] Yet even the Mexican consuls, journalists, government officials, and American assimilationists—who might be presumed to be sympathetic to the immigrants' plight—succumbed to the marginalizationists' rhetoric and began to believe that Mexicans would be better off in Mexico. While there was some criticism of the deportation process, especially for the most egregious removals such as those approved by Governor Johnson in Colorado or the warrantless roundups and raids in Los Angeles and other cities, few complained about the growing notion that Mexicans belonged in Mexico and should return there during hard times.[101] The temporary worker image initially offered something for everyone, including many immigrants. By the 1930s, however, it had become a convenient rationale for denying tens of thousands of immigrants the right to claim America as their home.[102]

Redefining Migratory Workers as Good Americans

One reason Mexicans were encouraged to leave the United States during the 1930s was that employers found a replacement source of labor ready to accept unsavory tasks and migratory jobs at low wages. In the 1920s, Americans linked the characteristics of the job with the people who performed them and viewed both the jobs and the people who filled them as lower class and not American. James Gregory explains "itinerancy itself was seen as a mark of failure." But during the Great Depression Americans found themselves needing this formerly undesirable employment.[103] Thus, while Americans tried to quit such jobs as quickly as possible, with most working on a migratory cycle for only a year or two, some Americans worked to redefine the jobs as dignified and worthy of being held by an American, rather than by a Mexican temporary worker.[104]

In 1940, the scholar George Gleason reported that at the beginning of the previous decade, "80 percent of the migrant workers were Mexicans and Filipinos" in California. He estimated that by 1935, "the complexion of the agricultural migrants has literally changed, so that 80 to 90 percent are now native white Americans." He explained that as the California newcomers were now a people "whose culture is similar to our own," he felt that the poor conditions of the migratory worker "must be promptly faced and wisely solved."[105] Agreeing with Gleason, U.S. legislators differentiated between Mexican workers who performed much of the migratory work in the 1920s and the new migrants. They wrote that the former Mexican laborers had been repatriated and that now "those who leave home . . . are predominantly normal, worth-while American people." In case there was any dispute about which Americans they referred to, the congressional authors explained that these new migratory workers included the "descendants of the oldest white families in the Southeastern and Eastern States."[106] Consequently, American scholars and officials attempted to redefine the previously maligned migratory jobs as well within the American tradition.

In the 1930s, various writers of federal and state government publications began to laud the character of transients and migratory laborers. David Cushman Coyle argued in the Works Progress Administration's *Depression Pioneers* that those who migrated internally were among the very best Americans due to their individualism, drive, and courage: "They are Americans in the old tradition, doing their best to fend for themselves." Coyle considered the new transient to be someone who had only recently fallen upon hard times, "superior to the run of the population," and more highly educated. One example was that of Jim Slade, who lost his job in the Youngstown steel mills after working there for five years. Upon hearing of opportunities in Flint, Michigan, Slade moved there and landed a job. Shortly afterward he was laid off and sought relief. According to Coyle, "Jim Slade can hardly be considered an undesirable citizen because he had the gumption to find himself a job in a distant city and then got left flat."[107] Yet before the depths of the Depression, few Americans would have applied the same logic to a *betabelero* or beet picker of Mexican descent who moved from Mexico or elsewhere in the United States to pick crops in the Michigan beet fields.

The Texas Transient Bureau reclaimed iconic American heroes to boost the dubious status of migratory workers. The bureau's *Alamo* publication highlighted the connections among Daniel Boone's intrepid spirit, movement, and the new transient workers. The most obvious of such connections was that of a sketch titled "Transients," in which the artist depicted Abraham Lincoln, Daniel Webster, and Sam Houston alongside "today's transient," who appeared to be a well-dressed white man.[108] A more curious juxtaposition in the same publication was that of an association of migratory people with American heroes like Davy Crockett, who fought at the Alamo. The authors argued "these heroes of the Alamo were transients."[109] Americans previously had not looked upon migration as something noble and patriotic, and instead disparaged such movement as uncivilized and intrinsic to Mexicans' character (see chapter 4). Yet Davy Crockett of the famed coonskin cap had himself been an emigrant from the United States to the then Mexican state of *Tejas*. The irony of this was apparently lost on the authors.

The trend of lauding the migratory worker continued throughout the 1930s. John Steinbeck, in his acclaimed novel *The Grapes of Wrath* (1936), sympathetically portrayed an "Okie" family uprooted through no fault of their own and forced to try their luck in California. Three years later, the success of this book launched a popular movie of the same name. Depression-era murals also valorized the strength and courage of white, working-class people. Although this short-lived era of praise did not result in an improvement in working conditions, it might have, had it endured, resulted in Americans rethinking the linkage of itinerant labor with being a failure, or foreign.[110]

As long as the economic depression continued, it would be difficult for people of Mexican descent to fit within or be recognized in the nation as any kind of American. Those who promoted the marginalization strategy had provided a space for Mexicans only at the bottom of society, as either subordinate Americans or temporary guests, doing work that few Americans wanted to do. The Depression removed even this lowly status as an opportunity since Americans then agreed to accept migratory work for low wages. With Mexicans safely out of sight, American politicians, government officials, and writers began to adjust and boost the image of migrant jobs and the people who performed them. But some forward-looking journalists and scholars wondered anew what would happen when the economy improved and once again there was "work no white man will do" at the proffered wages.[111] They were right to wonder, for during the Second World War that time would arrive and result in the welcoming of Mexicans, once again, as only temporary workers.

Notes

Introduction

1. For information on the medal, Theodore Roosevelt's reaction, and his speech, see both "Another Surprise," *Los Angeles Times*, June 26, 1899, and "Farewell to His Troops," *San Francisco Chronicle*, June 26, 1899. For Roosevelt's changing view on statehood, see "Oklahoma Will Be the Only New State," *San Francisco Chronicle*, December 8, 1902. For his position on joint statehood, see *San Francisco Chronicle*, January 3, 1903. For information on his godson, the christening, and his visit, see "Sergeant's Son," *Boston Daily Globe*, May 6, 1903; "Ask Roosevelt for Statehood," *Chicago Daily News*, May 6, 1903; "Mr. Roosevelt Tells New Mexico to Grow," *New York Times*, May 6, 1903; and "Mr. Roosevelt's Tour," *Independent*, May 14, 1903. Regarding the president's changing views, see Marion Dargan, "New Mexico's Fight for Statehood, 1895–1912, I," *New Mexico Historical Review* 14 (January 1939), 13; John Braeman, "Albert J. Beveridge and Statehood for the Southwest, 1902–1912," *Arizona and the West* 10 (Winter 1968), 320; and Jay J. Wagoner, *Arizona Territory, 1863–1912: A Political History* (Tucson: University of Arizona Press, 1970), 412. For the godson's behavior and the final quote in this paragraph, see "The President Having a 'Vociferous' Time," *Baltimore Sun*, May 7, 1903; all in *Proquest Historical Newspapers*.

2. I have been influenced by several historians who focus generally on U.S. national identity, including Lawrence H. Fuchs, *American Kaleidoscope: Race, Ethnicity, and the Civic Culture* (Hanover, NH: Wesleyan University Press, 1990); Gary Gerstle, *American Crucible: Race and Nation in the Twentieth Century* (Princeton, NJ: Princeton University Press, 2001); John Higham, *Strangers in the Land: Patterns of American Nativism, 1860–1925* (New Brunswick, NJ: Rutgers University Press, 1998); and Rogers M. Smith, *Civic Ideals: Conflicting Visions of Citizenship in U.S. History* (New Haven, CT: Yale University Press, 1997). Other historians have influenced my understanding of how the state works and how it racialized people of Mexican descent. In particular, see Linda Gordon, *The Great Arizona Orphan Abduction*

(Cambridge: Harvard University Press, 1999), 77, 143–46; and Ian Haney López, *White by Law: The Legal Construction of Race* (New York: New York University Press, 1998), 61 and chap. 2.

3. Regarding the association of the New Mexico and/or Arizona territories with America's expanding empire, see Pablo Mitchell, *Coyote Nation: Sexuality, Race, and Conquest in Modernizing New Mexico* (Chicago: University of Chicago Press, 2005), 4. Also see Kristin L. Hoganson, *Fighting for American Manhood: How Gender Politics Provoked the Spanish-American and Philippine-American Wars* (New Haven, CT: Yale University Press, 1998), 1–4 and 12–14; and Paul A. Kramer, *The Blood of Government: Race, Empire, the United States and the Philippines* (Chapel Hill: University of North Carolina Press, 2006), 4–7, 11–15.

4. Matthew Frye Jacobson, *Barbarian Virtues: The United States Encounters Foreign Peoples at Home and Abroad, 1876–1917* (New York: Hill and Wang, 2000), 247.

5. I borrow the term "gatekeeping" from Erika Lee, "The Chinese Exclusion Example: Race, Immigration, and American Gatekeeping, 1882–1924," *Journal of American Ethnic History* 21, no. 3 (Spring 2002), 36–62, esp. 37–38.

6. For some recent works focused specifically on people of Mexican descent and U.S. national identity, see Gabriela F. Arredondo, *Mexican Chicago: Race, Identity, and Nation, 1916–39* (Chicago: University of Illinois Press, 2008); Katherine Benton-Cohen, *Borderline Americans: Racial Divisions and Labor War in the Arizona Borderlands* (Cambridge: Harvard University Press, 2009); Alicia Schmidt Camacho, *Migrant Imaginaries: Latino Cultural Politics in the U.S.-Mexico Borderlands* (New York: New York University Press, 2008); Eric V. Meeks, *Border Citizens: The Making of Indians, Mexicans and Anglos in Arizona* (Austin: University of Texas Press, 2007); Mitchell, *Coyote Nation*; Anthony Mora, *Border Dilemmas: Racial and National Uncertainties in New Mexico, 1848–1912* (Durham, NC: Duke University Press, 2011); John M. Nieto-Phillips, *The Language of Blood: The Making of Spanish-American Identity in New Mexico, 1880s-1930s* (Albuquerque: University of New Mexico Press, 2004); and George J. Sánchez, *Becoming Mexican American: Ethnicity, Culture, and Identity in Chicano Los Angeles, 1900–1945* (New York: Oxford University Press, 1993). Laura Gómez addresses how people of Mexican descent in New Mexico fit within the nation, but concentrates more on the creation of what she deems the Mexican American race and the development of their off-white status, in *Manifest Destinies: The Making of the Mexican American Race* (New York: New York University Press, 2007).

7. Many historians and sociologists refer to strategies of incorporation with slightly different definitions and labels. The strategies I use differ from sociologists Alejandro Portes and Rubén Rumbaut's concept of segmented assimilation, which is an encompassing theory for how immigrants who entered in distinct time periods experienced assimilation—either into the mainstream or as part of the underclass—depending on a variety of factors, including the immigrants' background, government response, and the host society's reception. I see pluralism and marginalization as strategies created or modified by historical agents in a specific time and place as part of their efforts to achieve statehood and the incorporation of territorial residents into the polity. See Portes and Rumbaut, *Legacies: The Story of the Immigrant Second Generation* (Berkeley: University of California Press, 2001), 45. Regarding pluralism, Russell Kazal finds that "vernacular pluralism" originated in the early twentieth century and predated intellectuals Horace Kallen and Randolph Bourne's discussion of this concept; see

Kazal, "The Lost World of Pennsylvania Pluralism: Immigrants, Regions, and the Early Origins of Pluralist Ideologies in America," *Journal of American Ethnic History* 27 (Spring 2008), 7–9. Laura Gómez (*Manifest Destinies*, 10) refers to a "dominant view" held by those in Congress and the national press, which considered people of Mexican descent inferior, and a "progressive" one in which Euro Americans emphasized the Spanish heritage of New Mexican elites as a strategy for attaining statehood. For clarity, I prefer to use *exclusion* and *pluralism*, to coincide with terms more commonly used for other immigrant groups.

8. See Katherine Benton-Cohen (*Borderline Americans*, 7–8, 142–43) regarding the importance of the stability of the home and family life and Pablo Mitchell (Mitchell, *Coyote Nation*, 120–21) regarding modernity and "bodily comportment" influencing definitions of whiteness, citizenship, and being American. I see these factors as contributing to one's class status in the community, which is then conflated with whiteness and racial status. As for the connection between class and racialization of people of Mexican descent, see A. Yvette Huginnie, "'Mexican Labour' in a 'White Man's Town': Racialism, Imperialism, and Industrialization in the Making of Arizona, 1840–1905," in Peter Alexander and Rick Halpern, eds., *Racializing Class, Classifying Race: Labour and Difference in Britain, the USA and Africa* (New York: St Martin's Press, 2000), 33–34; Tomás Almaguer, *Racial Fault Lines: The Historical Origins of White Supremacy in California* (Berkeley: University of California Press, 1994), 72 and chap. 2; and Albert Camarillo, *Chicanos in a Changing Society: From Mexican Pueblos to American Barrios in Santa Barbara and Southern California, 1848–1930* (Cambridge: Harvard University Press, 1979).

9. For an example of Germans using pluralism, see Russell A. Kazal, *Becoming Old Stock: The Paradox of German-American Identity* (Princeton: Princeton University Press, 2004).

10. On the dominance of white nationalisms and how those deemed or constructed as nonwhite were viewed as un-American, see Nicholas De Genova who states that while various groups helped to build the nation-state, the dominant understanding of U.S. national identity was one "synonymous with racial whiteness," in De Genova, ed., *Racial Transformations: Latinos and Asians Remaking the United States* (Durham, NC: Duke University Press, 2006), 11–12. Given the era, it is perhaps not surprising to see anything other than white nationalisms being touted by those seeking a space in the American nation; I found few sources for working-class people of Mexican descent and recent immigrants who might have had other ideas on how and whether they wanted to integrate into the United States. Some Americans spoke in a language of "civic nationalism," but this, Gary Gerstle finds (*American Crucible*, 8), was often applied in exclusionary ways if people did not conform as expected to dominant society.

11. See the discussions of cultural citizenship in William V. Flores and Rina Benmayor, eds., *Latino Cultural Citizenship: Claiming Identity, Space and Rights* (Boston: Beacon Press, 1997), 44–46. Arredondo (*Mexican Chicago*, 80–82, 148–53, 172) sees pan-Americanism as declining during the Great Depression due to the constrained flow of travel and ideas in that era. George Sánchez (*Becoming Mexican American*, 12–13) finds a Mexican American identity being created in the 1930s and 1940s. For flexible nationalism, see Camacho, *Migrant Imaginaries*, 4, 25. For more on Mexican identity, see Zaragosa Vargas, *Proletarians of the North: A History of Mexican Industrial*

Workers in Detroit and the Midwest, 1917–1933 (Berkeley: University of California Press, 1993), 151, 157.

12. The residents in the territories were to be granted citizenship automatically one year after the treaty went into effect, unless they opted to retain Mexican citizenship and made this declaration formally, or moved to Mexico. People of Mexican descent were considered white for the purpose of suffrage, whereas Pueblo Indians, who had been able to vote as Mexican citizens, had this right removed after the Treaty of Guadalupe Hidalgo since the U.S. government considered Pueblos wards of the state. See Nieto-Phillips, *Language of Blood*, 37–40, 47, 52–58, 76. See also Articles VIII and IX of the Treaty of Guadalupe Hidalgo in Richard Griswold del Castillo, *The Treaty of Guadalupe Hidalgo: A Legacy of Conflict* (Norman: University of Oklahoma Press, 1990), 189–90; Frederick Merk, *Manifest Destiny and Mission in American History: A Reinterpretation* (New York: Alfred A. Knopf, 1963), 256–57, and chaps. 5 and 7.

13. President Lincoln signed the Organic Act (1863) establishing the Territory of Arizona to prevent secession. There were few serious attempts at statehood until the late nineteenth and early twentieth centuries; see Robert W. Larson, *New Mexico's Quest for Statehood, 1846–1912* (Albuquerque: University of New Mexico Press, 1968), 89, 116–33, 302.

14. Many scholars today agree that the United States is, and was, an empire; see Julian Go, "Chains of Empire, Projects of State: Political Education and U.S. Colonial Rule in Puerto Rico and the Philippines," *Comparative Studies in Society and History*, 42 (Apr. 2000), 333–62; Go, *American Empire and the Politics of Meaning: Elite Political Cultures in the Philippines and Puerto Rico during U.S. Colonialism* (Durham, NC: Duke University Press, 2008), 5–6; Gary Y. Okihiro, "Colonial Vision, Racial Visibility: Racializations in Puerto Rico and the Philippines during the Initial Period of U.S. Colonization," in De Genova, *Racial Transformations*, 24–25; Sally Engle Merry, *Colonizing Hawai'i: The Cultural Power of Law* (Princeton, NJ: Princeton University Press, 2000), 23–30; Kramer, *Blood of Government*, 11–18; Walter L. Williams, "United States Indian Policy and the Debate over Philippine Annexation: Implications for the Origins of American Imperialism," *Journal of American History* 66 (Mar. 1980), 810–83; Ann Laura Stoler, "Intimidations of Empire" in Ann Laura Stoler, ed., *Haunted by Empire: Geographies of Intimacy in North American History* (Durham, NC: Duke University Press, 2006), 1–22, esp. 9–11; and Linda Gordon, "Internal Colonialism and Gender," in Ann Laura Stoler, ed., *Haunted by Empire: Geographies of Intimacy in North American History* (Durham, NC: Duke University Press, 2006), 427–51., esp. 430–34.

15. For legislators' views, see "Power of Congress Most Remarkable," *Los Angeles Times*, January 11, 1901, *Proquest Historical Newspapers*; for the opinion of the U.S. attorney general, see H. K. Carroll, "The Territorial System for Our New Possessions," *Outlook*, December 23, 1899; for the views of the commissioner of Puerto Rico, see him qtd. in Lauren L. Basson, *White Enough to Be American? Race Mixing, Indigenous People, and the Boundaries of State and Nation* (Chapel Hill: University of North Carolina Press, 2008), 133–34. On May 27, 1901, the Supreme Court ruled that the Philippines would be considered an "unincorporated territory," a distinction that presumed that the incorporated territories would eventually be admitted as states; for more on this and the court's decision see Merk, *Manifest Destiny and Mission*, 256–58.

16. Quote in U.S. House committee report, repr. in *Congressional Record*, 57 Cong., 2nd. sess. (December 10, 1902), 180. Although the debates over statehood started immediately after the Mexican–American War, the majority of the people within the territories did not support self-government until the end of the nineteenth century; see Nieto-Phillips, *Language of Blood*, 79–80; Larson, *New Mexico's Quest for Statehood*, 195, 202; Mark E. Pry, "Arizona and the Politics of Statehood, 1889–1912" (PhD diss., Arizona State University, 1995), 56; and Karen Underhill Mangelsdorf, "The Beveridge Visit to Arizona in 1902," *Journal of Arizona History* 28, no. 3 (Fall 1987), 243–60, esp. 248. The omnibus bill included proposals for the statehood of Arizona, New Mexico, Oklahoma, and the Indian Territory. As a result of a congressional tour, the Beveridge Report (1902) recommended that Oklahoma and the Indian Territory be combined—to allow for Anglo control—into one state and that the other proposals be rejected. Oklahoma became a state in 1907; for more on this history, see David A. Chang, *The Color of the Land: Race, Nation, and the Politics of Land Ownership in Oklahoma, 1832–1929* (Chapel Hill: University of North Carolina Press, 2010).

17. Historians Robert Larson (*New Mexico's Quest for Statehood*) and Mark Pry ("Arizona and the Politics of Statehood") write on territorial history but concentrate mostly on the political debates over statehood rather than on how it affected American identity or how people of Mexican descent contributed to the debates. More recently, historians have begun to examine the place and role of people of Mexican descent during the late territorial/early statehood years. For New Mexico, see Gómez, *Manifest Destinies*; Nieto-Phillips, *Language of Blood*; Mitchell, *Coyote Nation*; Charles Montgomery, *The Spanish Redemption: Heritage, Power, and Loss on New Mexico's Upper Rio Grande* (Berkeley: University of California Press, 2002); and Mora, *Border Dilemmas*. For Arizona, see Benton-Cohen, *Borderline Americans*; Gordon, *Great Arizona Orphan Abduction*; and Meeks, *Border Citizens*.

18. The restrictions for the Chinese were initially placed on laborers before later applying to all Chinese immigrants. See Aristide R. Zolberg, *A Nation by Design: Immigration Policy in the Fashioning of America* (New York: Russell Sage Foundation, 2006), 188–92; and Daniel Kanstroom, *Deportation Nation: Outsiders in American History* (Cambridge: Harvard University Press, 2007), 133, 155, 210.

19. Influential works on temporary workers include Donna R. Gabaccia, "Is Everywhere Nowhere?: Nomads, Nations, and the Immigrant Paradigm of United States History," *Journal of American History* 86, no. 3 (1999), 1115–34; Cindy Hahamovitch, "Creating Perfect Immigrants: Guestworkers of the World in Historical Perspective," *Labor History* 44, no. 1 (2003), 69–94; Hahamovitch, *The Fruits of Their Labor: Atlantic Coast Farmworkers and the Making of Migrant Poverty, 1870–1945* (Chapel Hill: University of North Carolina Press, 1997); Gunther Peck, *Reinventing Free Labor: Padrones and Immigrant Workers in the North American West, 1880–1930* (New York: Cambridge University Press, 2000); Michael J. Piore, *Birds of Passage: Migrant Labor and Industrial Societies* (Cambridge: Cambridge University Press, 1979); Mark Wyman, *Round-Trip to America: The Immigrants Return to Europe, 1880–1930* (Ithaca, NY: Cornell University Press, 1996); Wyman, *Hoboes, Bindlestiffs, Fruit Tramps, and the Harvesting of the West* (New York: Hill and Wang, 2010).

20. Several historians note the transition from predominantly European to Mexican labor and decreasing fear of Europeans due to their declining numbers. See Benton-Cohen, *Borderline Americans*; Kathleen Mapes, *Sweet Tyranny* (Champaign-Urbana:

University of Illinois Press, 2009); and Jim Norris, *North for the Harvest: Mexican Workers, Growers, and the Sugar Beet Industry* (St. Paul: Minnesota Historical Press, 2009).

21. For more on the *Rodríguez* decision and later related cases, see Patrick D. Lukens, *A Quiet Victory for Latino Rights: FDR and the Controversy over "Whiteness"* (Tucson: University of Arizona Press, 2012), 110–14 and chap. 6.

22. For other historians' research on the second *bracero* program, see Kitty Calavita, *Inside the State: The Bracero Program, Immigration, and the INS* (New York: Routledge, 1992); Deborah Cohen, *Braceros: Migrant Citizens and Transnational Subjects in the Postwar United States and Mexico* (Chapel Hill: University of North Carolina, 2011); Barbara A. Driscoll, *The Tracks North: The Railroad Bracero Program of World War II* (Austin: University of Texas, 1999); and Gilbert González, *Guest Workers or Colonized Labor?: Mexican Labor to the United States* (Boulder, CO: Paradigm, 2005). For more on the first *bracero* program, see Mark Reisler, *By the Sweat of Their Brow: Mexican Immigrant Labor in the United States, 1900–1940* (Westport, CT: Greenwood Press, 1976), 24–48; Manuel García y Griego, "The Importation of Mexican Contract Laborers to the United States, 1942–1964: Antecedents, Operation, and Legacy," in Peter G. Brown and Henry Shue, eds., *The Border That Joins: Mexican Migrants and U.S. Responsibility* (Totowa, NJ: Rowman and Littlefield, 1983), 49–98; and Mapes, *Sweet Tyranny*, 122–42.

23. For a discussion of the association of Mexicans as temporary workers, see Reisler, *By the Sweat of Their Brow*, 24–48. Camille Guerin-Gonzales makes the connection more explicit in *Mexican Workers, American Dreams: Immigration, Repatriation and California Farm Labor, 1900–1939* (New Brunswick, NJ: Rutgers University Press, 1994), chap. 2, esp. 45. Many others also note the associations made between Mexicans and temporary workers; see Devra Weber, *Dark Sweat, White Gold: California Farm Workers, Cotton, and the New Deal* (Berkeley: University of California Press, 1994), 8; Abraham Hoffman, *Unwanted Mexican Americans in the Great Depression: Repatriation Pressures, 1929–1939* (Tucson: University of Arizona Press, 1974), 16–17; Piore, *Birds of Passage*, 3, 51–52, 77, 81–82; and Sánchez, *Becoming Mexican American*, 189. Also see Kathleen Mapes's recent study on sugar beet workers in the Midwest (*Sweet Tyranny*, 6–10 and chaps. 3 and 5), in which she notes the growers' and the state's involvement in creating "Mexicans as workers but not as immigrants." I agree but stress more how many people worked to create the temporary worker image, not just the state and growers, and that this reality of a temporary worker—as Mapes notes, too—was often a fictional construct. See also Fuchs, *American Kaleidoscope*, 111, 121.

24. The most influential works on this include Mae M. Ngai, *Impossible Subjects: Illegal Aliens and the Making of Modern America* (Princeton, NJ: Princeton University Press, 2004), chaps. 1 and 2. Ngai asserts that Americans did not view Mexicans as alien before the 1920s—on the whole, this seems accurate but the statehood debates show much concern about how "American" people of Mexican descent were or could be. Alexandra Stern looks at restrictionism in a new way, arguing that the eugenics movement extended its influence in the 1920s and 1930s, especially with regard to Mexicans in the West. Eugenicists believed that the environment had no impact or effect on an individual and thus did not believe in assimilationist theories. They saw Mexicans as dirty, degraded, and less intelligent than Anglos, with no ability to

become American. Other Americans shared the eugenicists' ideas, interpreting the Mexicans' lack of cleanliness as inherent and as a reason to delouse and inspect them more thoroughly than most other immigrants. Concurring with Ngai's work, Stern uses this evidence as proof of the racialization process that affected Mexicans after World War I. See Stern, *Eugenic Nation: Faults and Frontiers of Better Breeding in Modern America* (Berkeley: University of California Press, 2005). See also the work of recent scholars who examine new aspects of the Mexican immigration restriction debates. Regarding concerns about how the health of Mexicans might affect Americans and restrictionist efforts, see Natalia Molina, *Fit to Be Citizens? Public Health and Race in Los Angeles, 1879–1939* (Berkeley: University of California Press, 2006). Clare Sheridan argues that competing ideas of citizenship and concerns about the immigrants' class status increased fears that they would damage the American standard of living and undermine democracy in "Contested Citizenship: National Identity and the Mexican Immigration Debates of the 1920s," *Journal of American Ethnic History* 21, no. 3 (Spring 2002), 3–35. Kathleen Mapes (*Sweet Tyranny*), who limits her study to the Midwest, argues that neither the capitalists nor restrictionists were very interested in assimilating the newcomers; instead the debate was over the immigrants' labor.

25. Earlier important works on restrictionism include that of Robert Divine, who finds concern about Mexican relations important in preventing restriction, and that of Lawrence Cardoso, who concurs but expands on Divine's work, showing that the United States wanted to keep Mexico stable by keeping the 'safety valve' of immigration open, which would reduce the likelihood of more revolutions in Mexico. He also adds that missionaries argued against immigration restriction since they thought that Americanization would improve the immigrants: even if Mexicans returned home, the immigrants would take a favorable impression of the United States back to Mexico and help to build and maintain good relations between the United States and Mexico. See Divine, *American Immigration Policy, 1924–1952* (New Haven, CT: Yale University Press, 1957); and Cardoso, *Mexican Emigration to the United States, 1897–1931* (Tucson: University of Arizona Press, 1980).

26. For more on the eugenics movement, see Stern, *Eugenic Nation*.

27. Hoffman (*Unwanted Mexican Americans in the Great Depression*, 2, 174–75) estimates that approximately 500,000 Mexicans were repatriated, voluntarily and involuntarily, in the 1930s.

28. Francisco E. Balderrama and Raymond Rodríguez, *Decade of Betrayal: Mexican Repatriation in the 1930s* rev. ed. (Albuquerque: University of New Mexico Press, 2006), 80–82. For another work on repatriation, see Guerin-Gonzales, *Mexican Workers, American Dreams*, esp. chaps. 4 and 5.

29. Few Africans entered the United States during this era. For quote, see Paul Spickard, *Almost All Aliens: Immigration, Race and Colonialism in American History and Identity* (New York: New York University Press, 2007), 129; and Gómez, *Manifest Destinies*, 3. For views on southern and eastern Europeans, see James R. Barrett and David Roediger, "Inbetween Peoples: Race, Nationality, and the 'New Immigrant' Working Class," *Journal of American Ethnic History* 16, no. 3 (Spring 1997), 3–44. Also see Thomas A. Guglielmo, *White on Arrival: Italians, Race, Color, and Power in Chicago, 1890–1945* (Oxford: Oxford University Press, 2003), 8–9.

30. The process followed by the pluralists is akin to what Smith (*Civic Ideals*, 2–3) describes. Smith explains that Americans followed an "ascriptive tradition" in which

they ascribed a status to people based on their race, religion, and sex, with Anglo-Saxon males at the top of the hierarchy, and then supported citizenship laws reflecting this. The *nativo* pluralists included themselves among Anglo Americans at the top of this hierarchy.

31. For other examples of European immigrants boosting their status in Arizona in relation to people of Mexican descent, see Benton-Cohen, *Borderline Americans*, 15–17; and Gordon, *Great Arizona Orphan Abduction*, 102, 115–16.

32. Regarding resolving capitalists' and workers' ongoing struggle, see Lisa Lowe, *Immigrant Acts: On Asian American Cultural Politics* (Durham, NC: Duke University Press, 1996), 12–13.

33. Representative John Box, an exclusionist Democrat representing East Texas, used this phrase of a swinging door. Although he used it to question whether Mexicans ever left the United States, stating "the swinging door is seen to swing in only one direction," I use it here to reference the idea of a door going both ways: in when Americans want Mexican labor and out when they do not. For the Box quote, see U.S. House of Representatives, Committee on Immigration and Naturalization, *Imported Pauper Labor and Serfdom in America: Statement of Honorable John C. Box*, Hearings, 67th Cong., 1st sess. (1921), 17. Quotation is from a reprint of *Dallas News*, February 1, 1921, in the abovementioned hearing.

Chapter One

1. In 1885 Otero was opposed to statehood as he initially believed, like many other businessmen of the territory, that New Mexico did not have sufficient resources to support a government. By the time he became governor, the expansion of railroads in the area along with the establishment of a public school system led him to change his mind. See Marion Dargan, "New Mexico's Fight for Statehood, 1895–1912, I," *New Mexico Historical Review* 14 (January 1939), 17–18, 24–29.

2. Thomas E. Sheridan, *Los Tucsonenses: The Mexican Community in Tucson, 1854–1941* (Tucson: University of Arizona Press, 1986), 52, 96, 111, 212; John S. Goff, *Arizona Biographical Dictionary* (Cave Creek: Black Mountain Press, 1983), 54; Alex G. Jácome, "Letter to the Editor," *Arizona Star*, April 29, 1970, in Biofile-Carlos Jácome, Arizona and Southwestern Biographical File, Special Collections, University of Arizona Library. For reference to his band and pioneer membership, see Kaye Lynn Briegel, "Alianza Hispano-Americana, 1894–1965: A Mexican American Fraternal Insurance Society" (PhD diss., University of Southern California, 1974), 40–41.

3. Mark E. Pry, "Arizona and the Politics of Statehood, 1889–1912" (PhD diss., Arizona State University, 1995), 5–7.

4. In 1904 the Supreme Court ruled on the Insular Cases and declared that the Philippines would be considered an "unincorporated territory," rather than incorporated like New Mexico and Arizona. This distinction presumed that the incorporated territories were on the path to statehood and would eventually be admitted. See Frederick Merk, *Manifest Destiny and Mission in American History: A Reinterpretation* (New York: Alfred A. Knopf, 1963), 256–58.

5. Historian Howard R. Lamar perceived territorial history in the context of empire and saw that Theodore Roosevelt and Senator Albert Beveridge viewed the Ari-

zona and New Mexico territories in the context of America's recent acquisitions from the Spanish-American War. See Howard R. Lamar, *The Far Southwest, 1846–1912: A Territorial History* (Albuquerque: University of New Mexico, Press, 2000), 5–6, 423, 425–26.

6. William V. Flores and Rina Benmayor, eds., *Latino Cultural Citizenship: Claiming Identity, Space, and Rights* (Boston: Beacon Press, 1997), 46.

7. Bartholomew H. Sparrow, *The Insular Cases and the Emergence of American Empire* (Lawrence: University of Kansas Press, 2006), 21–29; and Gary Lawson and Guy Seidman, *The Constitution of Empire: Territorial Expansion and American Legal History* (New Haven, CT: Yale University Press, 2004), 91–93, 106–9.

8. Besides Chinese immigrants, a few others were excluded in the late nineteenth century if they were prostitutes or criminals (1875) or "idiots," "lunatics," or "likely to become a public charge" (1882). See Daniel J. Tichenor, *Dividing Lines: The Politics of Immigration Control in America* (Princeton, NJ: Princeton University Press, 2002), 3.

9. For this distinction between white as a color, or a legal/social category, and race, especially for Italians, see Thomas A. Guglielmo, *White on Arrival: Italians, Race, Color, and Power in Chicago, 1890–1945* (Oxford: Oxford University Press, 2003), 8–9. For a discussion of how Anglo-Americans viewed southern and eastern European immigrants more generally, see James R. Barrett and David Roediger, "In-between Peoples: Race, Nationality, and the 'New Immigrant' Working Class," *Journal of American Ethnic History* 16, no. 3 (Spring 1997), 3–44.

10. Erika Lee explains how Chinese immigrants dressed as Mexicans and learned a few words of Spanish so that they could cross into the United States without attracting attention. See Erika Lee, *At America's Gate: Chinese Immigration during the Exclusion Era, 1882–1943* (Chapel Hill: University of North Carolina Press, 2003), 172. Regarding why officials did not pay much attention to Mexican immigrants, see Katherine Benton-Cohen, "Other Immigrants: Mexicans and the Dillingham Commission of 1907–1911," *Journal of American Ethnic History* 30, no. 2 (Winter 2011), 33–57.

11. Regarding unity around the question of statehood, see John M. Nieto-Phillips, *The Language of Blood: The Making of Spanish-American Identity in New Mexico, 1880s–1930s* (Albuquerque: University of New Mexico Press, 2004), 52–58, 79–80; Robert W. Larson, *New Mexico's Quest for Statehood, 1846–1912* (Albuquerque: University of New Mexico Press, 1968), 195, 202; Lamar, *Far Southwest*, 171, 432; Pry, "Arizona and the Politics of Statehood," 56; and Karen Underhill Mangelsdorf, "The Beveridge Visit to Arizona in 1902," *Journal of Arizona History* 28, no. 3 (Fall 1987), 243–60, esp. 248. Howard Lamar (*Far Southwest*, 432–33) explains that a few territorial residents continued to make efforts to undermine statehood during the first decade of the twentieth century but at the same time emphasizes that the residents began to view their status as a mark of "inferiority" and thus united for statehood.

12. The omnibus bill included proposals for the statehood of Arizona, New Mexico, and Oklahoma. The battles over Oklahoma revolved around the presence of American Indians, rather than people of Mexican descent, and took a different path from that of Arizona and New Mexico. Oklahoma became a state in 1907. For a full discussion of this debate, see David A. Chang, *The Color of the Land: Race, Nation, and the Politics of Land Ownership in Oklahoma, 1832–1929* (Chapel Hill: University of North Carolina Press, 2010).

13. For criteria on statehood, see Peter S. Onuf, *Statehood and Union: A History of the Northwest Ordinance* (Bloomington: Indiana University Press, 1987), 67; and George H. Alden, "The Evolution of the American System of Forming and Admitting New States into the Union," *Annals of the American Academy of Political and Social Science* 18 (November 1901), 88–89. For state statistics, see U.S. Bureau of the Census, *Abstract of the Twelfth Census, 1900*, 3rd ed. (Washington, DC, 1904). Larson (Larson, *New Mexico's Quest for Statehood*, 303–4) argues that nativism was the major reason for the long delay in statehood. Regarding a similar argument for Arizona, see Pry, "Arizona and the Politics of Statehood," 188. Howard Lamar (*Far Southwest*, 423–25, 427) sees three major reasons for the delay: the effects of the Spanish-American War on the debate (with nativism a factor here), natural resources, and progressivism. Yet Lamar also argues that Senator Beveridge, who was so instrumental in these debates, believed that many of the Southwestern denizens were incompatible with Anglo Americans due to their ethnicity and culture.

14. In 1900 the number of Arizonans who were Mexican-born was 14,172; this number doubled within the next decade, see Thomas E. Sheridan, *Arizona: A History* (Tucson: University of Arizona Press, 1995), 169. For estimates on the percentage of people of Mexican descent—and these are only estimates since the census did not record this at the time—see David R. Berman, *Reformers, Corporations, and the Electorate: An Analysis of Arizona's Age of Reform* (Niwot: University Press of Colorado, 1992), 8–9. Also see U.S. Senate, Committee on the Territories, *New Statehood Bill*, Rep. 2206, 57 Cong., 2nd sess. (1902), 14. Pueblo Indians, who had been able to vote under Mexican rule, had this right removed after the Treaty of Guadalupe Hidalgo; see Nieto-Phillips, *Language of Blood*, 47. Regarding people of Mexican descent not being permitted to vote, see Martha Menchaca, "Chicano Indianism: A Historical Account of Racial Repression in the United States," *American Ethnologist*, 20 (no. 4, 1993), 583–603, esp. 593. Other statistics are from the U.S. Bureau of the Census, *Abstract of the Twelfth Census, 1900*. And see Committee on the Territories, *New Statehood Bill*, 14; Karen Jean Underhill, "Albert J. Beveridge's Congressional Report on Arizona Territory in 1902" (master's thesis, University of Arizona, 1990), 45. In Arizona, intermarriage between people of Anglo and Mexican descent dropped from 22.8 percent in the 1870s to 9.1 percent in the decade of the 1890s, further reducing ways in which people of Mexican descent retained power, see Sheridan, *Los Tucsonenses*, 149. Also see Eric V. Meeks, *Border Citizens: The Making of Indians, Mexicans, and Anglos in Arizona* (Austin: University of Texas Press, 2007), 25–30.

15. The term *peon* has been used in many ways. The historian Friedrich Katz explains that during much of the nineteenth and twentieth centuries in Mexico, people used the word for agricultural workers and sometimes laborers in the mines. Katz himself applies an even narrower definition, using it only for permanent laborers on a hacienda who were indebted to the owner or *hacendado*. I believe that the exclusionists in the United States used this term in a general way for any worker of Mexican descent. See Katz, "Labor Conditions on Haciendas in Porfirian Mexico: Some Trends and Tendencies," *Hispanic American Historical Review* 54, no. 1 (February 1974), 2n3.

16. Mangelsdorf, "Beveridge Visit to Arizona," 244; and John Braeman, "Albert J. Beveridge and Statehood for the Southwest, 1902–1912," *Arizona and the West* 10 (Winter 1968), 313–42, esp. 340.

17. Braeman, "Albert J. Beveridge," 313–17.

18. For information on Beveridge's propensity to arrange for speakers who would help to prove his case against statehood, see Jesse de la Cruz, "Rejection Because of Race: Albert J. Beveridge and Nuevo Mexico's Struggle for Statehood, 1902–1903," *Aztlán* 7, no. 1 (1977), 81–82. For the first quotation, see Article, "Against a Minority," retyped from *Citizen*, February 4, 1903, Marion Dargan Papers, MSS 120 BC, box 10, file 11, Center for Southwest Research, General Library, University of New Mexico; see also the hand-copied editorial, *El Paso Herald*, January 16, 1909, in box 2, file 10. Also see Mangelsdorf, "Beveridge Visit to Arizona," 249. The authors of this report were referring, in this case, specifically to New Mexico. But they recommended against the admission of Arizona as well, because of the presence of people of Mexican descent in that territory and expressed concern about the large number of Mexicans they believed to be immigrating to Arizona. Committee on the Territories, *New Statehood Bill*, 5–9 (quote from p. 9) and 14–20.

19. 57th Cong., 2nd sess., *Congressional Record* (January 1903), 568.

20. Appendix to 57th Cong., 2nd sess., *Congressional Record* (February 4, 1903), 182.

21. For the "black legend" and its origins, see David J. Weber, *The Spanish Frontier in North America* (Cambridge: Harvard University Press, 1992), 336–41. Regarding its decline, see Phoebe S. Kropp, *California Vieja: Culture and Memory in a Modern American Place* (Berkeley: University of California Press, 2006), 28–30, 52–54.

22. Although exclusionists continued to express alarm at the number of southern and eastern Europeans (including Spaniards) who made their way to America's shores, they primarily feared Spaniards as representative of yet another among the "hordes" coming to the United States rather than holding specific fears about the Spaniards themselves who emigrated in small numbers relative to other southern and eastern Europeans.

23. 57th Cong., 2nd sess., *Congressional Record* (February 1903), 1642.

24. Appendix to 57th Cong., 2nd sess., *Congressional Record* (February 4, 1903), 182–84.

25. As historian Lawrence Glickman explains, many Anglo American workers since the end of the nineteenth century have argued that greater needs and demands (consumption rather than production) defined the American worker in contrast to those who subsisted on much lower wages. See Lawrence B. Glickman, *A Living Wage: American Workers and the Making of Consumer Society* (Ithaca: Cornell University Press, 1997). Another scholar, A. Yvette Huginnie, adds to our understanding of this by demonstrating how living conditions helped define racial categories. Huginnie finds that in late nineteenth-century Arizona, some Anglo Americans believed that people who willingly ate beans or lived in slum-like conditions could not be "white" since white people would not accept such an environment. See Huginnie, "'Mexican Labour' in a 'White Man's Town': Racialism, Imperialism, and Industrialization in the Making of Arizona, 1840–1905," in Peter Alexander and Rick Halpern, eds., *Racializing Class, Classifying Race: Labour and Difference in Britain, the USA and Africa* (New York: St Martin's Press, 2000), 33–34.

26. Letter from New England Shoe and Leather Association, June 2, 1902, Records of the U.S. House of Representatives, Record Group 233, file HR 57A-H26.4, National Archives, Washington, DC.

27. For Pablo Mitchell's discussion of a certain type of respectable living and comportment associated with whiteness, see Pablo Mitchell, *Coyote Nation: Sexuality, Race, and Conquest in Modernizing New Mexico* (Chicago: University of Chicago Press, 2005), 120–21.

28. For the quotation, see Committee on the Territories, *New Statehood Bill*, 9. For Anglo American views on Chinese people, see Alexander Saxton, *The Indispensable Enemy: Labor and the Anti-Chinese Movement in California* (Berkeley: University of California Press, 1971), 2.

29. 57th Cong., 2nd sess., *Congressional Record* (February 1903), 1641–42.

30. 57th Cong., 2nd sess., *Congressional Record* (January 1903), 525.

31. Morris P. Watson, "The People of New Mexico," *Outlook*, February 7, 1903.

32. 57th Cong., 2nd sess., *Congressional Record* (January–February 1903), 574. For more on language and national unity, see Senator Lodge discussing his views on the importance of having a shared language for national unity, 57th Cong., 2nd. sess., *Congressional Record* (Jan.-Feb. 1903), 1412.

33. Committee on the Territories, *New Statehood Bill*.

34. 57th Cong., 2nd sess., *Congressional Record* (January–February 1903), 1891.

35. Ibid., 530–31, 570, 1941.

36. Quoted in Jay J. Wagoner, *Arizona Territory, 1863–1912: A Political History* (Tucson: University of Arizona Press, 1970), 411.

37. This story and the analysis of Senator Knute Nelson's defense of dual allegiances was described in Matthew Frye Jacobson, *Barbarian Virtues: The United States Encounters Foreign Peoples at Home and Abroad, 1876–1917* (New York: Hill and Wang, 2000), 203–4.

38. Committee on the Territories, *New Statehood Bill*, 8.

39. Ibid., 18.

40. Ibid., 23–24. Bernard Rodey, New Mexico's delegate to Congress and an avid assimilationist, requested that this statehood supporter be interviewed.

41. 57th Cong., 2nd sess., *Congressional Record* (December 1902), 188–89.

42. While some assimilationists genuinely believed their statements about people of Mexican descent, others may have used such language primarily to achieve their goal of statehood. Evidence for their beliefs is in the following paragraphs in this chapter's main text as well as the corresponding footnotes. Some, like Arizona Delegate Marcus Smith, would later advocate marginalization.

43. *Nuevomexicanos* means New Mexicans of Mexican descent and was a term commonly used at the turn-of-the-century. *Nativos* was also a term used at the time and generally referred to native-born people of Mexican descent in the United States. For background on what being "Mexican" signified in this era, as well as notions about people viewed as having a mixed racial heritage, see Anthony Mora, *Border Dilemmas: Racial and National Uncertainties in New Mexico, 1848–1912* (Durham, NC: Duke University Press, 2011) .

44. Interview of Miguel A. Otero by William E. Curtis, El Trovar, Grand Cañon, Arizona, on July 1, 1905, 10, Otero Papers, MSS 21 BC, box 4, file 3, Center for Southwest Research, General Library, University of New Mexico.

45. For more on Otero's assimilationist views as compared to those of others of Mexican descent, see Doris Meyer, *Speaking for Themselves: Neomexicano Cultural Identity and the Spanish-Language Press, 1880–1920* (Albuquerque: University of New Mexico Press, 1996), 200.

46. Otero speech, July 4, 1902, Otero Papers, box 4, file 12. Interestingly, Anthony Mora describes how some people of Mexican descent in New Mexico may have celebrated the Fourth of July because it coincided with a festival for a saint. See Mora, *Border Dilemmas*, 131–32.

47. Despite this commendation, some *nuevomexicanos* alleged that Otero was dismissive of those who shared his racial background since he did not appoint *nuevomexicanos* to positions of authority or select any of them as delegates to a national Republican meeting in Chicago. They charged that he saw them as good enough only for manual labor, not people to have dinner with or to be treated as equals. For this, see "Otero y los Hispano-Americanos," *La Voz del Pueblo* (Las Vegas, NM), March 26, 1904. Regarding Otero and the flag, see Miguel Antonio Otero, *My Nine Years as Governor of the Territory of New Mexico, 1897–1906*, ed. Marion Dargan (Albuquerque: University of New Mexico Press, 1940), 73.

48. Letter from W. Atkinson, General Superintendent of Public Instruction for the Philippine Islands to Miguel Otero, Sept. 18, 1901, and letter from Gustave L. Solignac of law firm of Hartigan, Marple, and Solignac, Attorneys in Manila, Philippines to Miguel Otero, November 23, 1901, Otero Papers, box 1, file 12; Erin Murrah, "Miguel Antonio Otero: Destabilizing Identity in the West," *Western American Literature* 43 (Summer 2008), 131, 136.

49. "New Mexico Shows Much of Antique," c. 1903/1904, box 6, scrapbook, Otero Papers. The coat was given to Governor Otero's wife as a gift from one of the officers present at the surrender. World's Fairs visually displayed who was included and excluded in a nation as well as established hierarchies of peoples. See Robert W. Rydell, *All the World's a Fair: Visions of Empire at American International Expositions, 1876–1916* (Chicago: University of Chicago Press, 1984). World's Fairs also provided an opportunity to justify white supremacy; see Laura Wexler, "The Fair Ensemble: Kate Chopin in St. Louis in 1904" in Ann Laura Stoler, ed., *Haunted by Empire: Geographies of Intimacy in North American History* (Durham, NC: Duke University Press, 2006), 283–84.

50. Miguel Antonio Otero, *Otero: An Autobiographical Trilogy* (New York: Arno Press, 1974), 392–93; Otero interview, Otero Papers; Governor's Report to the Secretary of Interior, 1904, New Mexico Territorial Records, New Mexico State Records Center and Archives.

51. Delegate Bernard Shandon Rodey was often referred to as Bernard "Statehood" Rodey. 57th Cong., 2nd. sess., *Congressional Record* (March 1903), 2884.

52. U.S. House of Representatives, Committee on the Territories, *Statehood Bill, Hearings*, 57th Cong., 2nd sess. (1903), 2.

53. 57th Cong., 2nd. sess., *Congressional Record* (January 1903), 956.

54. Brichta was born in Mexico circa 1860 and shortly thereafter immigrated to Arizona. Brichta's mother was Mexican, and his father was French. When his father died, his mother later remarried a Scottish man, Augustus Brichta, who adopted her son. Brichta identified himself with the community of people of Mexican descent and was a founding member of Alianza Hispano-Americana along with Carlos Jácome. See Thomas Sheridan, *Los Tucsonenses*, 111, 179; "Bernabé Brichta" (HB HAY BIO BRI BER), Arizona Collection, Department of Archives and Manuscripts, University Libraries, Arizona State University, Tempe.

55. Letter from Miguel A. Otero to Senator Henry M. Teller (CO), August 1, 1906, Otero Papers, box 2, file 2.

56. Article re Otero's speech to Republican Territorial Convention, October 5, 1900, Otero Papers, box 6, scrapbook.

57. Harry H. Pierce, "Defends New Mexico," Letter to Editor, *Washington Post*, n.d., box 14019, file 58, L. Bradford Prince Papers, New Mexico Territorial Records, New Mexico State Records Center and Archives.

58. House Committee on the Territories, *House Joint Resolution No. 14: Approving the Constitutions Formed by the Constitutional Conventions of the Territories of New Mexico and Arizona, Hearings*, 62nd Cong., 1st sess. (1911), Record Group 233, file HR62A-D23, 49, National Archives, Washington, DC.

59. Committee on the Territories, *New Statehood Bill*, 63, 320–21.

60. Committee on the Territories, *House Joint Resolution No. 14*, 58.

61. Miguel Otero speech, "Mr. Toastmaster and Gentlemen," 1–2, n.d., c. 1899/1900, Otero Papers, box 4, file 13. There were 342 public schools in New Mexico in 1890: 143 taught lessons in English, 106 in Spanish, and 93 in both languages. See Nieto-Phillips, *Language of Blood*, 80.

62. In Puerto Rico, the federal government permitted the territory to use its revenue to educate the schoolchildren, but New Mexico had to send its revenue to the federal government. This is from the *Santa Fe New Mexican*, June 29, 1901, Dargan Papers. For Otero's comments, see Otero speech, "Mr. Toastmaster and Gentlemen," 1–2, Otero Papers.

63. "New Mexico's Brave Fight for Statehood," *Houston Daily Post*, September 20, 1903, Bernard Rodey Papers, MSS 175 BC, box 1, scrapbook. Center for Southwest Research. General Library, University of New Mexico, Albuquerque.

64. Senate Committee on the Territories, *Statehood for the Territories: Papers Relating to the Question of Statehood for the Territories*, 57th Cong., doc. 153 (January–February 1903), 13.

65. J. W. Knaebel, poem, Prince Papers, box 14019, file 58.

66. Committee on the Territories, *New Statehood Bill*, 96, passim; Thomas B. Catron Papers, New Mexico Political Papers, series 404, reel no. 2, Center for Southwest Research. General Library. The University of New Mexico. Albuquerque.

67. Interestingly, notwithstanding Delegate Rodey's assertions, he seemed reluctant to leave the learning of English up to the leaders of the Spanish-speaking community. Several years later, after he had been appointed by President Roosevelt to serve as Puerto Rico's liaison, he continued to submit articles to the Spanish-language press in New Mexico, urging Spanish speakers to learn English. Rodey himself was quite a linguist and knew several languages, including Spanish. Committee on the Territories, *New Statehood Bill*, 332; and Newspaper Clipping from St. Louis, MO, June 8, 1902, "New Mexico's Champion," Bernard Rodey Papers, box 1, scrapbook. Fernández-Gibert also defines Rodey as an assimilationist. See Arturo Fernández-Gibert, "*La Voz del Pueblo:* Texto, Identidad y Lengua en la Prensa Neomexicana, 1890–1911" (PhD diss., University of New Mexico, 2001), 389–98.

68. 57th Cong., 2nd sess., *Congressional Record* (January–February 1903), 775, 1942.

69. "New Mexico's Claims," *New York Daily Tribune*, January, 19 1903, Prince Papers, box 14019, file 58.

70. Petitions, Statehood Bill (January 13–14, 1903), Records of the Senate, Record Group 46, file SEN 57A-K16, National Archives, Washington, DC.

71. 58th Cong., 2nd sess., *Congressional Record* (Apr. 1904), 5148; and Otero, *Otero*, 392–93.

72. For an example, see Watson, "People of New Mexico."

73. Committee on the Territories, *Statehood Bill, Hearings*, 10.

74. Draft of Otero's autobiography, 283–84, Dargan Papers, box 5, file 1.

75. Otero, *Otero*, 64.

76. *Speech of Honorable LeBaron Bradford Prince of New Mexico, Trans-Mississippi Congress: Statehood for New Mexico, Cripple Creek*, CO, July 19, 1901, 7–8. This reference material is available at http://books.google.com/books?id=iwcVAAAAYAAJ&pg=PA1&lpg=PA1&dq=le+baron+bradford+prince+statehood+for+new+mexico+speech+colorado&source=bl&ots=uf4cDmNBFO&sig=o197hS0TRsCOxxbAifVbL1Fzbhg&hl=en&sa=X&ei=1hjnUeu6BbDl4APSuoCADA&ved=0CDYQ6AEwAw#v=onepage&q=le%20baron%20bradford%20prince%20statehood%20for%20new%20mexico%20speech%20colorado&f=false

77. Committee on the Territories, *New Statehood Bill*, 331–32; Committee on the Territories, *House Joint Resolution No. 14*, 50.

78. Ibid., 52.

79. "Governor Otero and New Mexico," repr. from the *Denver Republican*, n.d., c. June, 1901, Otero Papers, box 6, scrapbook.

80. *Congressional Record*, 57th Cong., 2nd sess., House, Appendix (Jan. 28, 1903), 154.

81. Gary Gerstle, *American Crucible: Race and Nation in the Twentieth Century* (Princeton, NJ: Princeton University Press, 2001), 27, 41–42.

82. Dargan, "New Mexico's Fight for Statehood, 1895–1912, I," 13; Braeman, "Albert J. Beveridge," 320; and Wagoner, *Arizona Territory*, 412.

83. "New Mexico's Good Points Overlooked," *Pittsburgh Times*, May 26, 1903, Rodey Papers, box 1, scrapbook.

84. Watson, "People of New Mexico."

85. Article, retyped, "Not Fit for Citizenship," *Daily Evening Telegraph* (Philadelphia), December 13, 1902, Dargan Papers, box 10, file 6.

86. Phylis Cancilla Martinelli, *Undermining Race: Ethnic Identities in Arizona Copper Camps, 1880–1920* (Tucson: University of Arizona, 2009), chap. 6; and Rodolfo F. Acuña, *Corridors of Migration: The Odyssey of Mexican Laborers, 1600–1933* (Tucson: University of Arizona Press, 2007), 112–18.

87. In 1903, Mexican and Italian miners led a major strike in the Clifton and Morenci mines of Arizona, mining areas without any support, other than rhetoric, from the Western Federation of Miners, from which they had been excluded. Although ultimately unsuccessful, the mines shut down and forced the Arizona governor to request federal troops to provide peace as former miners strode through towns bearing their weapons. See Thomas E. Sheridan, *Arizona: A History* (Tucson: University of Arizona Press, 1995), 171–72. Also see Linda Gordon, *The Great Arizona Orphan Abduction* (Cambridge: Harvard University Press, 1999), 102, 115–16.

88. Acuña, *Corridors of Migration*, 128–30; and Michael C. Meyer, William L. Sherman, and Susan M. Deeds, *The Course of Mexican History*, 6th ed. (Oxford: Oxford University Press, 1999), 472–74.

89. In the early 1880s William Gillette Ritch, the head of New Mexico's new Bureau of Immigration—whose role was to encourage people from other parts of the nation to settle there—was partially responsible for the suggestion to name the territory

Montezuma since he created the myth that the Aztec emperor Montezuma had initially resided in Santa Fe before following an eagle in 1325 CE to Tenochtitlán, the site of present-day Mexico City. See Nieto-Phillips, *Language of Blood*, 122–23. For more on naming the state Montezuma, see "New Mexico's Claims," *New York Daily Tribune*, January 19, 1903, and "Letters to Constitutional Convention," New Mexico Territorial Records, reel 38, New Mexico State Records Center and Archives. Also see reprinted article in the *New York Evening Post* from Albert E. Pillsbury in the *Boston Post*, November 19, 1908 in Dargan Papers.

Chapter Two

A version of this chapter was previously published as "'I Am an American': Anglos, Mexicans, *Nativos*, and the National Debate over Arizona and New Mexico Statehood," in *Pacific Historical Review* 80, no. 3 (August 2011): 430–67.

1. Octaviano Larrazolo Papers, MSS BC 614, boxes 1 and 2, Center for Southwest Research, University Libraries, University of New Mexico; Box 14, Edna Fergusson Papers, MSS 45, Center for Southwest Research, University Libraries, University of New Mexico; *El Independiente* (Las Vegas, NM), August 31, 1911, Larrazolo Papers, Boxes 1 and 2.

2. Ramón A. Gutiérrez, *When Jesus Came, the Corn Mothers Went Away: Marriage, Sexuality, and Power in New Mexico, 1500–1846* (Stanford: Stanford University Press, 1991), 103–4, 176–206; Eric V. Meeks, *Border Citizens: The Making of Indians, Mexicans and Anglos in Arizona* (Austin: University of Texas Press, 2007), 24–25; Quotation is from John M. Nieto-Phillips, *The Language of Blood: The Making of Spanish-American Identity in New Mexico, 1880s-1930s* (Albuquerque: University of New Mexico Press, 2004), 13–14; also see 9, 15–49.

3. For more on property loss, see Phillip B. Gonzales, *Forced Sacrifice as Ethnic Protest: The Hispano Cause in New Mexico and the Racial Attitude Confrontation of 1933* (New York: New York University Press, 2001), 20–21; and María E. Montoya, *Translating Property: The Maxwell Land Grant and the Conflict over Land in the American West, 1840–1900* (Lawrence: University of Kansas Press, 2002), 4–5.

4. Charles Montgomery sees Anglos accepting a Spanish American identity to cover up for taking *nativos*' land in the courts, whereas Sarah Horton believes that *nativos* asserted this identity as a method of resistance. I see this assertion as *both* resistance and an identity fully embraced by elite *nativos*. Anglos accepted it because they recognized *nativos*' power and saw how it might help them to attain statehood. See Phillip B. Gonzales, "Whither *Nuevomexicanos:* The Career of a Southwestern Intellectual Discourse, 1907–2004," *Social Sciences Journal* 43, no. 2 (2006), 273–86; Sarah Horton, "Where Is the 'Mexican' in "New Mexican"?: Enacting History, Enacting Dominance in Santa Fe Fiesta," *Public Historian* 23 (Autumn 2001), 41–54; Charles Montgomery, *The Spanish Redemption: Heritage, Power, and Loss on New Mexico's Upper Rio Grande* (Berkeley: University of California Press, 2002), 57. Anthony Mora notes the creation of a New Mexican identity as a way to defuse the "race" issue by providing a more neutral label that Euro Americans could use to promote statehood to outsiders, or as a way for Mexican Americans to claim space in the terri-

tory. This is an interesting view, but I found that *nativo, hispano-americano,* and their equivalents in English were used frequently in the Spanish- and English-language press, and that much overt discussion about the racial heritage of the population in the territories continued. See Mora, *Border Dilemmas: Racial and National Uncertainties in New Mexico, 1848–1912* (Durham, NC: Duke University Press, 2011), chaps. 5 and 6. Nieto-Phillips explains that while there are few extant sources from nonliterate *nuevomexicanos,* oral histories confirm that they also proclaimed and supported the idea of a Spanish American identity; see Nieto-Phillips, *Language of Blood,* 2, 80–92, esp. 84–85; John-Michael Rivera, *The Emergence of Mexican America: Recovering Stories of Mexican Peoplehood in U.S. Culture* (New York: New York University Press, 2006), 51–81; Phillip B. Gonzales, "'History Hits the Heart: Albuquerque's Great Cuartocentenario Controvery, 1997–2005," in Phillip B. Gonzales, ed., *Expressing New Mexico: Nuevomexicano Creativity, Ritual and Memory* (Tucson: University of Arizona Press, 2007), 207–32, esp. 209–10.

5. Regarding the development of a stronger Spanish American identity, see Phillip B. Gonzales, "*La Junta de Indignación:* Hispano Repertoire of Collective Protest in New Mexico, 1884–1933," *Western Historical Quarterly* 31 (Summer 2000), 164–65. Arturo Fernández-Gibert finds the newspaper *La Voz del Pueblo* consistently using *hispano americano* (Spanish American) after 1903; see Fernández-Gibert, "*La Voz del Pueblo*: Texto, Identidad y Lengua en la Prensa Neomexicana, 1890–1911" (PhD diss., University of New Mexico, 2001), 331–32.

6. For more on the black legend and its origins, see David J. Weber, *The Spanish Frontier in North America* (New Haven, CT: Yale University Press, 1992), 336–41. For its decline, see Phoebe S. Kropp, *California Vieja: Culture and Memory in a Modern American Place* (Berkeley: University of California Press, 2006), 28–30. Regarding Helen Hunt Jackson's *Ramona,* see Nieto-Phillips, *Language of Blood,* 151.

7. For Anglos' growing use of Spanish history to promote the territory, see Nieto-Phillips, *Language of Blood,* 118–42, esp. 131–32.

8. In 1900, there were only 7,050 people identified as Spanish in the United States; see Campbell J. Gibson and Emily Lennon, "Historical Census Statistics on the Foreign-Born Population of the United States: 1850–1990," Working Paper No. 29 (U.S. Bureau of the Census, Population Division, 2011), Table 4, "Region and Country or Area of Birth of the Foreign-Born Population, With Geographic Detail Shown in Decennial Census Publications of 1930 or Earlier: 1850 to 1930 and 1960 to 1990," http://www.census.gov/population/www/documentation/twps0029/tab04.html.

9. Initially, Miguel Antonio Otero had emphasized assimilation over pluralism, but pluralism became more pronounced during the final years of the statehood battles so he shifted with the political climate. By the 1940s the "Caucasian strategy," a phrase used by historian Thomas Guglielmo, became more common and was one of the major ways in which Mexican Americans fought for civil rights; see Guglielmo, "Fighting for Caucasian Rights: Mexicans, Mexican Americans and the Transnational Struggle for Civil Rights in World War II Texas," *Journal of American History* 92 (Mar. 2006), 1212–37. The literature on whiteness is extensive. I remain most influenced by those historians who have looked to how both the state and class status affected racial categorization, including Tomás Almaguer, *Racial Fault Lines: The Historical Origins of White Supremacy in California* (Berkeley: University of California Press, 1994); Albert Camarillo, *Chicanos in a Changing Society: From Mexican Pueblos*

to American Barrios in Santa Barbara and Southern California, 1848–1930 (Cambridge: Harvard University Press, 1979); Linda Gordon, *The Great Arizona Orphan Abduction* (Cambridge: Harvard University Press, 1999), 77, 143–46; and A. Yvette Huginnie, "'Mexican Labour' in a 'White Man's Town': Racialism, Imperialism, and Industrialization in the Making of Arizona, 1840–1905," in Peter Alexander and Rick Halpern, eds., *Racializing Class, Classifying Race: Labour and Difference in Britain, the USA and Africa* (New York: New York University Press, 2000), 33–34. I also admire Peter Kolchin's essay on whiteness, in which he reminds us to consider how markers of difference other than race—such as class and culture—are important and contribute to constructions of race: "Whiteness Studies: The New History of Race in America," *Journal of American History,* 89 (June 2002), 154–73.

10. See Horace Kallen, "Democracy vs. the Melting Pot: A Study in American Nationality," *The Nation*, 100 (1915), 218–20. For Kallen's background, see Matthew Frye Jacobson, *Barbarian Virtues: The United States Encounters Foreign Peoples at Home and Abroad, 1876–1917* (New York: Hill and Wang, 2000), 209.

11. For more on Governor Otero's distance from his heritage, see Genaro M. Padilla, *My History, Not Yours: The Formation of Mexican American Autobiography* (Madison: University of Wisconsin Press, 1993), 34–35.

12. U.S. Senate, Committee on the Territories, *New Statehood Bill*, 100–1, qtd. in M.G. Cunniff, "The Last of the Territories," *World's Work* 11 (Jan., 1906), 7115.

13. Committee on the Territories, *New Statehood Bill*, 20, 35, 41.

14. A. Gabriel Meléndez, *So All Is Not Lost: The Poetics of Print in Nuevomexicano Communities, 1834–1958* (Albuquerque: University of New Mexico Press, 1997), 63–132; "El Estado in Dudo," *La Voz del Pueblo*, November 22, 1902. All translations, unless otherwise noted, are mine from Spanish into English.

15. Although such newspapers had a vested interest in Spanish, they would not continue to print such articles if their readers disagreed, see "La Admision de Nuevo Mexico," *El Labrador* (Las Cruces, NM), December 5, 1902.

16. *La Voz del Pueblo*, August 5, 1911, repr. in Fernández-Gibert, "*La Voz del Pueblo*," 382; "Admit the Territories," *Omaha World-Herald*, Jan. 23, 1903.

17. "El Idioma Castellano," *La Voz del Pueblo*, December 24, 1904; "Defensa de Nuestra Idioma," *La Voz del Pueblo*, February 25, 1911; "Cuando Será Estado Nuevo México?" *La Voz del Pueblo*, February 16, 1908.

18. See Fernández-Gibert, "*La Voz del Pueblo*," chap. 7. Erlinda Gonzales-Berry argues that *nuevomexicanos* emphasized the benefits of Spanish over language rights because they feared such arguments would harm the statehood effort. See Erlinda Gonzales-Berry, "Which Language Will Our Children Speak?" in Erlinda Gonzales-Berry and David R. Maciel, eds., *The Contested Homeland: A Chicano History of New Mexico* (Albuquerque: University of New Mexico Press, 2000), 161–89; Quotation is from *La Voz Del Pueblo*, February 25, 1911, repr. in Fernández-Gibert, "*La Voz del Pueblo*," 415–16, my translation.

19. Quoted in Charles S. Maier, *Among Empires: American Ascendancy and Its Predecessors* (Cambridge: Harvard University Press, 2006), 31.

20. "La Villania Arizoniana," *La Voz del Pueblo*, March 13, 1909; Miguel Antonio Otero, *Otero: An Autobiographical Trilogy* (New York: New York University Press, 1974), 214; Bernard Rodey Papers, MSS 175 BC, box 1, scrapbook, newspaper clip-

ping, no source, n.d., Center for Southwest Research, University Libraries, University of New Mexico.

21. Octaviano Larrazolo speech, Coronado Commemorative Convention, Albuquerque, New Mexico, October 9, 1907, Larrazolo Papers, box 1, file 11. The concept of building collective memories is from George Lipsitz, see a discussion of this in William V. Flores, "Citizens vs. Citizenry: Undocumented Immigrants and Latino Cultural Citizenship," in William V. Flores and Rina Benmayor, eds., *Latino Cultural Citizenship: Claiming Identity, Space and Rights* (Boston: Beacon Press, 1997), 255–78, esp. 266–68.

22. For information on Benjamin Read, see Doris Meyer, *Speaking for Themselves: Neomexicano Cultural Identity and the Spanish-Language Press, 1880–1920* (Albuquerque: University of New Mexico Press, 1996), 193–205.

23. "Triunfo de la Justicia," *La Revista de Taos*, January 27, 1911. For more on Read, see Meyer, *Speaking for Themselves*, 183–206; "George Washington Armijo," in Rose Díaz and Jan Dodson Barnhart, eds., *Hispanic Heroes: Portraits of New Mexicans Who Have Made a Difference* (Albuquerque: University of New Mexico Press, 1992): 9–17.

24. John L. Cowan, "Two More Stars for Old Glory," *Pacific Monthly*, 22 (September 1909), 232; part of Roosevelt's speech was qtd. in Otero, *Otero*, 323.

25. For this concept of "collaborating elites" who worked to support empire in the Philippines and thereby prove fitness for self-government, see Paul A. Kramer, *The Blood of Government: Race, Empire, the United States and the Philippines* (Chapel Hill: University of North Carolina Press, 2006), 19, 29–30.

26. Gonzales, *Expressing New Mexico*, 214. Regarding intimate relations, see Gutiérrez, *When Jesus Came, the Corn Mothers Went Away*, 103–4, 207–40.

27. Cunniff, "Last of the Territories," 7115.

28. Jay J. Wagoner, *Arizona Territory, 1863–1912: A Political History* (Tucson: University of Arizona Press, 1970), 97, 457, 485; Howard Lamar, *The Far Southwest: A Territorial History, 1846–1912* (Albuquerque: University of New Mexico Press, 2000), 412; U.S. Senate, Committee on the Territories, *Statehood for the Territories: Papers Relating to the Question of Statehood for the Territories*, 57 Cong., Doc. 153 (January–February 1903).

29. Huginnie, "'Mexican Labour' in a 'White Man's Town,'" 33–34.

30. Committee on the Territories, *New Statehood Bill*, 320–21, 337, 372; U.S. House of Representatives, Committee on the Territories, *Further Hearings on Statehood Bill* 58th Cong., 2nd sess. (December 1903–January 1904), 12–13, 16–24; U.S. House of Representatives, Committee on the Territories, *Statehood Bill, Hearings*, 57th Cong., 2nd sess. (1903) 15; Appendix to 57th Cong., 2nd sess. *Congressional Record* (February 9, 1903), 166; *Congressional Record*, 58 Cong., 2nd sess. (April 1904), 5139.

31. House Committee on the Territories, *Statehood for Arizona and New Mexico, Hearings*, 59 Cong., 1st sess. (1906), 18–19, 24–25.

32. Letter from the Bar Association of Arizona to Senator Charles W. Fairbanks of Indiana, December 31, 1904, in Senate Documents and Petitions on Statehood Bill, Sen. 58A-K7, National Archives, Washington, DC.

33. "Is This a Square 'Deal'?," *Arizona Republican* (Phoenix), December 6, 1905. For other such political cartoons, see Richard Melzer, "New Mexico in Caricature:

Images of the Territory on the Eve of Statehood," *New Mexico Historical Review,* 62 (no. 4, 1987), 335–60, esp. 340 and 358. For more on how Americans viewed Mexicans as a mixed race, and further gender analysis with regard to the need to protect white women's morality by the passing of anti-miscegenation laws, see Rosa Linda Fregoso, *MeXicana Encounters: The Making of Social Identities on the Borderlands* (Berkeley: University of California Press, 2003), 63, 132–38. Also see Peggy Pascoe regarding how Americans came to view interracial marriage as unnatural and immoral, and its connection with protecting the purity of the white race, in *What Comes Naturally: Miscegenation Law and the Making of Race in America* (Oxford: Oxford University Press, 2009), 2–3, 6, 12.

34. U.S. House of Representatives, Committee on the Territories, *Further Hearings on Statehood Bill,* 58th Cong., 2nd sess. (December 1903–January 1904), 19, 70–71, 73.

35. U.S. House of Representatives, Committee on the Territories, *Statehood for Arizona and New Mexico, Hearings* (January–February, 1909), 60th Cong., 2nd sess., 36–42; Governor Richard Sloan's views are qtd. in Charles Moreau Harger, "Our Two New States," *Outlook,* January 28, 1911, 165–76, esp. 171.

36. Quoted in Miguel Tinker Salas, *In the Shadow of the Eagles: Sonora and the Transformation of the Border during the Porfiriato* (Berkeley: University of California Press, 1997), 248; Thomas E. Sheridan, *Los Tucsonenses: The Mexican Community in Tucson, 1854–1941* (Tucson: University of Arizona Press, 1986), 102–12, 120–22. For examples in Velasco's newspaper, see "Repatriación de Mexicanos," *El Fronterizo* (Tucson, AZ), May 12, 1904, and "Los Peones Mexicanos," *El Fronterizo,* March 7, 1908, Arizona Historical Society, Tucson. There are few extant copies of this paper. See David G. Gutíerrez, *Walls and Mirrors: Mexican Americans, Mexican Immigrants, and the Politics of Ethnicity in the American Southwest* (Berkeley: University of California Press, 1995), 56–65.

37. For more on the AHA, see Sheridan, *Los Tucsonenses,* 102–13, 120–22; and Kaye Lynn Briegel, "Alianza Hispano-Americana, 1894–1965: A Mexican American Fraternal Insurance Society" (PhD diss., University of Southern California, 1974). Also see Linda Gordon (*Great Arizona Orphan Abduction,* 134–35, 226–27), who explains that most of the organization's members were workers and that one of the Clifton-Morenci strike leaders, Abrán Salcido, was president of the AHA chapter in the area, but as she also notes, separate organizations were created to organize labor; the AHA was not directly involved.

38. "Repatriación de Mexicanos"; "Los Peones Mexicanos."

39. Meeks, *Border Citizens,* 105; Sheridan, *Los Tucsonenses,* 110–12, 120–23.

40. Joint statehood passed in 1906, but Senator Joseph Foraker (Republican, Ohio) attached an amendment requiring that a majority of each territory's residents approve it. Arizonans overwhelming rejected this 16,265 to 3,141, whereas New Mexicans supported it 26,195 to 14,735 (many *nativo* districts opposed it); historians show that those who voted for jointure in New Mexico did so to enhance their chances for single statehood, knowing that Arizonans would reject it. Mark E. Pry, "Arizona and the Politics of Statehood, 1889–1912" (PhD diss., Arizona State University, 1995), 191; and Wagoner, *Arizona Territory,* 432–33, 439, 470–71.

41. This description of adobe homes as un-American is akin to Pablo Mitchell's discussion of a certain type of respectable living and comportment associated with whiteness. See Pablo Mitchell, *Coyote Nation: Sexuality, Race, and Conquest in*

Modernizing New Mexico (Chicago: University of Chicago Press, 2005), 120–21. J. W. Babcock, "Statehood Rights of Arizona and New Mexico," *Independent*, March 1, 1906, 505–8; M. G. Cunniff, "Last of the Territories," *World's Work* 11 (January, 1906), 7115; John S. Goff, *Arizona Biographical Dictionary* (Cave Creek, AZ: Black Mountain Press, 1983), 26.

42. Harger, "Our Two New States," 169.

43. Thomas E. Sheridan, *Arizona: A History* (Tucson: University of Arizona Press, 1995), 178–79.

44. Lamar, *Far Southwest*, 431.

45. New Mexico Governor George Curry and New Mexico Delegate William Andrews lobbied to strip Senator Beveridge's amendment from the bill; they feared they would have to answer to *nativos*, and pay a political price if they failed. See Lamar, *Far Southwest*, 431; and Pry, "Arizona and the Politics of Statehood," 219.

46. New Mexico Constitutional Convention, *Proceedings of the Constitutional Convention of the Proposed State of New Mexico* (October 3–November 21, 1910), 9–10, 12, 25–43. Law Library, Library of Congress.

47. U.S. Senate, *New Mexico Constitution*, 61st Cong., 3rd sess. (Washington, DC, 1911), 9–10, 25–43; Gonzales-Berry, "Which Language Will Our Children Speak?" 173–74.

48. New Mexico Constitutional Convention, *Proceedings*, 115–17.

49. Ibid., 289 for Montoya's comment. For Read's views, see Meyer, *Speaking for Themselves*, 202. For the view of *El Tiempo*, see "Viva Nuevo Mexico!" *El Tiempo* (Las Cruces, NM), January 7, 1911; For Otero's view, see Otero Speech, Taos County (NM), January, 1911, p. 3, Otero Papers, box 4, file 12, Center for Southwest Research, General Library, University of New Mexico, Albuquerque. New Mexicans approved the constitution in 1911, 31,742 to 13,399, and became a state in 1912, see Senate, *New Mexico Constitution*, 6; for the background of the state's politicians, see Phillip B. Gonzales and Ann Massman, "Loyalty Questioned: *Nuevomexicanos* in the Great War," *Western Historical Quarterly* 75 (November 2006), 629–66; for the continued adulation of Spanish culture, see Montgomery, *Spanish Redemption*, 109–10.

50. Senate Committee on the Territories, "An Act Enabling the People of New Mexico and Arizona to Form a Constitution and State Government," Report 454, 61st Cong., 2nd sess. (1910), 4–6. Regarding Anglo domination, see Sheridan, *Los Tucsonenses*, 121–22.

51. Arizona Constitutional Convention, *Minutes of the Constitutional Convention of the Territory of Arizona* (Phoenix, 1910), 22–24; John S. Goff, ed., *Records of the Arizona Constitutional Convention of 1910* (Phoenix: Supreme Court of Arizona, 1991), 21–24, 1358–84, 1389, 1391–92, 1396; see also Proposition 145 in this document at 732, 1383. For more on intermarriage, see Gordon, *Great Arizona Orphan Abduction*, 143–46; Katherine Benton-Cohen, *Borderline Americans* (Cambridge: Harvard University Press, 2009), 159–60; and Fregoso, *MeXicana Encounters*, 63.

52. Proposition 91, in Goff, *Records of the Arizona Constitutional Convention*, 825–27, 1374. For Democrats' fears and the letter to Governor Hunt, see Pry, "Arizona and the Politics of Statehood," 272–74, esp. 273.

53. Pry, "Arizona and the Politics of Statehood," 272; Propositions 15 and 73, in Goff, *Records of the Arizona Constitutional Convention*, 1065, 1181; Meeks, *Border Citizens*, 36–43.

54. "Constitution Signers," Arizona Statehood, 1911–12 (HAV-22), Arizona Collection, Department of Archives and Manuscripts, University Libraries, Arizona State University, Tempe, Arizona.

55. This chapter ends in 1912 but questions the optimistic rendering of assimilation by Joel Perlmann who argues that Mexican immigrants eventually fit within the body politic much as other European groups had; see Joel Perlmann, *Italians Then, Mexicans Now: Immigrant Origins and the Second-Generation Progress, 1890–2004* (New York: Russell Sage, 2004), 3–4, 124. The marginalization strategy suggests another pattern for how working-class immigrants were incorporated into the United States and one more in line with that found by Thomas Macias, *Mestizo in America: Generations of Mexican Ethnicity in the Suburban Southwest* (Tucson: University of Arizona Press, 2006), 10, 98.

Chapter Three

1. See Thomas E. Sheridan, *Los Tucsonenses: The Mexican Community in Tucson, 1854–1941* (Tucson: University of Arizona Press, 1986), 169–78; James D. McBride, "The Liga Protectora Latina: A Mexican American Benevolent Society in Arizona," *Journal of the West* 14 (4) (1975), 82–90; Eric V. Meeks, *Border Citizens: The Making of Indians, Mexicans, and Anglos in Arizona* (Austin: University of Texas Press, 2007), 94–96, and 105–7; and Karen Jean Underhill, "Albert J. Beveridge's Congressional Report on Arizona Territory in 1902" (master's thesis, University of Arizona, 1990), 143–44, 260.

2. Samuel Bryan, "Mexican Immigrants in the United States," *Survey*, September 7, 1912, 726–30. Katherine Benton-Cohen explains that some reasons why Mexican immigrants were ignored were that Americans perceived them much as they did workers in other colonies. Because Mexicans worked primarily in internal colonies—American territories—in places in which they held few rights, and that others perceived their labor as a local or regional issue since they were concentrated in the Southwest. She finds the tolerance of Mexican workers akin to that of Americans accepting nonwhite labor in other colonies such as Filipino labor in the Philippines and native Hawaiian labor in Hawai'i. See Benton-Cohen, "Other Immigrants: Mexicans and the Dillingham Commission of 1907–1911," *Journal of American Ethnic History* 30, no. 2 (Winter 2011), 33–57. Patrick Ettinger also shows the lack of interest in Mexican immigration in the first decade of the twentieth century but notes that at the border they were still inspected and that 1,000–3,000, were denied entry annually. See Ettinger, *Imaginary Lines: Border Enforcement and the Origins of Undocumented Immigration, 1882–1930* (Austin: University of Texas Press, 2009), chap. 5.

3. Mark Reisler further notes that these exemptions also did not apply for people from Canada, Cuba, or Newfoundland. Mark Reisler, *By the Sweat of Their Brow: Mexican Immigrant Labor in the United States, 1900–1940* (Westport, CT: Greenwood Press, 1976), 12. Technically, as early as 1891, Mexicans could be denied entry for being "likely to become a public charge" if they did not have sufficient funds when they crossed the border. New York officials exercised this regulation vigorously in their crowded ports, weeding out potential burdens, but in the developing Southwest few inspectors enforced this provision as they anticipated that the newcomers would

secure employment quickly. In addition, while labor laws prohibited contracting with potential employees before they emigrated, railroads and other corporations frequently worked around this law and recruited workers directly from Mexico. At times, the United States and Mexican governments negotiated formal agreements to permit contract arrangements in specific industries. Presidents William Taft and Porfirio Díaz did just this in 1909, allowing for 1,000 Mexicans to pick sugar beets in the fields of Colorado and Nebraska. This information may be found in Manuel García y Griego, "The Importation of Mexican Contract Laborers to the United States, 1942–1964: Antecedents, Operation, and Legacy," in Peter G. Brown and Henry Shue, eds., *The Border That Joins: Mexican Migrants and U.S. Responsibility* (Totowa, NJ: Rowman and Littlefield, 1983), 55.

4. U.S. Department of Commerce and Labor, *Annual Report*, from the Commissioner General of Immigration (Washington, DC: Government Printing Office, 1906), 67.

5. Victor S. Clark, "Mexican Labor in the United States," *Bulletin of the Bureau of Labor* 78 (Washington, DC: Government Printing Office, 1908), 466–522, quotations at 511.

6. President Díaz achieved his objective by improving transportation networks and repossessing much of the land formerly held in common by indigenous communities and the Catholic Church. These acquisitions permitted him to resell the land to investors interested in pursuing cash crops for higher profits than those possible by growing food staples for subsistence living. The improved transit and land repossession destabilized rural communities such that people there could not compete with more affordable products coming from distant markets. See Gilbert G. González, *Culture of Empire: American Writers, Mexico, and Mexican Immigrants, 1880–1930* (Austin: University of Texas Press, 2004), 107.

7. Gilbert González argues that Mexico's expanding market economy and relationship with the United States had more to do with encouraging immigration to *el norte* than the Mexican Revolution. This is likely correct, but the Revolution did spur some migration as a result of erratic farm production and violence, which forced people off haciendas. See González, *Culture of Empire*, chap. 4; and Reisler, *By the Sweat of Their Brow*, 111. Another reason Mexicans moved to the United States between 1910 and 1918 was because the production of corn and beans in Mexico declined dramatically due to the unstable farm production of the Revolution years, which resulted in soaring food prices, far beyond the reach of workers' stagnant wages. Consequently, few could resist the lure of higher pay ranging from $1 to $3 per day for farming jobs and approximately $5 daily in the copper mines of the United States. See Lawrence A. Cardoso, "Labor Emigration to the Southwest," in George C. Kiser and Martha Woody Kiser, eds., *Mexican Workers in the United States: Historical and Political Perspective* (Albuquerque: University of New Mexico Press, 1979), 16–18.

8. For more information on the Newlands Reclamation Act and its effects, see Patricia Nelson Limerick, *The Legacy of Conquest: The Unbroken Past of the American West* (New York: W. W. Norton, 1987), 136. For a comparison of U.S. and Mexican wages, see Reisler, *By the Sweat of Their Brow*, 3–5, 14–15.

9. See González, *Culture of Empire*; and Reisler, *By the Sweat of Their Brow*, 111.

10. Figures from González, *Culture of Empire*, 112–13; and Cardoso, "Labor Emigration to the Southwest," 19. See also Linda B. Hall and Don M. Coerver, *Revolution*

on the Border: The United States and Mexico, 1910–1920 (Albuquerque: University of New Mexico Press, 1988), 7–9, 127, 133.

11. Hall and Coerver, *Revolution on the Border*, 7–8, 130–41; and Rodolfo F. Acuña, *Corridors of Migration: The Odyssey of Mexican Laborers, 1600–1933* (Tucson: University of Arizona Press, 2007), 149, 168.

12. The origins of the Literacy Act date to 1887 when the economist Edward Bemis recommended that immigrants read or write in their native language before being accepted into the United States. A few years later, the proposal's popularity grew after Senator Henry Cabot Lodge (Republican, MA) recognized it as a convenient tool for denying entry of southern and eastern European immigrants, whom he considered unassimilable. Joining together with members of the Immigration Restriction League in Boston, Samuel Gompers of the American Federation of Labor, and a growing number of Western restrictionists, Senator Lodge worked feverishly to transform the literacy test into law. Although many congressmen, particularly Republicans, favored the measure, they had expanding constituencies of naturalized Americans and feared electoral retribution. Even so, the requirement almost became law several times before being vetoed by presidents Cleveland, Taft, and then Wilson. But with war on the horizon and an intensified nationalism sweeping the country, the forces against immigration eventually proved strong enough to override President Wilson's second veto on February 5, 1917. See Daniel J. Tichenor, *Dividing Lines: The Politics of Immigration Control in America* (Princeton, NJ: Princeton University Press, 2002), 138–40.

13. 42 Stat. 5, 8 USC 229. The test could be administered in a variety of ways, but generally U.S. officials showed the immigrants 30–40 words in their native language on a note card that they then had to read aloud. An interpreter would then translate for the immigration official. In more remote areas, the inspectors often handed the immigrants cards that required them to follow certain commands such as removing their hat, touching their right hand to their left shoulder, and so forth. The inspector kept an English-language version and knew the order in which the immigrants should perform the actions. These details and more may be found in the U.S. Department of Labor, *Annual Report*, from the Commissioner General of Immigration (Washington, DC: Government Printing Office, 1917), xiv.

14. The Literacy Act also established an Asiatic Barred Zone that excluded people from India, Polynesia, Afghanistan, Asiatic Russia, Burma, Indochina, Thailand, and Arabia from emigrating. See Bill Ong Hing, *Defining American through Immigration Policy* (Philadelphia: Temple University Press, 2004), 46, 60–61.

15. Cardoso, "Labor Emigration to the Southwest," 16–18. See also Otey M. Scruggs, "The First Mexican Farm Labor Program," *Arizona and the West* 2 (Winter 1960), 320. The State Department reassured reticent Mexicans that they would not be drafted for service unless they became U.S. citizens. President Venustiano Carranza of Mexico explained this to his constituents as well. Even so, the fear of being drafted reduced immigration during the war years. See Jaime R. Aguila, "Protecting 'México de Afuera': Mexican Emigration Policy, 1876–1928" (PhD diss., Arizona State University, 2000), 108–9.

16. U.S. House of Representatives, Committee on Immigration and Naturalization, *Temporary Admission of Illiterate Mexican Laborers, Hearings*, 66th Cong., 2nd sess. (1920), 200, 262.

17. U.S. Department of Labor, *Annual Report*, from the Commissioner General of Immigration (Washington, DC: Government Printing Office, 1920), 7–8. Wilson amended this circular a few days later to include Canadians willing to work in Maine, to relieve a labor shortage there. This exemption was rescinded in 1918. See Commissioner-General, Immigration to All Commissioners of Immigration, December 21, 1918, Immigration and Naturalization Service, Record Group 85, Entry 9, file 54261/202, National Archives, Washington, DC.

18. Commissioner General, Immigration to All Commissioners of Immigration, Inspectors in Charge, etc., May 23, 1917, Record Group 85, Entry 9, file 54261/202.

19. The ongoing war needs combined with growers' and other executives' intense lobbying initially convinced Secretary Wilson to expand and extend the departmental waivers beyond their original confines. He briefly approved exemptions for Mexican workers to work in lignite mines or do maintenance-of-way jobs on railroads in June 1918, only to then later exclude them from these same industries. Secretary Wilson later extended the existing policies and order while awaiting a decision from Congress. The last extension ended on March 2, 1921, although it took some time to send the workers home. See U.S. Department of Labor, *Annual Report* (1920), 7–8.

20. Figures from González, *Culture of Empire*, 112–13; Cardoso, "Labor Emigration to the Southwest," 19. See also Hall and Coerver, *Revolution on the Border*, 127, 133.

21. Charles Gibson and Benjamin Keen, "Trends of United States Studies in Latin American History," *American Historical Review* 62 (July 1957), 855–77, esp. 859.

22. Helen Delpar, *Enormous Vogue of Things Mexican: Cultural Relations between the United States and Mexico, 1920–1935* (Tuscaloosa: University of Alabama Press, 1992), 8.

23. Cecil Robinson sees the image of Mexico, Mexicans, and the Southwest as changing from more negative stereotypes to more romanticized ones in the late nineteenth century and early twentieth century. I agree, but think that in the 1910s and early 1920s, Americans romanticized more the Mexicans and Mexican Americans who they believed to be influenced by Spain and of "Spanish descent," rather than those who they did not see as having this heritage. See Robinson, *With the Ears of Strangers: The Mexican in American Literature* (Tucson: University of Arizona Press, 1971), chap 5.

24. Hall and Coerver, *Revolution on the Border*, 128–31, 135–36. Note that these authors find that 90 percent of the immigrants entering the United States between 1910 and 1920 had no skill or profession. See also Reisler, *By the Sweat of Their Brow*, 131–33; and statistics suggesting the greater poverty of later arrivals in "The Mexican 'Invaders' of El Paso," *Survey*, July 8, 1916, 380–82.

25. A Spanish American identity had been prevalent in California and some parts of Texas as well, but many of those claimants had since lost much economic and political power through the loss of their property. Other people of Mexican descent then referred to these former ranch owners as *los tuvos*, or "has-beens." From David Montejano, *Anglos and Mexicans in the Making of Texas, 1836–1986* (Austin: University of Texas Press, 1987), 113–15. For information on the decline of the *californios*' political power, see Albert Camarillo, *Chicanos in a Changing Society: From Mexican Pueblos to American Barrios in Santa Barbara and Southern California, 1848–1930* (Cambridge: Harvard University Press, 1979), 41–46. The statistics on where the immigrants moved to are from Hall and Coerver, *Revolution on the Border*, 135–36.

26. U.S. Department of Labor, *Annual Report* (1920), 7–8, 429–30.

27. Jorge Durand, Douglas S. Massey, and Chiara Capoferro, "The New Geography of Mexican Immigration," in Victor Zuñiga and Rubén Hernández-León, eds., *New Destinations: Mexican Immigration in the United States* (New York: Russell Sage Foundation, 2005), 5.

28. Mentioned in John Chávez, *The Lost Land: The Chicano Image of the Southwest* (Albuquerque: University of New Mexico Press, 1984), 92.

29. Edith Shatto King, "My Mexican Neighbors," *Survey*, March 3, 1917, 624–26. Quotations on p. 624.

30. Committee on Immigration and Naturalization, *Temporary Admission*, 113 (quotations), 116–17.

31. For examples in Arizona, see Tomás O. Belada, "Los Braceros y El Costo de la Vida," *El Tucsonense* (Tucson, AZ), February 19, 1920; and F.S. Moreno, ed., *El Tucsonense*, January 1, 1920. David Gutiérrez argues that there were conflicts between Mexican immigrants and Mexican Americans; see Gutiérrez, *Walls and Mirrors: Mexican Americans, Mexican Immigrants, and the Politics of Ethnicity* (Berkeley: University of California Press, 1995), 56–65. For other general information on the tensions between Mexican Americans and Mexican immigrants, see Chávez, *Lost Land*, 83–84.

32. See Meeks, *Border Citizens*, 96–97; and Miguel Tinker Salas, *In the Shadow of the Eagles: Sonora and the Transformation of the Border during the Porfiriato* (Berkeley: University of California Press, 1997), 26–27.

33. Gabriela Arredondo also notes Mexicans' disinterest in naturalizing in Chicago and sees it as due to Mexico's growing revolutionary nationalism combined with pressures to assimilate, as well as the increasing recognition by Mexicans that Americans did not regard them as Americans. See Gabriela F. Arredondo, *Mexican Chicago: Race, Identity, and Nation, 1916–39* (Chicago: University of Illinois Press, 2008), 8–10, 80–104, 157–58.

34. Patrick Lukens similarly explains Mexican Americans' reasons for assimilation although he concentrates on a later time period. See Patrick D. Lukens, *A Quiet Victory for Latino Rights: FDR and the Controversy over "Whiteness"* (Tucson: University of Arizona Press, 2012), 10–15.

35. Alex G. Jácome [son of Carlos Jácome], Letter to the Editor," *Arizona Star*, April 29, 1970.

36. Sheridan, *Los Tucsonenses*, 102–12, 166–79; Carlos C. Jácome, Clippings Files, Arizona Historical Society, Tucson; Meeks, *Border Citizens*, 94–96.

37. Bradford Luckingham, *Minorities in Phoenix: A Profile of Mexican American, Chinese American, and African American Communities, 1860–1992* (Tucson: University of Arizona Press, 1994), 28–34 (quotation on 34).

38. Committee on Immigration and Naturalization, *Temporary Admission*, quotation from 17–18; see also 14, 41, 82, 87, 113–15, 160.

39. See George J. Sánchez, *Becoming Mexican American: Ethnicity, Culture, and Identity in Chicano Los Angeles, 1900–1945* (New York: Oxford University Press, 1993), 87–107; and Sarah Deutsch, *No Separate Refuge: Culture, Class, and Gender on an Anglo-Hispanic Frontier in the American Southwest, 1880–1940* (New York: Oxford University Press, 1987), 110–21. Also see Cybelle Fox for a recent work on reformers' frustration and even complicity in promoting the idea of people of Mexican

descent as being dependent and undeserving charity cases: *Three Worlds of Relief: Race, Immigration, and the American Welfare State from the Progressive Era to the New Deal* (Princeton, NJ: Princeton University Press, 2012), 14–16, chap 4.

40. For more on the rise and spread of the eugenics movement in many parts of the country, see Alexandra Minna Stern, *Eugenic Nation: Faults and Frontiers of Better Breeding in Modern America* (Berkeley: University of California Press, 2005), 5–6. Also see John Higham, *Strangers in the Land: Patterns of American Nativism, 1860–1925* (New Brunswick, NJ: Rutgers University Press, 1998), 150–57, 313–14.

41. This stipulation would remain part of Arizona's state law until 1972, even after federal law declared such provisions illegal in the 1965 Voting Rights Act. See Luckingham, *Minorities in Phoenix*, 48.

42. Luckingham, *Minorities in Phoenix*, 28–31; and Meeks, *Border Citizens*, 102, 109.

43. Charles H. Harris, III, and Louis R. Sadler, *The Border and the Revolution: Clandestine Activities of the Mexican Revolution: 1910–1920* (Silver City, NM: High-Lonesome Books, 1988), 71–75, 101–9. Eric Meeks (*Border Citizens*, 103–6) finds that the 1915 strike in Ray involved many Mexicans. The local press (including the Spanish-language periodicals) criticized their efforts at improving their labor conditions by calling them bandits; they tried to discredit them by linking them with the "Plan de San Diego" mentioned in the text.

44. Colleen O'Neill, "Domesticity Deployed: Gender, Race, and the Construction of Class Struggle in the Bisbee Deportation," *Labor History* 34, nos. 2–3 (1993), 256–58, 271–72. Also see Meeks, *Border Citizens*, 102–3, 269; and Thomas E. Sheridan, *Arizona: A History* (Tucson: University of Arizona Press, 1995), 180–86, 215–16. For a more recent work on the Bisbee Deportation, see Katherine Benton-Cohen, *Borderline Americans* (Cambridge: Harvard University Press, 2009), chap. 7.

45. Committee on Immigration and Naturalization, *Temporary Admission*, 192. For other information on this first *bracero* program, see Cardoso, "Labor Emigration to the Southwest," 16–18. See also Otey M. Scruggs, "First Mexican Farm Labor Program," *Arizona and the West* 2 (Winter 1960), 320. Also see Reisler, *By the Sweat of Their Brow*, chaps. 2 and 3; and Meeks, *Border Citizens*, 109–14.

46. Committee on Immigration and Naturalization, *Temporary Admission*, 251.

47. Ibid., 116–17, 269, 275.

48. Ibid., 3–10; quotation on 87–88.

49. Committee on Immigration and Naturalization, *Temporary Admission*, 150, 189, 228–36. For information on how the Dingley Tariff of 1897 started the growth of the domestic sugar beet industry and how the first laborers were primarily Belgians, German-Russians, and then Japanese immigrants before the industry turned to Mexican workers, see Reisler, *By the Sweat of Their Brow*, 87–88. Also for a more recent work addressing the sugar beet industry and Mexican workers, see Kathleen Mapes, *Sweet Tyranny* (Urbana: University of Illinois Press, 2009), 34–36.

50. Committee on Immigration and Naturalization, *Temporary Admission*, 142.

51. Ibid., 254–59; quotation on 258.

52. Ibid., 33; quotation, 88.

53. Ibid., 33, 163.

54. In 1917, the exclusionists succeeded in reducing European and Asian immigration by passing the Literacy Act. In that same legislation, they prevailed in excluding

more Asians from entry by designating an Asiatic Barred Zone, which stipulated that people who lived within it would be prevented from immigrating to the United States.

55. Meeks, *Border Citizens*, 89–93; Sheridan, *Arizona: A History*, 178–79.

Chapter Four

A version of this paragraph (along with chapter 6 of this book), was published in "Strange Bedfellows: American Growers and Mexican Immigrants in the United States, 1926 to 1930," in Armand Colin, ed., *Monde(s). Histoire, Espaces, Relations*, no. 3 (June 2013), 213–235. See http: //www.monde-s.com/ and http://www.armand-colin .com/revue/37/1/modes-historie-espaces-relations.php.

1. Ross R. Rice, *Carl Hayden: Builder of the American West* (Lanham, MD: University Press of America, 1994), 5, 15, 19–21, 32–33, 39–40, 46–47, 66.

2. For general information on transience see James N. Gregory, *American Exodus: Dust Bowl Migration and Okie Culture in California* (Oxford: Oxford University Press, 1989), 78–81. For the debates about transient men in Arizona statehood, see Mark E. Pry, "Arizona and the Politics of Statehood, 1889–1912" (PhD diss., Arizona State University, 1995). See also primary sources, which demonstrate that legislators in favor of statehood emphasized the stability and settled nature of people of Mexican descent, in U.S. Senate, Committee on the Territories, *Statehood for the Territories: Papers Relating to the Question of Statehood for the Territories*, 57th Cong., doc. 153 (January–February 1903), 9–10; and U.S. Senate, Committee on the Territories, *New Statehood Bill, Hearing before the Subcommittee on Territories*, 57th Cong., 2nd sess. (1902), 90. Katherine Benton-Cohen also makes the argument that some employers preferred hiring family men as they saw them as less prone to initiate protests of working conditions in *Borderline Americans* (Cambridge: Harvard University Press, 2009), 138. Also see Mark Wyman, who finds that transient men of all backgrounds were "eagerly recruited—warmly welcome—then cast off," in *Hoboes: Bindlestiffs, Fruit Tramps, and the Harvesting of the West* (New York: Hill and Wang, 2010), 7.

3. Mae Ngai argues that after the 1924 restriction acts were imposed upon Europeans, Mexicans became associated with foreignness/alienness and illegality. I see this as occurring earlier and more in the guise of their temporary status. See Mae M. Ngai, *Impossible Subjects: Illegal Aliens and the Making of Modern America* (Princeton, NJ: Princeton University Press, 2004), chaps. 1 and 2. For an extensive discussion of the connection between Mexicans and temporary workers, see Camille Guerin-Gonzales, *Mexican Workers, American Dreams: Immigration, Repatriation, and California Farm Labor, 1900–1939* (New Brunswick, NJ: Rutgers University Press, 1994), chap. 2, esp. 45. Many others also note the connections that were made between Mexicans and temporary workers; see Devra Weber, *Dark Sweat, White Gold: California Farm Workers, Cotton, and the New Deal* (Berkeley: University of California Press, 1994), 8; Gregory, *American Exodus*, 68; Abraham Hoffman, *Unwanted Mexican Americans in the Great Depression: Repatriation Pressures, 1929–1939* (Tucson: University of Arizona Press, 1974), 16–17; Michael J. Piore, *Birds of Passage: Migrant Labor and Industrial Societies* (Cambridge: Cambridge University Press, 1979), 3, 51–52, 77, 81–82; and George J. Sánchez, *Becoming Mexican American: Ethnicity, Culture, and Identity in Chicano Los Angeles, 1900–1945* (New York: Oxford University

Press, 1993), 189. Also see Kathleen Mapes's recent study on sugar beet workers in the Midwest in which she notes the growers' and the state's involvement in creating "Mexicans as workers but not as immigrants." I agree but stress more how many people worked to create the temporary worker image, not just the state and growers, and that this reality of a temporary worker—as Mapes notes, too—was often a fictional construct. See my chapters 5 and 6, as well as this one. Mapes, *Sweet Tyranny* (Urbana: University of Illinois Press, 2009), 6–10, and esp. chaps. 3 and 5.

4. Patrick Ettinger, *Imaginary Lines: Border Enforcement and the Origins of Undocumented Immigration, 1882–1930* (Austin: University of Texas Press, 2009), 125.

5. Victor S. Clark, "Mexican Labor in the United States," *Bulletin of the Bureau of Labor* 78 (Washington, DC: Government Printing Office, 1908), 467, 496.

6. Ibid., 482, 485.

7. U.S. Department of Commerce and Labor, *Annual Report*, from the Commissioner General of Immigration (Washington, DC: Government Printing Office, 1911), 120–21.

8. Quoted in Gilbert G. González, *Culture of Empire: American Writers, Mexico, and Mexican Immigrants, 1880–1930* (Austin: University of Texas Press, 2004), 81.

9. Samuel Bryan, "Mexican Immigrants in the United States," *Survey*, September 7, 1912, 726–30.

10. The Chinese Exclusion Act passed in 1882, was extended in 1892, and made permanent in 1904. In 1907, President Theodore Roosevelt negotiated the Gentlemen's Agreement with Japan to restrict Japanese laborers from immigrating to the United States. See Bill Ong Hing, *Defining American through Immigration Policy* (Philadelphia: Temple University Press, 2004), 36–44. Senators Henry Cabot Lodge (Republican, MA) and William P. Dillingham (Republican, VT) were placed in charge of an investigation on immigration as part of a political compromise to get Lodge to drop the literacy requirement from a bill in 1907. See Daniel J. Tichenor, *Dividing Lines: The Politics of Immigration Control in America* (Princeton, NJ: Princeton University Press, 2002), 124–27.

11. U.S. Senate Committee on Immigration, *Reports of the Immigration Commission, Immigrants in Industries* (Washington, DC: Government Printing Office, 1911), pt. 25, 2: 682–83.

12. Ibid., 690.

13. Ibid., 682.

14. See Theda Skocpol, *Protecting Soldiers and Mothers: The Political Origins of Social Policy in the United States* (Cambridge: Belknap Press of Harvard University Press, 1992), 57–60.

15. W.B. Wilson, Secretary of Labor, to Representative Claude Hudspeth (TX), June 7, 1919, Immigration and Naturalization Service, Record Group 85, Entry 9, file 54261/202I, National Archives, Washington, DC.

16. Actually this resolution was somewhat different, providing for the admission of otherwise inadmissible Mexicans in the southwestern states of Texas, California, Arizona, and New Mexico, areas that presumably faced a shortage of laborers to harvest cotton and food crops.

17. U.S. House of Representatives, Committee on Immigration and Naturalization, *Temporary Admission of Illiterate Mexican Laborers, Hearings*, 66th Cong., 2nd sess. (1920), 263–75; quotation on 265.

18. Ibid., 189–92, 196.

19. Again, Camille Guerin-Gonzales (*Mexican Workers, American Dreams*, 45) states that this perception had existed before, but here I am emphasizing some of the connections and how this image grew and spread.

20. Committee on Immigration and Naturalization, *Temporary Admission of Illiterate Mexican Laborers*, 36.

21. Ibid., 87–88.

22. Ibid., 3–14.

23. "Los braceros y el costo de la vida," *El Tucsonense* (Tucson, AZ), February 19, 1920. Quotation from "Brillante éxito fue el segundo banquete del 'Club Comercial Hispano-Americano,'" *El Tucsonense*, April 20, 1920, my translation.

24. Servando I. Esquivel, Asociación de Jóvenes, El Paso, "The Immigrant from Mexico," *Outlook*, May 19, 1920, 131.

25. "Mexican Invaders Relieving Our Farm-Labor Shortage," *Literary Digest*, July 17, 1920, 53–54.

26. J. Blaine Gwin, "The New Mexican Immigration," *Survey*, August 3, 1918, 492.

27. J. Blaine Gwin, "Back and Forth to Mexico," *Survey*, October 6, 1917, 9–10.

28. Mark A. Reisler, *By the Sweat of Their Brow: Mexican Immigrant Labor in the United States, 1900–1940* (Westport, CT: Greenwood Press, 1976), 111–12. Also see F. Arturo Rosales, *!Pobre Raza!: Violence, Justice, and Mobilization among México Lindo Immigrants, 1900–1936* (Austin: University of Texas Press, 1999), chap. 3.

29. See Helen Delpar, *Enormous Vogue of Things Mexican: Cultural Relations between the United States and Mexico, 1920–1935* (Tuscaloosa: University of Alabama Press, 1992), 12–14; and Fernando Saúl Alanis Enciso, "No cuenten conmigo: La pólitica de repatriación del gobierno mexicano y sus nacionales en estados unidos, 1910–1928," *Mexican Studies/Estudios Mexicanos* 19 (Summer 2003), 406.

30. Gabriela F. Arredondo, *Mexican Chicago: Race, Identity, and Nation, 1916–39* (Chicago: University of Illinois Press, 2008), 90–104, 135–42.

31. U.S. Senate Committee on Immigration, *Reports of the Immigration Commission*, 58, 231, 690.

32. Eric V. Meeks, *Border Citizens: The Making of Indians, Mexicans, and Anglos in Arizona* (Austin: University of Texas Press, 2007), 72.

33. Regarding low naturalization rates, see Reisler, *By the Sweat of Their Brow*, 111; and G. Bromley Onnam, "The Mexican in Los Angeles from the Standpoint of the Religious Forces of the City," *Annals of the American Academy* 93 (January 1921), 130–33.

34. See Zaragosa Vargas, *Proletarians of the North: A History of Mexican Industrial Workers in Detroit and the Midwest, 1917–1933* (Berkeley: University of California Press, 1993), 58, 67–68. Regarding the existence of the tent camps, see Committee on Immigration and Naturalization, *Temporary Admission of Illiterate Mexican Laborers*, 195; see also Eric Vaughn Meeks, "Border Citizens: Race, Labor, and Identity in South-Central Arizona, 1910–1965" (PhD diss., University of Texas at Austin, 2001), 106–7.

35. U.S. Department of Labor, *Annual Report*, from the Commissioner General of Immigration (Washington, DC: Government Printing Office, 1921), 7.

36. Note that Pablo Mitchell also makes a linkage between being American and being modern, as well as having a certain type of bodily comportment, in *Coyote Nation: Sexuality, Race, and Conquest in Modernizing New Mexico, 1880–1920* (Chicago: University of Chicago Press, 2005), 176–77.

37. Michael Piore (*Birds of Passage*, 81) believes it was almost inevitable for temporary workers to remain in the United States and establish permanent communities. Camille Guerin-Gonzales (*Mexican Workers, American Dreams*, 78) and Devra Weber (*Dark Sweat, White Gold*, 44–46, 77–78) find that permanent communities were being formed.

38. U.S. House of Representatives, Committee on Immigration and Naturalization, *Imported Pauper Labor and Serfdom in America: Statement of Honorable John C. Box*, Hearings, 67th Cong., 1st sess. (1921), 17. Quotation is from a reprint of *Dallas News*, February 1, 1921, in the abovementioned hearing.

39. U.S. Department of Labor, *Annual Report* (1921), 7.

40. Committee on Immigration and Naturalization, *Temporary Admission of Illiterate Mexican Laborers*, 39.

41. Ibid., 106–7.

42. Reisler, *By the Sweat of Their Brow*, 49–56.

43. Supervisory Inspector at El Paso to Commissioner General, Immigration, January 28, 1920, Immigration and Naturalization Service, Record Group 85, Entry 9, file 54261/202.

44. W.H. Knox, Arizona Cotton Growers' Association to Supervisory Inspector at El Paso, March 2, 1921, U.S. Immigration and Naturalization Service, Record Group 85, Entry 9, file 55091/6.

45. Supervisory Inspector at Denver to Commissioner General, Immigration, December 6, 1921, U.S. Immigration and Naturalization Service, Record Group 85, Entry 9, file 55091/6. Regarding how the statute of limitations for deportation under the likely to become a public charge clause was extended to five years under the Burnett-Smith Act of 1917, see Ngai, *Impossible Subjects*, 59.

46. U.S. Department of Labor, *Annual Report*, from the Commissioner General of Immigration (Washington, DC: Government Printing Office, 1920), 442.

47. W.P. Mansfield, Office of Inspector, Denver to Commissioner General, Immigration, August 13, 1919, U.S. Immigration and Naturalization Service, Record Group 85, Entry 9, file 54261/202H.

48. E. L. Flannery to Supervising Inspector, El Paso, June 2, 1919, U.S. Immigration and Naturalization Service, Record Group 85, Entry 9, file 54261/202H.

49. Supervising Inspector, El Paso to Commissioner General of Immigration, August 13, 1919, and from the Department of Labor to Commissioner General, Immigration, August 30, 1919 in U.S. Immigration and Naturalization Service, Record Group 85, Entry 9, file 54261/202I in National Archives. Again, regarding the presumed stability of family men, see Benton-Cohen, *Borderline Americans*, 138.

50. U.S. Department of Labor, *Annual Report* (1920), 428.

51. J. M. Waterhouse, Spreckels Sugar Company Representative, to George Harris, Acting Supervising Inspector, El Paso, April 23, 1918, U.S. Immigration and Naturalization Service, Record Group 85, Entry 9, file 54321/181.

52. Reisler, *By the Sweat of Their Brow*, 41, 49–50.

53. For two examples of this, see article in *Denver Post*, January 19, 1922, and letter from Charles M. Johnston, Department of State, February 11, 1921, U.S. Immigration and Naturalization Service, Record Group 85, Entry 9, file 55091/6.

54. Inspector at Ellis Island to Commissioner General, Immigration, February 22, 1921, U.S. Immigration and Naturalization Service, Record Group 85, Entry 9, file 55091/6.

55. "Los mexicanos sin trabajo serán regresados," *El Tucsonense*, February 22, 1921.

56. Manuel García y Griego, "The Importation of Mexican Contract Laborers to the United States, 1942–1964: Antecedents, Operation, and Legacy," in Peter G. Brown and Henry Shue, eds., *The Border That Joins: Mexican Migrants and U.S. Responsibility* (Totowa, NJ: Rowman and Littlefield, 1983), 49–98, esp. 52–53.

57. See "Se llega a un acuerdo para repatriar a los 'Cottonpickers'," *El Tucsonense*, February 8, 1921; and Charles Johnston, Department of State to Assistant Commissioner General, Immigration, February 11, 1921, U.S. Immigration and Naturalization Service, Record Group 85, Entry 9, file 55091/6.

58. Francisco Pereda, Mexican Consul to William Hale Thompson, Mayor of the City of Chicago, April 25, 1921, U.S. Immigration and Naturalization Service, Record Group 85, Entry 9, file 55091/6.

59. Letter from Willows to Fieser, Division Manager of Red Cross, May 3, 1921, U.S. Immigration and Naturalization Service, Record Group 85, Entry 9, file 55091/6.

60. W. H. Robb, Fort Worth Welfare Association to C.N. Adar, American Federation of Labor, April 6, 1921, U.S. Immigration and Naturalization Service, Record Group 85, Entry 9, file 55091/6.

61. Inspector in Charge, Detroit, Michigan, to Commissioner General of Immigration, in U.S. Immigration and Naturalization Service, Record Group 85, Entry 9, file 55091/6.

62. Ibid.

63. For a reference to repatriation from Los Angeles in the 1920s, see Manuel García y Griego, "The Importation of Mexican Contract Laborers to the United States, 1942–1964." Chapter 7 of the present volume discusses the larger repatriation drives of the 1930s.

64. Article in *Denver Post*, January 19, 1922, U.S. Immigration and Naturalization Service, Record Group 85, Entry 9, file 55091/6.

65. Office of Inspector in Midwest to Commissioner General, Immigration, February 5, 1921, in U.S. Immigration and Naturalization Service, Record Group 85, Entry 9, file 55091/6.

66. Cybelle Fox also shows how there was a growing association between Mexicans and dependence and explains why social reformers began to believe this and promote this idea to others in *Three Worlds of Relief: Race, Immigration, and the American Welfare State from the Progressive Era to the New Deal* (Princeton, NJ: Princeton University Press, 2012), chap. 4.

67. "La falta de trabajo entre el elemento mexicano," *El Tucsonense*, January 29, 1921.

68. Alianza Hispano Americana Organo Oficial, July 10, 1921, Alianza Hispano-Americana, MS 597, Box 3, F17, Arizona Historical Society, Tucson.

69. Letter from Denver Office of Inspections to Commissioner General, Immigration, December 6, 1921, U.S. Immigration and Naturalization Service, Record Group 85, Entry 9, file 55091/6.

70. Ibid.

71. Reisler, *By the Sweat of Their Brow*, 53.

72. Committee on Immigration and Naturalization, *Temporary Admission of Illiterate Mexican Laborers*, 257.

73. I agree with Cybelle Fox (Fox, *Three Worlds of Relief*, chap. 4) that many reformers had become disenchanted with assimilation for people of Mexican descent and that some worked willingly to repatriate them, but some reformers (perhaps, more of them than she allows for) continued to believe that Mexicans could be assimilated and worked to assist them as best they could.

Chapter Five

1. I am indebted to the historians who have previously investigated immigration restriction debates generally, as well as to those who have studied Mexican restriction debates more specifically: John Higham focuses on Asian and European immigration and then concludes that restrictionists lost steam and energy after 1924, whereas Robert Divine argues that Mexicans were not restricted for fear of angering Mexico. Robert Lipshultz provides a detailed analysis of the debates and believes that Mexican restriction failed because Americans chose to concentrate first on expelling or decreasing European and Asian immigrants. Lawrence Cardoso expands on Divine's work, showing that the United States wanted to keep Mexico stable by keeping the "safety valve" of immigration open. American policy makers felt it would reduce the likelihood of more revolutions in Mexico. Cardoso also adds that missionaries argued against immigration restriction since they believed that Americanization would improve the immigrants. Even if they returned home, as they suspected they would, the immigrants would take a favorable impression of the United States back to Mexico, helping to build and maintain good relations between the United States and Mexico. See Higham, *Strangers in the Land: Patterns of American Nativism, 1860–1925* (New Brunswick, NJ: Rutgers University Press, 1998); Divine, *American Immigration Policy, 1924–1952* (New Haven, CT: Yale University Press, 1957); Lipshultz, "American Attitudes toward Mexican Immigration, 1924–1952" (master's thesis, University of Chicago, 1962); Cardoso, *Mexican Emigration to the United States, 1897–1931* (Tucson: University of Arizona Press, 1980). For a more recent work focused on sugar beet growers, see Kathleen Mapes, *Sweet Tyranny: Migrant Labor, Industrial Agriculture, and Imperial Politics* (Urbana: University of Illinois Press, 2009), esp. chaps. 3, 6, and 9.

2. Divine, *American Immigration Policy*, 54. For more on exclusionists' new focus on restricting Mexicans, see also Patrick D. Lukens, *A Quiet Victory for Latino Rights: FDR and the Controversy over "Whiteness"* (Tucson: University of Arizona Press, 2012), 33, 108.

3. Zaragosa Vargas, *Proletarians of the North: A History of Mexican Industrial Workers in Detroit and the Midwest, 1917–1933* (Berkeley: University of California Press, 1993), 145–54; and Gabriela F. Arredondo, *Mexican Chicago: Race, Identity, and Nation, 1916–39* (Chicago: University of Illinois Press, 2008), 21–22.

4. The total number of immigrants officially entering in 1924 was 706,896. The U.S. population in 1924 was 105,710,620. Mark Reisler, *By the Sweat of Their Brow: Mexican Immigrant Labor in the United States, 1900–1940* (Westport, CT: Greenwood Press, 1976), 152–53.

5. Albert W. Atwood, "Where Have the Miners Gone?" *Saturday Evening Post*, March 10, 1923. For more on the entwining of Mexicans with disease and their danger

for Americans, see Alexandra Minna Stern, *Eugenic Nation: Faults and Frontiers of Better Breeding in Modern America* (Berkeley: University of California Press, 2005); and Natalia Molina, *Fit to Be Citizens?: Public Health and Race in Los Angeles, 1879–1939* (Berkeley: University of California Press, 2006).

6. Quoted in Divine, *American Immigration Policy*, 53. The term *menace* was used to describe Mexicans in various articles and testimony. For one example, see Remsen Crawford, "The Menace of Mexican Immigration," *Current History* 31 (October 1930–March 1931), 902–7.

7. Francisco E. Balderrama and Raymond Rodríguez, *Decade of Betrayal: Mexican Repatriation in the 1930s* (Albuquerque: University of New Mexico Press, 1995), 18.

8. Reisler, *By the Sweat of Their Brow*, 173.

9. Cardoso, *Mexican Emigration to the United States*, 139.

10. U.S. Department of Labor, *Annual Reports*, from the Commissioner General of Immigration (Washington, DC: Government Printing Office, 1926–29).

11. U.S. House of Representatives, Committee on Immigration and Naturalization, *Western Hemisphere Immigration, Hearings*, 71st Cong., 2nd sess. (1930), 317.

12. For Hushing, see Committee on Immigration and Naturalization, *Western Hemisphere Immigration*, 366. For Foerster and Laughlin, see Reisler, *By the Sweat of Their Brow*, 206–8; and Divine, *American Immigration Policy*, 56–57.

13. Exclusionists may have been more willing to embrace Spanish Americans because of their recent success in restricting Spanish immigrants through the quota laws of 1921 and 1924.

14. A summary of Hoover's article is in "Mexican Immigration," *New York Times*, October, 1929 in Records of the Immigration and Naturalization Service, Record Group 85, Entry 9, file 55639/616, National Archives, Washington, DC.

15. Harry Hull, Commissioner to James K. Fisk, California Joint Immigration Committee, March 19, 1932; Secretary Davis to Hiram W. Johnson, Chair of Senate Committee, February 5, 1929, Immigration and Naturalization Service, Record Group 85, Entry 9, file 55639/617A.

16. "The Southwest's Immigration Problem," *New York Times*, November 10, 1926, *Proquest Historical Newspapers*.

17. Norman M. Blaney to Roy L. Garis, Vanderbilt University, December 24, 1929, in Immigration and Naturalization Service, Record Group 85, Entry 9, file 55639/616.

18. Chester H. Rowell, "Why Make Mexico an Exception?" *Survey*, May 1, 1931.

19. U.S. House of Representatives, Committee on Immigration and Naturalization, *Restriction of Immigration from Republic of Mexico*, Rep. 1594, 71st Cong., 2nd sess. (1930), 2, 6.

20. Committee on Immigration and Naturalization, *Western Hemisphere Immigration*, 323–25, quotation on 325. There was very little debate over Canadians as immigrants and potential Americans; most seemed to agree that they could become American and only extended the restriction to them so as not to offend Mexico. While the quotations shown emphasize the class status of the Canadians as a reason for belonging, many Canadian immigrants did have lower-class status and entered to take logging jobs in the Northeast. The presumption that Canadians were members of the white race contributed to the lack of controversy about them. People testifying in the restriction debates noted Canadians' ability to blend in and be the same as

other Americans within a generation or two. For information on Canadian immigration, see U.S. Department of Labor, *Annual Reports* (1926–29).

21. "Restrict the Peons," *Washington Post*, August 24, 1926, *Proquest Historical Newspapers*.

22. Committee on Immigration and Naturalization, *Western Hemisphere Immigration*, 318.

23. Rosa Linda Fregoso, *MeXicana Encounters: The Making of Social Identities on the Borderlands* (Berkeley: University of California Press, 2003), 116–17.

24. August Fast to Representative Albert Johnson, March 3, 1928, Records of the U.S. House of Representatives, Record Group 233, file HR70A-F14.3, National Archives, Washington, DC.

25. Committee on Immigration and Naturalization, *Western Hemisphere Immigration*, 317.

26. Ibid., 366–67. Also, regarding the importance of homeownership to being American and its inaccessibility for people of Mexican descent, see Katherine Benton-Cohen, *Borderline Americans* (Cambridge: Harvard University Press, 2009), 130–33, 142–46.

27. Romano Herrera to the Commissioner of Immigration, October 29, 1929, Immigration and Naturalization Service, Record Group 85, Entry 9, file 55639/617A.

28. Alfonso Fabila, *El problema de la emigracion de obreros y campesinos mexicanos* (Mexico City: Publicaciones de la secretaria de gobernacion, 1929), 12–13.

29. Secretaria de relaciones exteriores, *La migracion y proteccions de mexicanos en el extranjero* (Mexico City: Ministerio de relaciones exteriores, 1928), 17.

30. Reisler, *By the Sweat of Their Brow*, 228.

31. The *Literacy Digest* information is mentioned in Reisler, *By the Sweat of Their Brow*, 205. For the *Saturday Evening Post*, see Abraham Hoffman, *Unwanted Mexican Americans in the Great Depression: Repatriation Pressures, 1929–1939* (Tucson: University of Arizona Press, 1974), 29.

32. The survey was apparently sponsored by Representatives John Box (Democrat, TX) and Thomas Jenkins (Republican, OH) of the House Immigration Committee with questionnaires sent to several thousand Americans, including merchants, teachers, and judges. Survey results are summarized in Crawford, "Menace of Mexican Immigration."

33. The term "Mexicanization" is from U.S. House of Representatives, Committee on Immigration and Naturalization, *Seasonal Agricultural Laborers from Mexico, Hearings*, 69th Cong., 1st sess. (1926), 35. For more on the expansion of "Little Mexicos," see Letter from Theodore Farmer to the Committee on Immigration, May 23, 1928, Immigration and Naturalization Service, Record Group 233, file HR 70A-H3.3.

34. George Horace Lorimer, ed., "Present and Future," *Saturday Evening Post*, March 15, 1930, 28.

35. T. J. O'Donnell from California to unnamed newspaper on April 7, 1930, in Immigration and Naturalization Service, Record Group 233, file HR 71A-F16.4, box 517. There were many voices stating that the immigrants had not left as initially claimed. See the various hearings on immigration, 1926–30, and letters to representatives. For one example, see letter from Alexander Hamilton Bolton, February 1928, to Representative Joseph Crail (Republican, CA) in Immigration and Naturalization Service, Record Group 233, file HR 70A-H3.3.

36. Pamphlet in Immigration and Naturalization Service, Record Group 233, file HR 71A-F16.4, box 517.

37. Reisler, *By the Sweat of Their Brow*, 156.

38. C. M. Goethe, "The Influx of Mexican Amerinds," *Eugenics* 2, no. 1 (1929), 9.

39. Committee on Immigration and Naturalization, *Restriction of Immigration from Republic of Mexico*, 6.

40. Committee on Immigration and Naturalization, *Western Hemisphere Immigration*, 258–59. J. C. Canales also says this on pp. 172–73 of the same hearings.

41. Ibid., 260.

42. Ibid., 180–81.

43. Telegram to William Green entered into testimony, ibid., 191. Also see Patrick Lukens (*A Quiet Victory for Latino Rights*, 94–99) who sees LULAC as for restricting Mexican immigrants but opposed to immigrant abuse and discrimination that might be directed at themselves as well.

44. "Are Texas-Mexicans 'Americans'?" *LULAC News*, p. 7, RM-142, Hayden Library, Arizona State University, Tempe, Arizona.

45. This fits with Thomas A. Guglielmo's recent findings in his article in the *Journal of American History* and may be considered an earlier version of what he refers to as the "Caucasian strategy," used by LULAC members and other Mexican Americans in 1940s Texas to fight for civil rights for all those who could claim this heritage. See Guglielmo, "Fighting for Caucasian Rights: Mexicans, Mexican Americans, and the Transnational Struggle for Civil Rights in World War II Texas," *Journal of American History* 92 (March 2006), 1212–37.

46. For missionary views, see Cardoso, *Mexican Emigration to the United States*, 119.

47. Robert N. McLean, "Mexican Workers in the United States," in *Proceedings of the National Conference of Social Work* (Chicago: University of Chicago Press, 1929), 531–38.

48. Don D. Lescohier, "The Vital Problem in Mexican Immigration," *Proceedings of the National Conference of Social Work* (Chicago: University of Chicago Press, 1927), 551; Charles A. Thomson, "Mexicans—an Interpretation," *Proceedings of the National Conference of Social Work* (Chicago: University of Chicago Press, 1928), 499–503; and Thomson, "Restriction of Mexican Immigration," *Journal of Applied Psychology* 11 (July–August 1927), 577.

49. Helen Walker, "Mexican Immigrants and American Citizenship," *Sociology and Social Research* 13, no. 5 (1929), 463–71.

50. James Hoffman Batten, "Southwest and Center: The Mexican Conference at Pomona," *Survey Midmonthly*, January 15, 1929, 475.

51. Cybelle Fox also finds that reformers became increasingly unsure about Mexicans' success with assimilating in the late 1920s. She sees most reformers as wanting to get rid of Mexicans—pointing to their allegedly disproportionate dependence on charity—I see more ambivalence among the reformers about what to do about the lack of assimilation. See Fox, *Three Worlds of Relief: Race, Immigration, and the American Welfare State from the Progressive Era to the New Deal* (Princeton. NJ: Princeton University Press, 2012), chap 4.

52. Committee on Immigration and Naturalization, *Seasonal Agricultural Laborers from Mexico*, 138–44. As the example suggests, only a small percentage of people of Mexican descent in Arizona possessed the financial wherewithal to buy a home,

a critical component of Americanism. See Katherine Benton-Cohen's study in which she finds only five elite Mexicans who were able to afford a home in the middle-class community of Warren, Arizona in *Borderline Americans*, 144, and her general discussion of the importance of homeownership to Americanism at 130–33 and 142–46.

53. For more on the fascination with Spanish heritage, see F. Arturo Rosales, "'Fantasy Heritage' Reexamined: Race and Class in the Writings of the Bandini Family Authors and Other Californios, 1828–1965," in Erlinda González Berry and Charles Tatum, eds., *Recovering the U.S. Hispanic Literary Heritage*, vol. 2 (Houston: Arte Público Press, 1996), 83–106.

54. This "vogue" is identified and described in Alfred Coester, "Why Spanish?" *Hispania* 7, no. 1 (1924), 21–29. Further evidence is from U.S. House of Representatives, Committee on Ways and Means, *Hearings on the Pacific Southwest Exposition*, 70th Cong. (1928), 6.

55. Cleve Hallenbeck, *Spanish Missions of the Old Southwest* (Garden City, NY: Doubleday, Page, 1926), v, 7–9, 15.

56. Sarah Bixby-Smith, *Adobe Days* (Cedar Rapids, IA: Torch Press, 1925), 81, 101, 121–25.

57. Committee on Immigration and Naturalization, *Western Hemisphere Immigration*, 152.

58. Devra Weber, *Dark Sweat, White Gold: California Farm Workers, Cotton, and the New Deal* (Berkeley: University of California Press, 1994), 39–41, 46, 240n81.

59. "El primer banquete del club latino fue un exìto," *El Tucsonense*, January 26, 1926. For more on Mexican Americans' conflicted views regarding Mexican immigrants and how they might be affected by an influx of newcomers, see David G. Gutiérrez, *Walls and Mirrors: Mexican Americans, Mexican Immigrants, and the Politics of Ethnicity in the American Southwest* (Berkeley: University of California Press, 1995).

60. Paul S. Taylor, *Mexican Labor in the United States: Valley of the South Platte, Colorado*, vol. 6, no. 2 (Berkeley: University of California Press, 1928), 212.

61. Paul S. Taylor, *Mexican Labor in the United States: Dimmit County, Winter Garden District, South Texas*, vol. 6, no. 5 (Berkeley: University of California Press, 1930), 432.

62. Ibid., 446.

63. Committee on Immigration and Naturalization, *Western Hemisphere Immigration*, 366.

64. Paul S. Taylor, *Mexican Labor in the United States: Chicago and the Calumet Region*, vol. 7, no. 2 (Berkeley: University of California Press, 1932), 112. Information collected from period 1928–29. Also, see Paul S. Taylor, *Mexican Labor in the United States: Imperial Valley*, vol. 6, no. 1 (Berkeley: University of California Press, 1928), 91.

65. Taylor, *Valley of the South Platte, Colorado*, 212–14.

Chapter Six

A version of this chapter was published as "Strange Bedfellows: American Growers and Mexican Immigrants in the United States, 1926 to 1930," in Armand Colin, ed., *Monde(s). Histoire, Espaces, Relations*, no. 3 (June 2013) 215–235. See http://www.monde-s.com/ and http://www.armand-colin.com/revue/37/1/mondes-histoire-espaces-relations.php.

1. For statistics on annual immigration, see U.S. Department of Labor, *Annual Reports*, from the Commissioner General of Immigration (Washington, DC: Government Printing Office, 1925–30). For information on the proposed immigration limits, see Mark Reisler, *By the Sweat of Their Brow: Mexican Immigration Labor in the United States, 1900–1940* (Westport, CT: Greenwood Press, 1976), 207; and Lawrence A. Cardoso, *Mexican Emigration to the United States, 1897–1931: Socioeconomic Patterns* (Tucson: University of Arizona Press, 1980), 137.

2. For the argument that restriction failed due to fears of offending Mexico, see Robert Divine, *American Immigration Policy, 1924–1952* (New Haven, CT: Yale University Press, 1957), 66. Mae Ngai explains that restriction never passed since increased enforcement made it unnecessary in *Impossible Subjects: Illegal Aliens and the Making of Modern America* (Princeton, NJ: Princeton University Press, 2004), 54–55. For more information on the final results of the proposed bills, see Cardoso, *Mexican Emigration to the United States*, 141.

3. For other historians' descriptions of how growers promoted Mexicans as only temporary workers, see James N. Gregory, *American Exodus: Dust Bowl Migration and Okie Culture in California* (Oxford: Oxford University Press, 1989), 68; Camille Guerin-Gonzales, *Mexican Workers, American Dreams: Immigration, Repatriation and California Farm Labor, 1900–1939* (New Brunswick, NJ: Rutgers University Press, 1994), chap. 2; Kathleen Mapes, *Sweet Tyranny* (Champaign-Urbana: University of Illinois Press, 2009), 6–9; Michael J. Piore, *Birds of Passage: Migrant Labor and Industrial Societies* (Cambridge: Cambridge University Press, 1979), 3, 51–52, 77, 81–82; George J. Sánchez, *Becoming Mexican American: Ethnicity, Culture, and Identity in Chicano Los Angeles, 1900–1945* (New York: Oxford University Press, 1993), 189; and Devra Weber, *Dark Sweat, White Gold: California Farm Workers, Cotton, and the New Deal* (Berkeley: University of California Press, 1994), 8.

4. California Farm Bureau Federation Resolution, Annual Meeting, November, 1929, Records of the Immigration and Naturalization Service, Record Group 85, Entry 9, file 55639/616, National Archives, Washington, DC.

5. Cardoso, *Mexican Emigration to the United States*, 85, 125–26.

6. Ibid., 85; Harry Schwartz, *Seasonal Farm Labor in the United States* (New York: Columbia University Press, 1945), 41–42; article in the *Washington Herald*, February 11, 1930, repr. in *Congressional Record*, 71st Cong., 2nd sess. (April 1930), 7137.

7. U.S. House of Representatives, Committee on Immigration and Naturalization, *Seasonal Agricultural Laborers from Mexico, Hearings*, 69th Cong., 1st sess. (1926), 62–64.

8. U.S. House of Representatives, Committee on Immigration and Naturalization, *Western Hemisphere Immigration, Hearings*, 71st Cong., 2nd sess. (1930), 91.

9. Committee on Immigration and Naturalization, *Seasonal Agricultural Laborers from Mexico*, 112.

10. In the first half of 1928, 32,000 Mexicans emigrated to the United States. Of these, 20,000 were male adults; the remainder were women and children. Agriculturalists hired them particularly to help with cotton, beet, and fruit crops. See Linna E. Bresette, *Mexicans in the United States: A Report of a Brief Survey* (Washington, DC: National Catholic Welfare Conference, 1929), 8–9, 12.

11. See C. M. Newman, American National Livestock Association to El Paso Chamber of Commerce, October 12, 1927, Records of the U.S. House of Representa-

tives, Record Group 233, file HR70A-F14.3, National Archives, Washington, DC; and Reisler, *By the Sweat of Their Brow,* 228.

12. Again, other historians have also noted the relationship Americans made between Mexicans and temporary work. See note 3 above.

13. "The Southwest's Immigration Problem," *New York Times,* November 10, 1926, *Proquest Historical Newspapers.*

14. See Louise Funston Shields, "Six New Irrigation Projects Nearing Completion in Mexico," *Los Angeles Times,* November 18, 1928; for vanishing over the border, "Mexican Migration, *Los Angeles Times,* May 2, 1929, *Proquest Historical Newspapers.*

15. "California's Farm Labor Situation One Calling for Careful Study," *Los Angeles Times,* May 2, 1926, *Proquest Historical Newspapers.*

16. Regarding Mexicans' use of the car to take seasonal jobs, see Weber, *Dark Sweat, White Gold,* 64.

17. R. G. Risser, California Vegetable Union to Representative W. E. Evans, December 21, 1928, U.S. House of Representatives, Record Group 233, file HR 70A-F14.3.

18. Committee on Immigration and Naturalization, *Western Hemisphere Immigration,* 222.

19. Statement from E. J. Walker, Executive Secretary, Central Chamber of Agriculture and Commerce (AZ), n.d., U.S. House of Representatives, Record Group 233, file HR 70-A-F14.3.

20. In 1917, Puerto Ricans became U.S. citizens per the Jones Act.

21. U.S. Senate, Committee on Immigration, *Restriction of Western Hemisphere Immigration, Hearings,* 70th Cong, 1st sess. (1928), 36–37.

22. George Perry, "Imported Porto Rican Laborers Suffering at Hands of Arizona Cotton Growers' Combine," *Pittsburgh Courier,* October 9, 1926.

23. Mary Wood to Representative Johnson (WA), November 14, 1927, U.S. House of Representatives, Record Group 233, file HR 70–A-F14.3.

24. From an Arizona paper, reprinted in George Perry, "Imported Porto Rican Laborers."

25. Ngai, *Impossible Subjects,* 96–97.

26. House Committee on Immigration and Naturalization, *Western Hemisphere Immigration,* 60–61, 244–46; "Mexican Labor Exclusion Bill Would Cause Influx of Filipino Population," Hayden Collection, MSS-1, Hayden Family Papers, box 580, file 2, Hayden Library, Arizona State University, Tempe. For one specific newspaper story regarding Mexicans and Filipinos and taxi-dance girls, see "Taxi-Dance Girls Start Filipinos on Wrong Foot," *Los Angeles Times,* February 2, 1930, *Proquest Historical Newspapers.*

27. Ventura County Farm Bureau to Representative Johnson, January 31, 1928, House of Representatives, Record Group 233, file HR 70A-F14.3. Cybelle Fox provides evidence showing that social workers in California feared Mexicans' dependence on charity. This is perhaps an example of growers contesting that image to suggest that Californians had more to fear from black workers. See Cybelle Fox, *Three Worlds of Relief: Race, Immigration, and the American Welfare State from the Progressive Era to the New Deal* (Princeton, NJ: Princeton University Press, 2012), chap. 4.

28. House Committee on Immigration and Naturalization, *Western Hemisphere Immigration,* 60.

29. Ibid., 209.
30. Ibid., 69.
31. George P. Clements to Representative Phil D. Swing (California), December 27, 1928, House of Representatives, Record Group 233, file HR 70A-F14.3.
32. House Committee on Immigration and Naturalization, *Western Hemisphere Immigration*, 139.
33. Committee on Immigration and Naturalization, *Seasonal Agricultural Laborers from Mexico*, 95.
34. Ibid., 46.
35. Ibid., 53.
36. House Committee on Immigration and Naturalization, *Western Hemisphere Immigration*, 61.
37. Committee on Immigration and Naturalization, *Seasonal Agricultural Laborers from Mexico*, 188.
38. "Declaration of Principles" from the Central Chamber of Agriculture and Commerce, El Paso Conference, November 18–19, 1927, U.S. House of Representatives, Record Group 233, file HR 70A-F14.3.
39. Resolution from the Anaheim Union Water Company, February 6, 1928, U.S. House of Representatives, Record Group 233, file HR 70A-F14.3.
40. Secretaría de relaciones exteriores, *La migración y protección de mexicanos en el extranjero* (Mexico City: Ministerio de relaciones exteriores, 1928), 11–13.
41. Committee on Immigration and Naturalization, *Seasonal Agricultural Laborers from Mexico*, 191.
42. Ibid., 94–95.
43. Ibid., 195.
44. Francisco E. Balderrama and Raymond Rodríguez, *Decade of Betrayal: Mexican Repatriation in the 1930s*, rev. ed. (Albuquerque: University of New Mexico, 2006), 38.
45. The word *guest*, a less pejorative euphemism for some of these words, was not used until a much later date.
46. One of many specific examples in the congressional hearings was S. Parker Friselle, the chairman of the Agriculture Committee of Fresno, California, County Chamber of Commerce, who described Mexican immigrants as "transient" and "homers," that "like the pigeon goes back to roost." Representative Roy Richard Woodruff from Michigan used words like "drift" to emphasize Mexicans' movement. See Committee on Immigration and Naturalization, *Seasonal Agricultural Laborers from Mexico*, 6, 8, 26. Other examples are Russell Bennett, editor of the *Holtville Tribune* in California, who referred to Mexicans as "mostly nomadic," and William Hushing, the legislative representative of the American Federation of Labor in Washington, DC, who described them as "a roving class." See House Committee on Immigration and Naturalization, *Western Hemisphere Immigration*, 317, 367.
47. Devra Weber shows how some Mexicans in California remained due to migrant schools, as well as indebtedness to company stores, in *Dark Sweat, White Gold*, 44.
48. For Chicago's population, see Gabriela F. Arredondo, *Mexican Chicago: Race, Identity, and Nation, 1916–39* (Chicago: University of Illinois Press, 2008), 28; and Bresette, *Mexicans in the United States*, 8–9. Emory S. Bogardus, "Mexican Immigrants and the Quota." *Sociology and Social Research* 12 (1928): 371–78.

49. James Hoffman Batten, "Southwest and Center: The Mexican Conference at Pomona," *Survey Midmonthly*, January 15, 1929, 475.

50. Helen W. Walker, "Mexican Immigrants and American Citizenship," *Sociology and Social Research* 13 (May–June 1929), 465–71; quotations from 467.

51. J. Francis Lemon, "The English-Mexican Class," *Hispania* 9 (October 1926), 248–50.

52. Some Mexican scholars and officials did see the loss of Mexicans as negative and thought it only enriched the North at the expense of Mexico. Others recognized that there were few opportunities in Mexico and that the remittances from the North contributed to the Mexican economy. See Cardoso, *Mexican Emigration to the United States*, 104–10.

53. Lore Diana Kuehnert, "Pernicious Foreigners and Contested Compatriots: Mexican Newspaper Debates over Immigration, Emigration and Repatriation, 1928–1936" (PhD diss., University of California–Riverside, 2002), 19, 28, 54–61.

54. Jaime R. Aguila, "Protecting 'México de Afuera': Mexican Emigration Policy, 1876–1928" (PhD diss., Arizona State University, 2000), 64–75, 211–12.

55. F. Arturo Rosales, *!Pobre Raza!: Violence, Justice, and Mobilization among México Lindo Immigrants, 1900–1936* (Austin: University of Texas Press, 1999), 36–44.

56. Ibid., 42–44, 78.

57. Sánchez, *Becoming Mexican American*, 109.

58. Kuehnert, "Pernicious Foreigners," 19, 28, 54–61, 78, 261–62.

59. See Benedict Anderson, *Imagined Communities: Reflections on the Origin and Spread of Nationalism*, rev. ed. (London: Verso, 1991), 6–7.

60. Kuehnert uses the term *hijos de México* in "Pernicious Foreigners," 267–70.

61. For quotation and his statistical interpretation, see Manuel Gamio, "Observations on Mexican Immigration into the United States," *Pacific Affairs* (August 1929), 463–69; quotation from 464. Also see Robert Redfield's summary of Gamio's work on Mexican immigration in 1926–27 in "The Antecedents of Mexican Immigration to the United States," *American Journal of Sociology* 35 (July 1929–May 1930), 433–38. And Cardoso, *Mexican Emigration*, 104.

62. Kuehnert, "Pernicious Foreigners," 254, 270, 288.

63. For more on the Mexican government's position, see Balderrama and Rodríguez, *Decade of Betrayal*, rev. ed., 163–64.

64. Ironically, this requirement was against U.S. laws, which prohibited people from emigrating to the United States if they had prearranged work contracts.

65. Enrique Santibañez, *Ensayo acerca de la inmigracion mexicana en los Estados Unidos* (San Antonio: Clegg Co., 1930), 98, 104–5. Quote is my trans. from p. 51.

66. See Cardoso, *Mexican Emigration to the United States*, 117.

67. Editorial from *El Heraldo de México*, repr. in *El Fronterizo* (Tucson, AZ), April 7, 1928.

68. Santibañez, *Ensayo*, 104–5.

69. *El Diario*, repr. in "Los Emigrantes," *El Tucsonense*, July 12, 1928.

70. Kuehnert, "Pernicious Foreigners," 54, 77, 261–62. Also, regarding the requests for assistance directed to Mexican consulates and the Mexican government's efforts to assist repatriates, see Balderrama and Rodríguez, *Decade of Betrayal*, rev. ed., 168–77.

71. Rosales, *¡Pobre Raza!*, 5; and Eric V. Meeks, *Border Citizens: The Making of Indians, Mexicans, and Anglos in Arizona* (Austin: University of Texas Press, 2007), 96–97.

72. Quoted in Cardoso, *Mexican Emigration to the United States*, 77.

73. Paul S. Taylor, *Mexican Labor in the United States: Chicago and the Calumet Region*, vol. 7, no. 2 (Berkeley: University of California Press, 1932), 275.

74. Ibid.

75. Rosales, *¡Pobre Raza!*, 5–7 and chap. 3.

76. The concept of the cosmic race celebrated *mestizaje* ("mixture") and the cultural mixing of Europeans and Native Americans. It signified that Mexican identity would henceforth be rooted in an Aztec or indigenous heritage and the creation of a new mixed race, the cosmic race, which would be superior to all existing ones. All Mexicans, then, theoretically, could see themselves in this more inclusive Mexican identity, which previously had emphasized a pure European heritage. Africans and Asians, however, were excluded from this national narrative and not recognized as being a part of the nation's history or current era. Also, the new ideology called for indigenous people to change their ways to coincide with those who had already melded their cultures and identity. See Zaragosa Vargas, *Proletarians of the North: A History of Mexican Industrial Workers in Detroit and the Midwest, 1917–1933* (Berkeley: University of California Press, 1993), 151, 157. See also Kuehnert, "Pernicious Foreigners," 11–12.

77. Regarding low naturalization rates, see Reisler, *By the Sweat of Their Brow*, 111.

78. Manuel Gamio, *El inmigrante mexicano: la historia de su vida, entrevistas completas, 1926–27*, ed. Devra Weber, Roberto Melville, and Juan Vicente Palermo (Mexico City: Regents of the University of California, 2002), 413–14.

79. Although immigrants felt emotionally connected to Mexico and dreamed or even planned to return, I am not suggesting that they did not try to organize and improve their conditions in the United States. Regarding their activism, see Weber, *Dark Sweat, White Gold*, esp. 8 and chaps. 3 and 7.

80. Weber, *Dark Sweat, White Gold*, 55–56.

81. *Corrido* quoted in Cardoso, *Mexican Emigration to the United States*, 76.

82. "A propósito de la emigración," *La Opinión* (Los Angeles), October 5, 1926.

83. Sánchez, *Becoming Mexican American*, 108–13; and Arredondo, *Mexican Chicago*, chap. 5.

84. *Congressional Record*, 71st Cong., 2nd sess. (1930), 7111.

85. "Mexican Labor Exclusion Bill Would Cause Influx of Filipino Population," Hayden Collection, MSS-1, Hayden Papers, box 580, file 2, Hayden Library, Arizona State University, Tempe.

86. Weber, *Dark Sweat, White Gold*, 63.

Chapter Seven

1. Hubert H. D'Autremont to Lewis Douglas, February 5, 1932, Lewis Douglas Papers, AZ 290, box 181, University of Arizona Library, Tucson. For more background on D'Autremont and his affiliation with the copper company, see Katherine Benton-

Cohen, *Borderline Americans: Racial Division and Labor War in the Arizona Borderlands* (Cambridge: Harvard University Press, 2009), 130. The title of this chapter refers to a common exclusionist slogan quoted in Paul S. Taylor, "More Bars against Mexicans?" *Survey* 64 (April 1930), 26.

2. Mae Ngai makes the argument that, due to increased restriction, Mexicans stayed longer in the United States rather than risking deportation or being prevented from re-entering the United States at a later date. See Ngai, *Impossible Subjects: Illegal Aliens and the Making of Modern America* (Princeton, NJ: Princeton University Press, 2004), chap. 2.

3. Hubert H. D'Autremont to Lewis Douglas, February 5, 1932; Lewis Douglas to Hubert H. D'Autremont, February 10, 1932; Harry E. Hull to Lewis Douglas, March 24, 1932; Hubert H. D'Autremont to Lewis Douglas, March 29, 1932; Lewis Douglas Papers, AZ 290, box 181.

4. See chapters 5 and 6 for more background on how growers persuaded Americans to view Mexicans as temporary workers. Although some areas of the country were already experiencing falling crop prices and depression, cotton prices continued to soar throughout the 1920s. In fact, many agriculturalists turned to cotton because of the higher prices. This cotton boom, however, did not benefit pickers, whose wages fell during the same period. See Carey McWilliams, *Factories in the Field: The Story of Migratory Farm Labor in California* (Boston: Little, Brown, 1939), 191–93; Devra Weber, *Dark Sweat, White Gold: California Farm Workers, Cotton, and the New Deal* (Berkeley: University of California Press, 1994) 21, 35–41, 215.

5. Camille Guerin-Gonzales discusses the construction of a myth that Mexicans were male temporary workers and that the reality was different. Although she does not elaborate on this in detail, she notes how this narrative was employed to expel Mexicans. She also discusses Mexican repatriation in California. See Guerin-Gonzales, *Mexican Workers, American Dreams: Immigration, Repatriation and California Farm Labor, 1900–1939* (New Brunswick, NJ: Rutgers University Press, 1994), 77–94, 98, 135–36.

6. Paul S. Taylor, *An American-Mexican Frontier: Nueces County, Texas* (Chapel Hill: University of North Carolina Press, 1934), 103–4. Also see Devra Weber (*Dark Sweat, White Gold,* 63–65), who shows that Mexicans traveled regular migratory routes, often traveling with family and friends.

7. U.S. House of Representatives, *Select Committee to Investigate the Interstate Migration of Destitute Citizens*, 76th Cong., 3rd sess. (1940–41), pt. 10, 3883.

8. Regarding growers' attempts to retain Mexican labor and the formation of Mexican communities and labor organizations in the United States, see Weber, *Dark Sweat, White Gold,* 44, 57–78, 85. Regarding Midwestern growers paying more—in lieu of transit to the border—to remain in urban areas nearby, see Gabriela F. Arredondo, *Mexican Chicago: Race, Identity, and Nation, 1916–39* (Chicago: University of Illinois Press, 2008), 24–25.

9. See "Population of the United States by Color or Race," Bureau of the Census, Department of Commerce (Washington, DC: Government Printing Office, 1931). Official figures for people of Mexican descent are notoriously inaccurate. The 1930 figure includes all people of Mexican descent except those deemed as members of the white race, which accounted for an additional 65,965. The 1920 statistic (700,541) is an estimate since Mexicans were not recorded separately from whites until the 1930

census. Neither decennial census accounts for the number of undocumented Mexican immigrants. Mae Ngai (*Impossible Subjects*, 131) estimates approximately 200,000 such immigrants arrived between 1908 and 1920 and an additional 100,000 annually throughout the 1920s.

10. Paul S. Taylor, "Mexicans North of the Rio Grande," *Survey*, May 1, 1931, 205.

11. Editor's note, "Now Is the Time to Take Stock" in Taylor, "Mexicans North of the Rio Grande," 135.

12. "Ban on Alien Inflow from Mexico Asked," *Tucson Daily Citizen*, January 27, 1931.

13. The 1924 Immigration Act authorized immigration officials to deport those whose only crime was to enter the country illegally for not coming in through an appropriate entrance station, paying the necessary fees, and passing medical and literacy exams. It eliminated the statute of limitations on illegal entry. This meant that if immigrants entered illegally after 1924, they could be deported whenever caught, regardless of their years in residency (this was what happened to Santiago Lopez, mentioned in the first paragraphs of this chapter). Later the 1929 Registry Act provided a method for immigrants to legalize their status. If they could prove continuous residency since 1921, and paid $20, they could get a certificate which would make them legal, allowing them to exit and re-enter the country without problem and begin the naturalization process if they wished. Between 1930 and 1940, 115,000 people took advantage of this law: over 80 percent of them were Canadian and European. Few Mexicans used this law either because they did not know about the act, could not provide sufficient proof, or could not pay the $20 fee. See Ngai, *Impossible Subjects*, 82.

14. From the General Department of Statistics in Mexico City in James Carl Gilbert, "A Field Study in Mexico of the Mexican Repatriation Movement" (master's thesis, University of Southern California, 1934), 19; Francisco E. Balderrama and Raymond Rodríguez, *Decade of Betrayal: Mexican Repatriation in the 1930s* (Albuquerque: University of New Mexico Press, 1995), 121–22; Abraham Hoffman, *Unwanted Mexican Americans in the Great Depression: Repatriation Pressures, 1929–1939* (Tucson: University of Arizona Press, 1974), 2.

15. Cybelle Fox, *Three Worlds of Relief: Race, Immigration, and the American Welfare State from the Progressive Era to the New Deal* (Princeton, NJ: Princeton University Press, 2012), 285 and chap. 4.

16. Only 16,000–20,000 immigrants from all areas of the world were deported each year in the early 1930s. One-third to one-half of all the immigrants deported in these years came from Mexico (in part because many other immigrant groups had been greatly restricted or excluded by 1924). While deportations were uncommon, the United States investigated 100,000 people each year, increasing Mexicans' fears of being removed. Deportations increased dramatically after the 1929 Deportation Act provided more funds for investigation and removal. From 1908 to 1920, the United States deported only 2,000–3,000 immigrants annually. See Francis F. Kane, "The Challenge of the Wickersham Deportations Report," *Journal of Law and Criminology* 23 (November–December 1932), 589; and Ngai, *Impossible Subjects*, 131.

17. Kane, "Challenge of the Wickersham Deportations Report," 591; U.S. Department of Labor, *Annual Report*, from the Commissioner General of Immigration (Washington, DC: Government Printing Office, 1932), 6, 73.

18. In 1932 the 1929 Deportation Act was amended to allow those who had been deported to re-apply one year later with the secretary of labor's permission. This was done to address hardship situations in which family members had been separated as a consequence of deportation. Those deported for cause, such as because they were deemed criminals or were anarchists, could not take advantage of this amendment. The 1929 Deportation Act also defined illegal entry as a misdemeanor with jail time and/or fines. A second illegal entry constituted a felony with greater jail time and fines. See Kane, "Challenge of the Wickersham Deportations Report," 604; for details on the Deportation Act, see Ngai, *Impossible Subjects*, 59–60.

19. Monthly statistics are from July 1931. See "Immigration from Mexico," Department of State, September 24, 1931, Carl Hayden Papers, MSS 001, box 654, folder 3, Arizona Collection, Department of Archives and Manuscripts, University Libraries, Arizona State University, Tempe.

20. Quote is from Justice Hughes in his decision against the Arizona law, which restricted the number of noncitizens employed by private companies; see Harold Fields, "Where Shall the Alien Work?" *Social Forces* 12 (December 1933), 213–21; quotation at 221.

21. Gilbert, "Field Study," 25.

22. Edna Ewing Kelley, "The Mexicans Go Home," *Southwest Review* 17 (April 1932), 305–7.

23. Mercedes Carrera de Velasco, *Los mexicanos que devolvió la crisis, 1929–1932* (Tlatelolco, México: Secretaría de relaciones exteriores, 1974), 75.

24. Senator Hayden advocated this even after increased penalties for illegal entry and greater funding for deportation had just been passed in the 1929 Deportation Act. See Newspaper clipping, "Congressional Records Show Hayden's Stand on Immigration and the Copper Tariff," December 26, 1930, Carl Hayden Papers, MSS 001, box 503, folder 54.

25. Harry Schwartz, *Seasonal Farm Labor in the United States* (New York: Columbia University Press, 1945), 62. James Gregory discusses how the composition of farm laborers changed after 1930 with 43 percent of whites engaged in farm labor in that year and 76 percent by 1940. Gregory further explains that these Okies and Arkies perceived movement and itinerancy as a sign of failure and considered these migrant jobs as ones for Mexicans and blacks rather than themselves. Consequently, they left migratory work after a year or two, preferring to stay in one place—even if they could not make much of a living in this way—and accept relief to fill in the seasonal gaps. See Gregory, *American Exodus: Dust Bowl Migration and Okie Culture in California* (Oxford: Oxford University Press, 1989), 58, 62, 68–70. Devra Weber also discusses the new American migrants and shows the ready supply of laborers in *Dark Sweat, White Gold*, 137–45.

26. Mark Reisler, *By the Sweat of Their Brow: Mexican Immigrant Labor in the United States, 1900–1940* (Westport, CT: Greenwood Press, 1976), 228.

27. Brodie was mistaken. The federal government did not deport 150,000 Mexicans in the early 1920s. While the Mexican government has statistics showing that approximately 100,000 Mexicans returned in the early 1920s, many of these immigrants repatriated themselves with the aid of the Mexican government or charitable organizations or at the expense of their employer if they were brought in via special exemptions approved by the U.S. Department of Labor. The federal government did

not obtain the authority to deport Mexicans solely for illegal entry until 1924. They could deport immigrants only if they had become a public charge within five years of their entry, or if they were anarchists or communists. J. C. Brodie to Franklin Delano Roosevelt, March 29, 1934, Records of the Immigration and Naturalization Service, Record Group 85, Entry 9, file 55739/674A, National Archives, Washington, DC.

28. Samuel T. Wright, Immigration Inspector to Inspector in Charge, Immigration and Naturalization Service, Tucson, April 9, 1934, Immigration and Naturalization Service, Record Group 85, Entry 9, file 55739/674A.

29. R. E. Pasters to U.S. Representative Lewis Douglas, March 16, 1931, and April 3, 1931, Lewis Douglas Papers, AZ 290, box 181; R. E. Pasters to Rep. Albert Johnson and Sen. Henry R. Ashurst, February 25, 1931, Records of the U.S. House of Representatives, Record Group 233, file HR 71A-F16.4, box 517, National Archives, Washington, DC.

30. Letter from W. L. Warren, August 14, 1933, Immigration and Naturalization Service, Record Group 85, Entry 9, file 55739/674A.

31. Cora West to President Roosevelt, August 6, 1933, Immigration and Naturalization Service, Record Group 85, Entry 9, file 55639/616A.

32. Ms. H. Hanshaw to President Roosevelt, August 11, 1933, Immigration and Naturalization Service, Record Group 85, Entry 9, file 55639/616A.

33. Balderrama and Rodríguez, *Decade of Betrayal*, 66.

34. Robert Frazer, Consul General, Mexico, D.F., to U.S. Secretary of State, January 28, 1931, State Department Records, Record Group 59, file 812.5511/107.

35. Robert N. McLean, "The Mexicans Return," *Nation*, August 24, 1932, 165.

36. Interestingly, a Spanish-language publication in Tucson slyly commented in a parenthetical that the mayor was a naturalized Arab. It is likely this was done to contrast his more recent American status with that of the newspaper's readers, many of whom were native-born Americans. See "No Solo a los Mexicanos Sino a los Hispano-Americanos se les Niega Trabajo," *El Tucsonense* (Tucson, AZ), June 17, 1930; and Thomas E. Sheridan, *Los Tucsonenses: The Mexican Community in Tucson, 1854–1941* (Tucson: University of Arizona Press, 1986), 216.

37. Fox, *Three Worlds of Relief*, 48, 285.

38. Harold Fields, "Where Shall the Alien Work?," 213–21.

39. Lawrence Leslie Waters, "Transient Mexican Agricultural Labor," *Southwestern Social Science Quarterly* 22 (June 1941), 49–66.

40. Amy Elizabeth Davis, "Deportation and the Border Blockade: How Western Conservatism Impacted Immigrant Sugar Beet Workers in Colorado between 1900 and 1940" (master's thesis, University of Oregon, 2003), 2, 61–68.

41. Ibid. Also see Sarah Deutsch, *No Separate Refuge: Culture, Class, and Gender on an Anglo-Hispanic Frontier in the American Southwest, 1880–1940* (New York: Oxford University Press, 1987), 165–66.

42. Although only between five and 13 percent of Mexican immigrants in the U.S. in 1910, 1920, and 1930 had become naturalized citizens (see Balderrama and Rodríguez, *Decade of Betrayal*, 20), Mexicans' extended duration in the United States—in that they settled and established lives there—made some believe they were citizens. See Davis, "Deportation and the Border Blockade," 61–68; "The Lesson of Mr. Johnson," enclosure in *El Universal* (Mexico City), May 11, 1935, U.S. State Department, Record Group 59, file 812.5511/170.

43. Davis, "Deportation and the Border Blockade," 3, 68–74.

44. Letter from Director of Friendly House, Placida Garcia Smith, to Maricopa County Board of Supervisors, July 11, 1933, Hugh C. Gilbert Papers, 1914–33, MS 1097, Arizona Historical Society, Tucson; Placida Garcia Smith biography, 80–81, Arizona Women Collection, Department of Archives and Manuscripts, University Libraries, Arizona State University, Tempe.

45. Dionicio Valdés, *Mexicans in Minnesota: The People of Minnesota* (St. Paul: Minnesota Historical Society, 2005), 9–18.

46. Rubén R. Lozano, "LULAC Subsidiaries," *LULAC News* 2 (October 1932), Chicano Collection, Department of Archives and Manuscripts, University Libraries, Arizona State University, Tempe.

47. Davis, "Deportation and the Border Blockade," 54–55.

48. Norman D. Humphrey, "Mexican Repatriation from Michigan: Public Assistance in Historical Perspective," *Social Service Review* 15 (September 1941), 511.

49. Adena Miller Rich, "Case Work in the Repatriation of Immigrants," *Social Service Review* 10 (December 1936), 601.

50. Remsen Crawford, "The Deportation of Undesirable Aliens," *Current History* 30 (September 1929), 1079.

51. Carey McWilliams, "The State of the Union: Getting Rid of the Mexican," *American Mercury* (1933), 322–24.

52. *LULAC News*, no. 10 (May 1932), RM-125, Hayden Library, Arizona State University, Tempe.

53. J. C. Brodie to Franklin Delano Roosevelt, September 30, 1933, Immigration and Naturalization Service, Record Group 85, Entry 9, file 55739/674A.

54. "Los mexicanos en E.U. perderemos," *El Tucsonense*, February 7, 1931.

55. Davis, "Deportation and the Border Blockade," 61–68.

56. Translation of *Excelsior* (Mexico City), February 9, 1931, included in letter from Robert Frazer, Consul General in Mexico to U.S. Secretary of State, February 18, 1931, U.S. State Department, Record Group 59, file 812.55/98, National Archives, College Park, MD.

57. Translation of *Excelsior*, February 11, 1931, ibid.

58. Mexican officials stopped supporting repatriation once they became more aware of the problems in 1932. See George J. Sánchez, *Becoming Mexican American: Ethnicity, Culture, and Identity in Chicano Los Angeles, 1900–1945* (New York: Oxford University Press, 1993), 216–24.

59. "Pierden su nacionalidad los mexicanos?," in "Notas Editoriales," *El Tucsonense*, October 2, 1930.

60. William P. Blocker, American Consul, to U.S. Secretary of State, January 3, 1931, U.S. State Department, Record Group 59, file 812.5511/102.

61. George Sánchez concludes that the Mexican government and sociologist Manuel Gamio supported Mexicans' temporary immigration to the United States and desired their eventual return in Sánchez, *Becoming Mexican American*, 113, 120–23.

62. Gilbert, "Field Study," 105–19. Camille Guerin-Gonzales also retells this story from Gilbert in *Mexican Workers, American Dreams*, 103–4. Also see Hoffman, *Unwanted Mexican Americans*, 139–41.

63. Emory Bogardus, "Mexican Repatriates," *Sociology and Social Research* 17 (November–December 1933), 170.

64. Statement by Ignacio L. Batiza, Mexican Consul in Detroit, to the Mexican *colonia*, October 13, 1932, Immigration and Naturalization Service, Record Group 85, Entry 9, file 55784/585; Mercedes Carrera de Velasco, *Los mexicanos que devolvio la crisis*, 67–68; Zaragosa Vargas, *Proletarians of the North: A History of Mexican Industrial Workers in Detroit and the Midwest, 1917–1933* (Berkeley: University of California Press, 1993), 170–86.

65. Vargas, *Proletarians of the North*," 170–86.

66. Report by Edward Anderson, American consul, Mexico, D.F., "Analysis of Mexican Migration Statistics: 1932–1936," November 11, 1938, U.S. State Department, Record Group 59, file 812.55/297.

67. Regarding shrinking *colonias* in which one merchant in southern California reported a 20 to 50 percent decline in business, see "35,000 Mexicans Leave California," *New York Times*, April 12, 1931, 5; Kelley, "The Mexicans Go Home," 308; Lore Diana Kuehnert, "Pernicious Foreigners and Contested Compatriots: Mexican Newspaper Debates over Immigration, Emigration and Repatriation, 1928–1936" (PhD diss., University of California-Riverside, 2002), 261–62.

68. See "Mexico Puts Bars on Immigration," *New York Times*, February 17, 1934, U.S. State Department, Record Group 59, file 812.5511/154.

69. "The Lesson of Mr. Johnson," *El Universal*, May 11, 1935, U.S. State Department, Record Group 59, file 812.5511/170.

70. Bogardus, "Mexican Repatriates," 172.

71. Gilbert, "Field Study," 157–58.

72. Sánchez, *Becoming Mexican American*, 213.

73. See Rich, "Case Work," 569–605; Hoffman, *Unwanted Mexican Americans*, 39–65; Balderrama and Rodríguez, *Decade of Betrayal*, 63–82.

74. See Hoffman, *Unwanted Mexican Americans*, 39–65; Balderrama and Rodríguez, *Decade of Betrayal*, 50–66; C.P. Visel to Secretary of Labor, March 19, 1931, Immigration and Naturalization Service, Record Group 85, Entry 9, file 55739/674A.

75. N. D. Collaer to District Director, U.S. Immigration Service, El Paso, n.d., Lewis Douglas Papers, AZ 290, box 181.

76. John L. Zurbrick to Commissioner-General of Immigration, October 20, 1932; John L. Zurbrick to Mexican Consul, Ignacio Batiza, November 23, 1932; Edward J. Shaughnessy, Acting Commissioner-General to John L. Zurbrick, October 27, 1932, Immigration and Naturalization Service, Record Group 85, Entry 9, file 55784/585.

77. Harry E. Hull to District Director of Immigration in Detroit, November 18, 1932, Immigration and Naturalization Service, Record Group 85, Entry 9, file 55784/585.

78. "Congressman Douglas to Aid Return of Yaquis to Valley," *Star*, May 26, 1931, Lewis Douglas Clippings, Arizona Historical Society, Tucson.

79. John S. Littell, "Trend of Migratory Movements in Mexico," July 20, 1934, 6, U.S. State Department, Record Group 59, file 812.55/225.

80. See "Back to the Homeland," *Survey* (January 1933); "Guitars Strum as 400 Mexicans Start Home," Immigration and Naturalization Service, Record Group 85, Entry 9, file 55784/585; "Send Them Home," *Express*, February 13, 1931 as noted in Hoffman's *Unwanted Mexican Americans*, 55; and "Jobless Latins to Be Sent to Homes," *Tucson Daily Citizen*, January 8, 1931.

81. Kelley, "Mexicans Go Home," 303–11.

82. "Guitars Strum as 400 Mexicans Start Home."

83. Taylor, "Mexicans North of the Rio Grande," 205.

84. Humphrey, "Mexican Repatriation from Michigan," 502, 505, 511.

85. Ibid., 502, 507–12.

86. Valdés, *Mexicans in Minnesota*, 9–18.

87. Case of Celia and Belen Vasquez in Lewis Douglas Papers and letters to Arthur A. Heredia, August 8, 1932; August 9, 1932 and letter to Inspector-in-Charge, Nogales, AZ, November 8, 1932, Lewis Douglas Papers, AZ 290, box 181. Francisco Balderrama and Raymond Rodríguez (*Decade of Betrayal*, rev. ed., 64) also discuss how a Mexican consul in Arizona complained about the pressure placed upon Mexicans to voluntarily depart the country.

88. Information in a letter reprinted from a Mexican immigrant (with name removed) to President Herbert Hoover, n.d., in Kane, "Challenge of the Wickersham Deportations Report," 606.

89. See William V. Flores and Rina Benmayor, eds., *Latino Cultural Citizenship: Claiming Identity, Space, and Rights* (Boston: Beacon Press, 1997), 46.

90. Statement by Tiburcio Navarro to A. A. Spurgeon, Inspector-in-Charge, Immigration and Naturalization Service, June 29, 1934, Immigration and Naturalization Service, Record Group 85, Entry 9, file 55739/674A. For more examples and information on the repatriation experience, see Balderrama and Rodríguez, *Decade of Betrayal*, rev. ed., 119–51.

91. "Guitars Strum as 400 Mexicans Start Home."

92. R. W. Gangewere, U.S. Immigrant Inspector to District Director of Immigration, Detroit, November 29, 1932, Immigration and Naturalization Service, Record Group 85, Entry 9, file 55784/585. For other similar stories, see Balderrama and Rodríguez, *Decade of Betrayal*, rev. ed., 232–64.

93. Rich, "Case Work," 604; Gilbert, "Field Study," 67, 70, 140.

94. Quoted in Gilbert, "Field Study," 67, 70, 140.

95. Ibid., 5, 8, 38, 53–55, 63, 137, 160; and Osgood Hardy, "Los Repatriados," *Pomona College Magazine* (January 1933), 71–73

96. Gamio's research and conclusions are discussed in Gilbert, "Field Study," 5.

97. Agnes K. Hanna, "Social Services on the Mexican Border," *Proceedings of the National Conference of Social Work* (Chicago: University of Chicago Press, 1935), 698.

98. H. M. Brown to Frances Perkins, Secretary of Labor, March 14, 1933, Immigration and Naturalization Service, Record Group 85, Entry 9, file 55639/616A.

99. William A. Carlson, Chair, Board of County Commission, Greeley, CO, to Commissioner-General of Immigration, Harry E. Hull, n.d., c. 1933, Immigration and Naturalization Service, Record Group 85, Entry 9, file 55639/616A.

100. Gabriela Arredondo (Arredondo, *Mexican Chicago*, 92–107) also discusses the impact of discrimination on Mexican immigrants in Chicago in the 1920s and 1930s and argues that it contributed to their development of a "Mexican" identity, via various celebrations and parades, as the diverse Mexican community tried to counteract the discrimination they experienced by unifying around their status as Mexicans. This fits with my argument here in that I show how discriminatory treatment and nostalgia for Mexico contributed to the growing image of Mexicans as only temporarily in

the United States, yet the nostalgia the immigrants felt did not mean that they wanted to return to Mexico.

101. For some examples of criticism, see "Smuggled Over Mexican Line," *Tucson Star,* November 15, 1933, Aliens Ephemera Clippings File, Arizona Historical Society, Tucson; Jane Perry Clark, "Aliens in the Deportation Dragnet," *Current History* 36 (April 1932), 27–31; Zaragosa Vargas, *Labor Rights Are Civil Rights: Mexican American Workers in Twentieth-Century America* (Princeton, NJ: Princeton University Press, 2005), 54; Hoffman, *Unwanted Mexican Americans,* 77–80. Lawrence Cardoso also notes how difficult it was for many to criticize repatriation in *Mexican Emigration,* 148.

102. Camille Guerin-Gonzales (*Mexican Workers, American Dreams,* 74–75) notes the link between the myth of Mexicans' temporary status and the ease, then, of removing them. My analysis differs in that it shows how various groups developed and promoted this image and then used its creation to help to bring about Mexicans' removal.

103. Regarding the transition from Mexican to white labor, see Gregory, *American Exodus,* 58–70, quotation from 69; and Devra Weber, *Dark Sweat, White Gold,* 137–61. James Gregory (*American Exodus,* 94, 98, 115) finds that the new white migrants experienced the same conditions as Mexican workers. He adds that while supporters of the New Deal took it upon themselves to expose the conditions of migrant laborers—although he does not elaborate why they felt so motivated—and to advocate for improvements, few changes were made. Also see Weber, *Dark Sweat, White Gold,* 161. In Arizona, Eric V. Meeks finds Anglos beginning to outnumber Mexicans in the cotton fields in the mid-1930s, although they quickly were selected for positions with more status than Mexican workers; see Meeks, *Border Citizens: The Making of Indians, Mexicans and Anglos in Arizona* (Austin: University of Texas Press, 2007), 118–23.

104. James Gregory (*American Exodus,* 32, 67–87, 94–98) demonstrates that white people did not like the migratory life and left it quickly. He also explains that New Dealers often served as advocates for the migrant workers, although he saw that little changed as a consequence of the greater awareness of migrants' plight. Devra Weber (*Dark Sweat, White Gold,* 189) also notes that little changed in workers' situations, especially after Americans' attention turned to the brewing war in Europe. Gregory finds that some communities did not want white Americans working in the fields as they tended to stick around after the harvest season and became dependent upon relief, causing residents to resent the increased tax burden.

105. David Cushman Coyle, Works Progress Administration, *Depression Pioneers* (Washington, DC: Government Printing Office, 1939), 9, 18; *Select Committee,* pt. 8, 2996.

106. U.S. House of Representatives, *Preliminary Report of the Select Committee to Investigate the Interstate Migration of Destitute Citizens,* 76th Cong., 3rd sess. (1941), 9.

107. Coyle, *Depression Pioneers,* 10, 13, 18–19.

108. Sketch, "Transients," *The Alamo,* December 5, 1934, 1.

109. "The Eternal Transient," *The Alamo,* May 8, 1934, 1.

110. James Gregory (*American Exodus,* 111–13) interprets John Steinbeck's novel differently in that he sees that even while it brought awareness to the problems of migratory labor, it resulted in Americans viewing the "Okie" as uneducated and degen-

erate. Yet, the sympathetic portrayal of the Joad family, amidst an increase in efforts to laud the American worker, put a more positive spin on migratory labor than had previously existed. For the lack of much change in workers' situation, see James Gregory, *American Exodus*, 98; and Devra Weber, *Dark Sweat, White Gold*, 189. For more on the promotion of the American worker, see Gary Gerstle, *American Crucible: Race and Nation in the Twentieth Century* (Princeton, NJ: Princeton University Press, 2001), 153–54 and 179–81.

111. Robert N. McLean, "The Mexican Returns," *Nation* 24 (August 1932), 166.

Bibliography

Primary Sources

Manuscript Collections

ARIZONA HISTORICAL SOCIETY, TUCSON

Alianza Hispano-Americana Collection.
Aliens Ephemera Clippings Files.
Douglas, Lewis. Clippings File.
Gilbert, Hugh C. Papers. 1914–33.
Jácome, Carlos C. Ephemera File.
Jácome, Katie Hughes. Papers.
Tucson Biographical Files.

CENTER FOR SOUTHWEST RESEARCH, ZIMMERMAN LIBRARY, UNIVERSITY OF NEW MEXICO, ALBUQUERQUE

Catron, Thomas B. Papers.
Dargan, Marion. Papers.
Fergusson, Edna. Papers.
Larrazolo, Octaviano. Papers.
Luna, Solomon. Papers.
New Mexico Constitution Collection.
Otero, Miguel A. Papers.
Rodey, Bernard S. Papers.

DEPARTMENT OF ARCHIVES AND MANUSCRIPTS, UNIVERSITY LIBRARIES, ARIZONA STATE UNIVERSITY, TEMPE

Arizona Collection.
Brichta, Bernabé. Biography. Chicano Research Collection.
García Smith, Placida. Biography. Arizona Women Collection.
Hayden [Carl] Family Papers. Arizona Collection.
Hunt, George W. P. Papers. Arizona Collection.
LULAC Records. Chicano Research Collection.
Young, George U. Papers. Arizona Collection.

FRAY ANGÉLICO CHÁVEZ HISTORY LIBRARY, PALACE OF THE GOVERNORS, SANTA FE

Vertical files.

NEW MEXICO STATE RECORDS CENTER AND ARCHIVES, SANTA FE

Governors' Papers.
Prince, L. Bradford. Papers.
Territorial Archives of New Mexico.

SPECIAL COLLECTIONS, UNIVERSITY OF ARIZONA LIBRARY, TUCSON

Arizona Constitutional Convention Papers.
Cameron, Ralph Henry. Papers.
Douglas, Lewis. Papers.
Hunt, George W. P. Scrapbooks.
Jácome, Carlos C. Biofile. Arizona and Southwestern Biographical File.
Smith, Marcus A. Papers.

U.S. NATIONAL ARCHIVES AND RECORDS ADMINISTRATION

U.S. House of Representatives. Record Group 233. Washington, DC: National Archives.
U.S. Immigration and Naturalization Service. Record Group 85. Washington, DC: National Archives.
U.S. Senate. Record Group 46. Washington, DC: National Archives.
U.S. State Department. Record Group 59. College Park, MD: National Archives.

Newspapers and Periodicals

ENGLISH-LANGUAGE PAPERS AND PERIODICALS

Alamo
American Federationist
American Mercury

American Review of Reviews
Arizona Democrat (Phoenix)
Arizona Gazette (Phoenix)
Arizona Republican (Phoenix)
Arizona Star (Tucson)
Christian Century
Commoner
Commonwealth
Daughters of the American Revolution Magazine
Denver Post
Foreign Affairs
Independent
Literary Digest
Los Angeles Times
Nation
Nation's Business
New Republic
New York Daily Tribune
New York Times
North American Review
Omaha (NE) World-Herald
Outlook
Out West
Pacific Monthly
Pittsburgh Courier
Santa Fe New Mexican
Saturday Evening Post
Southwest Review
Sunset
Survey
Survey Midmonthly
Tucson Daily Citizen
Tucson Star
Washington Post
World Tomorrow
World's Work

SPANISH-LANGUAGE PAPERS

El Independiente (Las Vegas, NM)
El Fronterizo (Tucson, AZ)
El Labrador (Las Cruces, NM)
El Mosquito (Tucson, AZ)
El Nacional (Chicago, IL)
El Tiempo (Las Cruces, NM)
El Tucsonense (Tucson, AZ)
La Opinión (Los Angeles, LA)

La Revista de Taos (Taos, NM)
La Voz del Pueblo (Las Vegas, NM)

Government Publications

U.S. GOVERNMENT SERIAL PUBLICATIONS

Congressional Digest.

Congressional Record.

U.S. Bureau of Naturalization. *Annual Reports*, of the Commissioner of Naturalization to the Secretary of Labor. Washington, DC: Government Printing Office.

U.S. Department of Commerce and Labor. *Annual Reports*, from the Commissioner General of Immigration. Washington, DC: Government Printing Office.

U.S. Department of Labor. *Annual Reports*, from the Commissioner General of Immigration. Washington, DC: Government Printing Office.

OTHER GOVERNMENT RECORDS AND REPORTS

Arizona Constitutional Convention. *Minutes of the Constitutional Convention of the Territory of Arizona*. Phoenix: Phoenix Printing Co., 1910.

Brown, Malcolm, and Orin Cassmore. *Migratory Cotton Pickers in Arizona*. Works Progress Administration. Washington, DC: Government Printing Office, 1939.

Carleton, H. A. R., and E. S. Downey, eds. *The Nomad, California Transient Service: Progress and Methods of Approach*. San Francisco: Transient Publication Project, 1935.

Carrera de Velasco, Mercedes. *Los mexicanos que devolvió la crisis, 1929–1932*. Tlatelolco, México: Secretaría de relaciones exteriores, 1974.

Clark, Victor S. "Mexican Labor in the United States." *Bulletin of the Bureau of Labor* 78 (1908): 466–522.

Coyle, David Cushman. *Depression Pioneers*. Works Progress Administration. Washington, DC: Government Printing Office, 1939.

Fabila, Alfonso. *El problema de la emigracion de obreros y campesinos mexicanos*. Mexico City: Publicaciones de la secretaria de gobernacion, 1929.

Foerster, Robert F. *The Racial Problems Involved in Immigration from Latin America and the West Indies to the United States*. U.S. Department of Labor. Washington, DC: Government Printing Office, 1925.

Goff, John S. ed., *Records of the Arizona Constitutional Convention of 1910*. Phoenix: Supreme Court of Arizona, 1991.

New Mexico Constitutional Convention. *Proceedings of the Constitutional Convention of the Proposed State of New Mexico*. October 3–November 21, 1910. Law Library, Library of Congress.

Secretaría de relaciones exteriores. *La migración y protección de mexicanos en el extranjero*. Mexico City: Ministerio de relaciones exteriores, 1928.

U.S. House of Representatives. *Preliminary Report of the Select Committee to Investigate the Interstate Migration of Destitute Citizens*. 76th Cong., 3rd sess., 1941.

——. *Select Committee to Investigate the Interstate Migration of Destitute Citizens.* 76th Cong., 3rd sess., 1940–41.

U.S. House of Representatives, Committee on Immigration and Naturalization. *Admission of Mexican and other Alien Laborers into Texas and Other States.* Washington, DC: Government Printing Office, 1920.

——. *Immigration from the Countries of the Western Hemisphere, Hearings.* 70th Cong., 1st sess., 1928.

——. *Immigration from Countries of the Western Hemisphere, Hearings.* 71st Cong., 2nd sess., 1930.

——. *Immigration from Countries of the Western Hemisphere, Hearings.* 72nd Cong., 1st sess., 1931.

——. *Immigration from Latin America, the West Indies, and Canada, Hearings.* 68th Cong., 2nd sess., 1930.

——. *Immigration from Mexico, Hearings.* 71st Cong., 2nd sess., 1930.

——. *Imported Pauper Labor and Serfdom in America: Statement of Honorable John C. Box, Hearings.* 67th Cong., 1st sess., 1921.

——. *Restriction of Immigration from Republic of Mexico.* Rep. 1594, 71st Cong., 2nd sess., 1930.

——. *Seasonal Agricultural Laborers from Mexico, Hearings.* 69th Cong., 1st sess., 1926.

——. *Temporary Admission of Illiterate Mexican Laborers, Hearings.* 66th Cong., 2nd sess., 1920.

——. *Western Hemisphere Immigration, Hearings.* 71st Cong., 2nd sess., 1930.

U.S. Department of Commerce, Bureau of the Census. *Abstract of the Twelfth Census, 1900,* 3rd ed. Washington, DC: Government Printing Office, 1904.

U.S. Department of Commerce and Labor. "Population of the United States by Color or Race." Washington, DC: Government Printing Office, 1931.

U.S. House of Representatives, Committee on the Territories. *Admission of Certain Territories into the Union.* Rep. 1309, 57th Cong., 1st sess., 1902.

——. *Annual Report of the Department of the Interior: Governor of New Mexico.* Doc. 5, 59th Cong., 2nd sess., 1906–7.

——. *Constitutions of New Mexico and Arizona.* Rep. 33, 62nd Cong., 1st sess., 1911.

——. *Further Hearings on Statehood Bill.* 58th Cong., 2nd sess., December 1903–January 1904.

——. *House Joint Resolution No. 14, Hearings.* 62nd Cong., 1st sess., 1911.

——. *Statehood Bill, Hearings.* 57th Cong., 2nd sess., 1903.

——. *Statehood for Arizona and New Mexico, Hearings.* 59th Cong., 1st sess., 1906.

——. *Statehood for Arizona and New Mexico, Hearings.* 60th Cong., 2nd sess., 1909.

——. *Statehood for Arizona and New Mexico, Hearings.* 61st Cong., 2nd sess., 1910.

——. *Statehood for the Territories.* Rep. 2335, 58th Cong., 2nd sess., 1904.

——. *Statehood for the Territories.* Rep. 496, 59th Cong., 1st sess., 1906.

——. *Statehood for the Territories.* Rep. 2079, 60th Cong., 2nd sess., 1909.

——. *Statehood for the Territories.* Rep. 152, 61st Cong., 2nd sess., 1910.

U.S. House of Representatives, Committee on Ways and Means. *Hearings on the Pacific Southwest Exposition.* 70th Cong., 1928.

U.S. Senate, Committee on Immigration. *Admission of Mexican Agricultural Laborers, Hearings*. 66th Cong., 2nd sess., 1920.

——. *Emergency Immigration Legislation, Hearings*. 66th Cong., 3rd sess., 1921.

——. *Reports of the Immigration Commission, Immigrants in Industries*. 61st Cong., 3rd sess. Washington, DC: Government Printing Office, 1911.

——. *Restriction of Western Hemisphere Immigration, Hearings*, 70th Cong., 1st sess., 1928.

——. *To Subject Certain Immigrants Born in Countries of the Western Hemisphere to the Quota Under the Immigration Law*. Rep. 1343, 70th Cong., 2nd sess., 1928.

U.S. Senate, Committee on the Territories. *An Act Enabling the People of New Mexico and Arizona to Form a Constitution and State Government, Etc*. Rep. 454, 61st Cong., 2nd sess., 1910.

——. *Admission of Territories of Arizona and New Mexico*. Rep. 100, 62nd Cong., 1st sess., 1911.

——. *Hearing before the Committee on Territories in Relation to S. J. Res. Nos. 2, 9*. 62nd Cong., 1st sess., 1911.

——. *Hearings before the Committee on Territories. on H.J. Res. 14*. 62nd Cong., 1st sess., 1911.

——. *H.R. 18166* (amended version). Calendar No. 388. 61st Cong., 2nd sess., 1910.

——. *Joint Statehood for New Mexico and Arizona*. Doc. 254, 59th Cong., 1st sess., 1906.

——. *New Mexico Constitution*. 61st Cong., 3rd sess., Washington, DC: Government Printing Office, 1911.

——. *New Statehood Bill: Hearings before the Subcommittee on Territories*. 57th Cong., 2nd sess., 1902.

——. *New Statehood Bill*. Rep. 2206, 57th Cong., 2nd sess., 1902.

——. *Protest against Union of Arizona with New Mexico*. 59th Cong., 1st sess., 1906.

——. *Statehood. Hearings*. 61st Cong., 2nd sess., 1910.

——. *Statehood for the Territories: Papers Relating to the Question of Statehood for the Territories*. Doc. 153, 57th Cong., January–February 1903.

Secondary Sources

Acuña, Rodolfo F. *Corridors of Migration: The Odyssey of Mexican Laborers, 1600–1933*. Tucson: University of Arizona Press, 2007.

——. *Occupied America: A History of Chicanos*, 3rd ed. New York: Harper and Row, 1988.

Aguila, Jaime R. "Protecting 'México de Afuera': Mexican Emigration Policy, 1876–1928." PhD diss., Arizona State University, 2000.

Alden, George H. "The Evolution of the American System of Forming and Admitting New States into the Union." *Annals of the American Academy of Political and Social Science* 18 (November 1901): 469–79.

Almaguer, Tomás. "Ideological Distortions and Recent Chicano Historiography: The Internal Colonial Model and Chicano Historical Interpretation." *Aztlán* 18, no. 1 (Spring 1987): 7–28.

——. *Racial Fault Lines: The Historical Origins of White Supremacy in California*. Berkeley: University of California Press, 1994.

Anderson, Benedict. *Imagined Communities: Reflections on the Origin and Spread of Nationalism*, rev. ed. London: Verso, 1991.

Aron, Stephen, and Jeremy Adelman. "From Borderlands to Borders: Empires, Nation-States, and the Peoples in Between in North American History." *American Historical Review* 104, no. 3 (1999): 814–41.

Arredondo, Gabriela F. *Mexican Chicago: Race, Identity, and Nation, 1916–39*. Chicago: University of Illinois Press, 2008.

Balderrama, Francisco E. *In Defense of La Raza: The Los Angeles Mexican Consulate and the Mexican Community, 1929 to 1936*. Tucson: University of Arizona Press, 1982.

Balderrama, Francisco E., and Raymond Rodríguez. *Decade of Betrayal: Mexican Repatriation in the 1930s*. Albuquerque: University of New Mexico Press, 1995.

———. *Decade of Betrayal: Mexican Repatriation in the 1930s*, rev. ed. Albuquerque: University of New Mexico Press, 2006.

Barrera, Mario. *Race and Class in the Southwest: A Theory of Racial Inequality*. South Bend, IN: University of Notre Dame Press, 1979.

Barrett, James R., and David Roediger. "Inbetween Peoples: Race, Nationality, and the 'New Immigrant' Working Class." *Journal of American Ethnic History* 16, no. 3 (Spring 1997): 3–44.

Basson, Lauren L. *White Enough to Be American? Race Mixing, Indigenous People, and the Boundaries of State and Nation*. Chapel Hill: University of North Carolina Press, 2008.

Behdad, Ali. *A Forgetful Nation: On Immigration and Cultural Identity in the United States*. Durham, NC: Duke University Press, 2005.

Benton-Cohen, Katherine. *Borderline Americans: Racial Divisions and Labor War in the Arizona Borderlands*. Cambridge: Harvard University Press, 2009.

———. "Other Immigrants: Mexicans and the Dillingham Commission of 1907–1911." *Journal of American Ethnic History* 30, no. 2 (Winter 2011): 33–57.

Berman, David R. *Reformers, Corporations, and the Electorate: An Analysis of Arizona's Age of Reform*. Niwot: University Press of Colorado, 1992.

Betten, Neil, and Raymond A. Mohl. "From Discrimination to Repatriation: Mexican Life in Gary, Indiana during the Great Depression." *Pacific Historical Review* 42 (August 1973): 370–88.

Bixby-Smith, Sarah. *Adobe Days*. Cedar Rapids, IA: Torch Press, 1925.

Bloch, Louis. "Facts about Mexican Immigration before and since the Quota Restriction Laws." *Journal of the American Statistical Association* 24 (March 1929): 50–60.

Bloom, John Porter, ed. *The American Territorial System*. Athens: Ohio University Press, 1973.

Bogardus, Emory S. "Mexican Immigrants and the Quota." *Sociology and Social Research* 12 (1928): 371–78.

———. *The Mexican in the United States*. Los Angeles: University of Southern California Press, 1934.

———. "Mexican Repatriates." *Sociology and Social Research* 17 (November–December 1933): 169–76.

Boswell, Thomas D. "The Growth and Proportional Distribution of the Mexican Stock Population of the United States: 1910–1970." *Mississippi Geographer* 7, no. 1 (Spring 1979): 57–76.

Bowers, Claude G. *Beveridge and the Progressive Era.* New York: Literary Guild, 1932.

Braeman, John. *Albert J. Beveridge: American Nationalist.* Chicago: University of Chicago Press, 1971.

———. "Albert J. Beveridge and Statehood for the Southwest, 1902–1912." *Arizona and the West* 10 (Winter 1968): 313–42.

Bresette, Linna E. *Mexicans in the United States: A Report of a Brief Survey.* Washington, DC: National Catholic Welfare Conference, 1929.

Briegel, Kaye Lynn. "Alianza Hispano-Americana, 1894–1965: A Mexican American Fraternal Insurance Society." PhD diss., University of Southern California, 1974.

Brown, Peter G., and Henry Shue, eds. *The Border That Joins: Mexican Migrants and U.S. Responsibility.* Totowa, NJ: Rowman and Littlefield, 1983.

Burnett, Christina Duffy, and Burke Marshall, eds. *Foreign in a Domestic Sense: Puerto Rico, American Expansion, and the Constitution.* Durham, NC: Duke University Press, 2001.

Calavita, Kitty. *Inside the State: The Bracero Program, Immigration, and the INS.* New York: Routledge, 1992.

Camacho, Alicia Schmidt. *Migrant Imaginaries: Latino Cultural Politics in the U.S.-Mexico Borderlands.* New York: New York University Press, 2008.

Camarillo, Albert. *Chicanos in a Changing Society: From Mexican Pueblos to American Barrios in Santa Barbara and Southern California, 1848–1930.* Cambridge: Harvard University Press, 1979.

Cardenas, Gilbert. "Los Desarrigados: Chicanos in the Midwestern Region of the United States." *Aztlán* 7 (Summer 1976): 141–52.

Cardoso, Lawrence A. "Labor Emigration to the Southwest." In George C. Kiser and Martha Woody Kiser, eds., *Mexican Workers in the United States: Historical and Political Perspective.* Albuquerque: University of New Mexico Press, 1979.

———. *Mexican Emigration to the United States, 1897–1931: Socioeconomic Patterns.* Tucson: University of Arizona Press, 1980.

———. "La repatriación de braceros en época de Obregón: 1920–1923." *Historia Mexicana* 26, no. 4 (1977): 576–95.

Chang, David A. *The Color of the Land: Race, Nation, and the Politics of Land Ownership in Oklahoma, 1832–1929.* Chapel Hill: University of North Carolina Press, 2010.

Chávez, John R. *The Lost Land: The Chicano Image of the Southwest.* Albuquerque: University of New Mexico Press, 1984.

Clark, Jane Perry. "Aliens in the Deportation Dragnet." *Current History* 36 (April 1932): 27–31.

Coester, Alfred. "Why Spanish?" *Hispania* 7, no. 1 (1924): 21–29.

Cohen, Deborah. *Braceros: Migrant Citizens and Transnational Subjects in the Postwar United States and Mexico.* Chapel Hill: University of North Carolina, 2011.

Crawford, Remsen. "The Deportation of Undesirable Aliens." *Current History* 30 (September 1929): 1077–79.

———. "The Menace of Mexican Immigration." *Current History* 31 (October 1930–March 1931): 902–7.

Daniel, Cletus. *Bitter Harvest: A History of California Farmworkers, 1870–1941.* Berkeley: University of California Press, 1981.

Dargan, Marion. "New Mexico's Fight for Statehood, 1895–1912, I." *New Mexico Historical Review* 14 (January 1939): 1–33.

———. "New Mexico's Fight for Statehood, 1895–1912, II." *New Mexico Historical Review* 14 (April 1939): 121–42.

Davis, Amy Elizabeth. "Deportation and the Border Blockade: How Western Conservatism Impacted Immigrant Sugar Beet Workers in Colorado between 1900 and 1940." Master's thesis, University of Oregon, 2003.

Davis, Edward Everett. *The White Scourge.* San Antonio: Naylor Co., 1940.

Davis, James J. "Selective Immigration." *Forum* 70 (September 1923): 1857–65.

Davis, James J., et al. "'Quota-Mindedness' toward Mexico: Should the Policy Be Abandoned?" *Eugenics* 2 (November 1929): 18–21.

De Genova, Nicholas, ed. *Racial Transformations: Latinos and Asians Remaking the United States.* Durham, NC: Duke University Press, 2006.

de la Cruz, Jesse. "Rejection Because of Race: Albert J. Beveridge and Nuevo Mexico's Struggle for Statehood, 1902–1903." *Aztlán* 7, no. 1 (1976): 79–97.

De León, Arnoldo. *They Called Them Greasers: Anglo Attitudes toward Mexicans in Texas, 1821–1900.* Austin: University of Texas Press, 1983.

Delpar, Helen. *The Enormous Vogue of Things Mexican: Cultural Relations between the United States and Mexico, 1920–1935.* Tuscaloosa: University of Alabama Press, 1992.

Deutsch, Sarah. *No Separate Refuge: Culture, Class, and Gender on an Anglo-Hispanic Frontier in the American Southwest, 1880–1940.* New York: Oxford University Press, 1987.

Díaz, Rose, and Jan Dodson Barnhart, eds. *Hispanic Heroes: Portraits of New Mexicans Who Have Made a Difference.* Albuquerque: University of New Mexico Press, 1992.

Diego Ferreira, Zeferino, and Laura Cummings, eds. "Zeferino Diego Ferreira: The Life Story of a Villista/Zeferino Diego Ferreira: Historia Oral de una Villista." *Journal of the Southwest* 41, no. 1 (1999): 1–103.

Divine, Robert. *American Immigration Policy, 1924–1952.* New Haven, CT: Yale University Press, 1957.

Driscoll, Barbara A. *The Tracks North: The Railroad Bracero Program of World War II.* Austin: University of Texas, 1999.

Durand, Jorge, Douglas S. Massey, and Chiara Capoferro. "The New Geography of Mexican Immigration." In Victor Zuñiga and Rubén Hernández-León, eds., *New Destinations: Mexican Immigration in the United States.* New York: Russell Sage Foundation, 2005, 1–22.

Enciso, Fernando Saúl Alanis. "No cuenten conmigo: La pólitica de repatriación del gobierno mexicano y sus nacionales en estados unidos, 1910–1928." *Mexican Studies/Estudios Mexicanos* 19 (Summer 2003): 401–31.

Ettinger, Patrick. *Imaginary Lines: Border Enforcement and the Origins of Undocumented Immigration, 1882–1930.* Austin: University of Texas Press, 2009.

Fernández-Gibert, Arturo. "*La Voz del Pueblo:* Texto, Identidad y Lengua en la Prensa Neomexicana, 1890–1911." PhD diss., University of New Mexico, 2001.

Fields, Harold. "Where Shall the Alien Work?" *Social Forces* 12 (December 1933): 213–21.

Flores, William V., "Citizens vs. Citizenry: Undocumented Immigrants and Latino Cultural Citizenship." In William V. Flores and Rina Benmayor, eds., *Latino*

Cultural Citizenship: Claiming Identity, Space and Rights. Boston: Beacon Press, 1997, 255–78.

Flores, William V., and Rina Benmayor, eds. *Latino Cultural Citizenship: Claiming Identity, Space and Rights*. Boston: Beacon Press, 1997.

Foley, Neil. *Quest for Equality: The Failed Promise of Black-Brown Solidarity*. Cambridge: Harvard University Press, 2010.

——. *The White Scourge: Mexicans, Blacks, and Poor Whites in Texas Cotton Culture*. Berkeley: University of California Press, 1997.

Fox, Cybelle. *Three Worlds of Relief: Race, Immigration, and the American Welfare State from the Progressive Era to the New Deal*. Princeton, NJ: Princeton University Press, 2012.

Fregoso, Rosa Linda. *MeXicana Encounters: The Making of Social Identities on the Borderlands*. Berkeley: University of California Press, 2003.

Fuchs, Lawrence H. *The American Kaleidoscope: Race, Ethnicity, and the Civic Culture*. Hanover, NH: Wesleyan University Press, 1990.

Gabaccia, Donna R. "Is Everywhere Nowhere? Nomads, Nations, and the Immigrant Paradigm of United States History." *Journal of American History* 86, no. 3 (1999): 1115–34.

Galarza, Ernesto. "Life in the United States for Mexican People: Out of the Experience of a Mexican." In *Proceedings of the National Conference of Social Work*. Chicago: University of Chicago Press, 1929.

Gamio, Manuel. *El inmigrante mexicano: la historia de su vida, entrevistas completas, 1926–27*, edited by Devra Weber, Roberto Melville, and Juan Vicente Palermo. Mexico City: Regents of the University of California, 2002.

——. *The Mexican Immigrant, His Life Story*. Chicago: University of Chicago Press, 1931.

——. *Mexican Immigration to the United States*. Chicago: University of Chicago Press, 1930. Repr., New York: Dover, 1971.

——. "Observations on Mexican Immigration into the United States." *Pacific Affairs* 2, no. 8 (August 1929): 463–69.

García, Juan R. *Mexicans in the Midwest, 1900–1932*. Tucson: University of Arizona, 1996.

García, Mario. "Americanization and the Mexican Immigrant, 1880–1930." *Journal of Ethnic Studies* 6 (1978): 19–34.

——. *Desert Immigrants: The Mexicans of El Paso, 1880–1920*. New Haven, CT: Yale University Press, 1981.

——. *Mexican Americans: Leadership, Ideology, and Identity, 1930–1960*. New Haven, CT: Yale University Press, 1989.

García, Richard A. *Rise of the Mexican American Middle Class, San Antonio, 1929*. College Station: Texas A&M University Press, 1991.

García y Griego, Manuel. "The Importation of Mexican Contract Laborers to the United States, 1942–1964: Antecedents, Operation, and Legacy." In Peter G. Brown and Henry Shue, eds., *The Border That Joins: Mexican Migrants and U.S. Responsibility*. Totowa, NJ: Rowman and Littlefield, 1983, 49–98.

Gerstle, Gary. *American Crucible: Race and Nation in the Twentieth Century*. Princeton, NJ: Princeton University Press, 2001.

Gibson, Charles, and Benjamin Keen. "Trends of United States Studies in Latin American History." *American Historical Review* 62 (July 1957): 855–77.

Gilbert, James Carl. "A Field Study in Mexico of the Mexican Repatriation Movement." Master's thesis, University of Southern California, 1934.

Glickman, Lawrence B. *A Living Wage: American Workers and the Making of Consumer Society*. Ithaca, NY: Cornell University Press, 1997.

Go, Julian. *American Empire and the Politics of Meaning: Elite Political Cultures in the Philippines and Puerto Rico during U.S. Colonialism*. Durham, NC: Duke University Press, 2008.

———."Chains of Empire, Projects of State: Political Education and U.S. Colonial Rule in Puerto Rico and the Philippines." *Comparative Studies in Society and History* 42 (April 2000): 333–62.

Goethe, C. M. "The Influx of Mexican Amerinds." *Eugenics* 2 (January 1929): 6–9.

Goff, John S. *Arizona Biographical Dictionary*. Cave Creek, AZ: Black Mountain Press, 1983.

Gómez, Laura E. *Manifest Destinies: The Making of the Mexican American Race*. New York: New York University Press, 2007.

Gomez-Quiñones, Juan. *Mexican American Labor, 1790–1990*. Albuquerque: University of New Mexico Press, 1994.

Gonzales, Phillip B. *Forced Sacrifice as Ethnic Protest: The Hispano Cause in New Mexico and the Racial Attitude Confrontation of 1933*. New York: New York University Press, 2001.

———. "'History Hits the Heart' Albuquerque's Great Cuartocentenario Controvery, 1997–2005." In Phillip B. Gonzales, ed., *Expressing New Mexico: Nuevomexicano Creativity, Ritual and Memory*. Tucson: University of Arizona Press, 2007, 207–32.

———. "*La Junta de Indignación*: Hispano Repertoire of Collective Protest in New Mexico, 1884–1933." *Western Historical Quarterly*, 31 (Summer 2000).

———. "Whither *Nuevomexicanos*: The Career of a Southwestern Intellectual Discourse, 1907–2004." *Social Sciences Journal* 43, no. 2 (2006): 273–86.

Gonzales, Phillip B., and Ann Massman. "Loyalty Questioned: *Nuevomexicanos* in the Great War." *Western Historical Quarterly* 75 (November 2006): 639–49.

Gonzales-Berry, Erlinda. "Which Language Will Our Children Speak?" In Erlinda Gonzales-Berry and David R. Maciel, eds., *The Contested Homeland: A Chicano History of New Mexico*. Albuquerque: University of New Mexico Press, 2000, 161–89.

Gonzales-Berry, Erlinda, and David R. Maciel, eds. *The Contested Homeland: A Chicano History of New Mexico*. Albuquerque: University of New Mexico Press, 2000.

Gonzales-Berry, Erlinda, and Charles Tatum, eds. *Recovering the U.S. Hispanic Literary Heritage*, vol. 2. Houston: Arte Público Press, 1996.

González, Deena J. *Refusing the Favor: The Spanish-Mexican Women of Santa Fe, 1820–1880*. Oxford: Oxford University Press, 1999.

González, Gilbert G. *Culture of Empire: American Writers, Mexico, and Mexican Immigrants, 1880–1930*. Austin: University of Texas Press, 2004.

———. *Guest Workers or Colonized Labor? Mexican Labor to the United States*. Boulder, CO: Paradigm Publishers, 2005.

———. *Mexican Consuls and Labor Organizing: Imperial Politics in the American Southwest*. Austin: University of Texas Press, 1999.

Gordon, Linda. *The Great Arizona Orphan Abduction*. Cambridge: Harvard University Press, 1999.

———. "Internal Colonialism and Gender." In Ann Laura Stoler, ed., *Haunted by Empire: Geographies of Intimacy in North American History*. Durham, NC: Duke University Press, 2006, 427–51.

Grebler, Leo. "The Naturalization of Mexican Immigrants in the United States." *International Migration Review* 1 (1966): 17–32.

Gregory, James N. *American Exodus: Dust Bowl Migration and Okie Culture in California*. Oxford: Oxford University Press, 1989.

Griswold del Castillo, Richard. *The Treaty of Guadalupe Hidalgo: A Legacy of Conflict*. Norman: University of Oklahoma Press, 1990.

Guerin-Gonzales, Camille. *Mexican Workers, American Dreams: Immigration, Repatriation and California Farm Labor, 1900–1939*. New Brunswick, NJ: Rutgers University Press, 1994.

Guglielmo, Thomas A. "Fighting for Caucasian Rights: Mexicans, Mexican Americans, and the Transnational Struggle for Civil Rights in World War II Texas." *Journal of American History* 92 (March 2006): 1212–37.

———. *White on Arrival: Italians, Race, Color, and Power in Chicago, 1890–1945*. Oxford: Oxford University Press, 2003.

Gutiérrez, David G. "The Third Generation: Selections on Recent Chicano Historiography." *Mexican Studies/Estudios Mexicanos* 5, no. 2 (Summer 1989): 281–96.

———. *Walls and Mirrors: Mexican Americans, Mexican Immigrants, and the Politics of Ethnicity in the American Southwest*. Berkeley: University of California Press, 1995.

———, ed. *Between Two Worlds: Mexican Immigrants in the United States*. Wilmington, DE: Scholarly Resources, 1996.

Gutiérrez, Ramon A. *When Jesus Came, the Corn Mothers Went Away: Marriage, Sexuality and Power in New Mexico, 1500–1846*. Stanford: Stanford University Press, 1991.

Hahamovitch, Cindy. "Creating Perfect Immigrants: Guestworkers of the World in Historical Perspective." *Labor History* 44, no. 1 (2003): 69–94.

———. *The Fruits of Their Labor: Atlantic Coast Farmworkers and the Making of Migrant Poverty, 1870–1945*. Chapel Hill: University of North Carolina Press, 1997.

Hall, Linda B., and Don M. Coerver. *Revolution on the Border: The United States and Mexico, 1910–1920*. Albuquerque: University of New Mexico Press, 1988.

Hallenbeck, Cleve. *Spanish Missions of the Old Southwest*. Garden City, NY: Doubleday, Page and Co., 1926.

Hanna, Agnes K. "Social Services on the Mexican Border." In *Proceedings of the National Conference of Social Work*. Chicago: University of Chicago Press, 1935.

Hardy, Osgood. "Los Repatriados." *Pomona College Magazine* (January 1933): 71–73.

Harris, Charles H., III, and Louis R. Sadler. *The Border and the Revolution: Clandestine Activities of the Mexican Revolution: 1910–1920*. Silver City, NM: High-Lonesome Books, 1988.

Higbie, Frank Tobias. *Indispensable Outcasts: Hobo Workers and Community in the American Midwest, 1880–1930*. Urbana: University of Illinois Press, 2003.

Higham, John. *Strangers in the Land: Patterns of American Nativism, 1860–1925*. New Brunswick, NJ: Rutgers University Press, 1998.

Hing, Bill Ong. *Defining American through Immigration Policy.* Philadelphia: Temple University Press, 2004.

Hoffman, Abraham. "A Note on the Field Research Interviews of Paul S. Taylor for the Mexican Labor in the United States Monographs." *Pacific Historian* 20 (Summer 1976): 123–31.

——. *Unwanted Mexican Americans in the Great Depression: Repatriation Pressures, 1929–1939.* Tucson: University of Arizona Press, 1974.

Hoganson, Kristin L. *Fighting for American Manhood: How Gender Politics Provoked the Spanish-American and Philippine-American Wars.* New Haven, CT: Yale University Press, 1998.

Horsman, Reginald. *Race and Manifest Destiny: The Origins of American Racial Anglo-Saxonism.* Cambridge: Harvard University Press, 1981.

Horton, Sarah. "Where Is the 'Mexican' in "New Mexican"? Enacting History, Enacting Dominance in Santa Fe Fiesta." *Public Historian* 23 (Autumn 2001): 41–54.

Howland, Charles P., ed. *Survey of American Foreign Relations.* New Haven, CT: Yale University Press, 1929.

Hubbard, Howard A. "Arizona's Struggle against Joint Statehood." *Pacific Historical Review* 11 (1942): 415–23.

Huginnie, A. Yvette. " 'Mexican Labour' in a 'White Man's Town': Racialism, Imperialism, and Industrialization in the Making of Arizona, 1840–1905." In Peter Alexander and Rick Halpern, eds., *Racializing Class, Classifying Race: Labour and Difference in Britain, the USA and Africa.* New York: St Martin's Press, 2000.

Humphrey, Norman D. "Mexican Repatriation from Michigan: Public Assistance in Historical Perspective." *Social Science Review* 15 (September 1941): 497–513.

Hutchinson, Edward. *Legislative History of American Immigration Policy, 1790–1965.* Philadelphia: University of Pennsylvania, 1981.

Jacobson, Matthew Frye. *Barbarian Virtues: The United States Encounters Foreign Peoples at Home and Abroad, 1876–1917.* New York: Hill and Wang, 2000.

Jacoby, Karl. *Shadows at Dawn: A Borderlands Massacre and the Violence of History.* New York: Penguin Press, 2008.

Jones, Robert C., and Louis R. Wilson. *The Mexican in Chicago.* Chicago: University of Chicago Press, 1931.

Kane, Francis F. "The Challenge of the Wickersham Deportations Report." *Journal of Law and Criminology* 23 (November–December 1932): 575–613.

Kanstroom, Daniel. *Deportation Nation: Outsiders in American History.* Cambridge: Harvard University Press, 2007.

Katz, Friedrich. "Labor Conditions on Haciendas in Porfirian Mexico: Some Trends and Tendencies." *Hispanic American Historical Review* 54, no. 1 (February 1974): 1–47.

Kazal, Russell A. *Becoming Old Stock: The Paradox of German-American Identity.* Princeton, NJ: Princeton University Press, 2004.

——. "Revisiting Assimilation: The Rise, Fall, and Reappraisal of a Concept in American Ethnic History." *American Historical Review* 100, no. 2 (April 1995): 437–71.

Kinnicutt, Francis H. "Immigration." *Eugenics* 2 (December 1929): 34–35.

——. "Immigration." *Eugenics* 3 (February 1930): 76–77.

——. "Immigration: Stalemate in Congress." *Eugenics* 3 (July 1930): 279.

Kiser, George, and David Silverman. "Mexican Repatriation during the Great Depression." *Journal of Mexican American History* 3, no. 1 (1973): 139–64.

Knight, Alan. "Racism, Revolution, and *Indigenismo:* Mexico, 1910–1940." In Richard Graham, ed., *The Idea of Race in Latin America, 1870–1940.* Austin: University of Texas Press, 1990.

Kolchin, Peter. "*Whiteness* Studies: The New History of Race in America." *Journal of American History* 89 (June 2002): 154–73.

Kramer, Paul A. *The Blood of Government: Race, Empire, the United States and the Philippines.* Chapel Hill: University of North Carolina Press, 2006.

Kropp, Phoebe S. *California Vieja: Culture and Memory in a Modern American Place.* Berkeley: University of California Press, 2006.

Kuehnert, Lore Diana. "Pernicious Foreigners and Contested Compatriots: Mexican Newspaper Debates over Immigration, Emigration, and Repatriation, 1928–1936." PhD diss., University of California–Riverside, 2002.

Lamar, Howard Roberts. *The Far Southwest, 1846–1912: A Territorial History.* New Haven, CT: Yale University Press, 1966.

——. "The Reluctant Admission: The Struggle to Admit Arizona and New Mexico to the Union." In Robert G. Ferris, ed., *The American West: An Appraisal.* Santa Fe: Museum of New Mexico Press, 1963.

Larson, Robert W. *New Mexico's Quest for Statehood, 1846–1912.* Albuquerque: University of New Mexico Press, 1968.

Lawson, Gary, and Guy Seidman. *The Constitution of Empire: Territorial Expansion and American Legal History.* New Haven, CT: Yale University Press, 2004.

Lee, Erika. *At America's Gate: Chinese Immigration during the Exclusion Era, 1882–1943.* Chapel Hill: University of North Carolina Press, 2003.

——. "The Chinese Exclusion Example: Race, Immigration, and American Gatekeeping, 1882–1924." *Journal of American Ethnic History* 21, no. 3 (Spring 2002): 36–62.

Lemon, J. Francis. "The English-Mexican Class." *Hispania* 9 (October 1926): 248–50.

Leopard, Donald D. "Joint Statehood: 1906." *New Mexico Historical Review* 34 (October 1959): 241–47.

Lescohier, Don D. "The Vital Problem in Mexican Immigration." In *Proceedings of the National Conference of Social Work.* Chicago: University of Chicago Press, 1927.

Levenstein, Harvey A. "The AFL and Mexican Immigration in the 1920s: An Experiment in Labor Diplomacy." *Hispanic American Historical Review* 48 (May 1968): 206–19.

Limerick, Patricia. *The Legacy of Conquest: The Unbroken Past of the American West.* New York: W. W. Norton, 1987.

Lipshultz, Robert J. "American Attitudes toward Mexican Immigration, 1924–1952." Master's thesis, University of Chicago, 1962.

Lockwood, Frank C. *Pioneer Days in Arizona: From the Spanish Occupation to Statehood.* New York: Macmillan, 1932.

López, Ian Haney. *White by Law: The Legal Construction of Race.* New York: New York University Press, 1998.

Lowe, Lisa. *Immigrant Acts: On Asian American Cultural Politics.* Durham, NC: Duke University Press, 1996.

Luckingham, Bradford. *Minorities in Phoenix: A Profile of Mexican American, Chinese American, and African American Communities, 1860–1992*. Tucson: University of Arizona Press, 1994.

Lukens, Patrick D. *A Quiet Victory for Latino Rights: FDR and the Controversy over "Whiteness."* Tucson: University of Arizona Press, 2012.

Macias, Leonardo. "Mexican Immigration and Repatriation during the Great Depression." Master's thesis, Arizona State University, 1992.

Macias, Thomas. *Mestizo in America: Generations of Mexican Ethnicity in the Suburban Southwest*. Tucson: University of Arizona Press, 2006.

Maier, Charles S. *Among Empires: American Ascendancy and Its Predecessors*. Cambridge: Harvard University Press, 2006.

Mangelsdorf, Karen Underhill. "The Beveridge Visit to Arizona in 1902." *Journal of Arizona History* 28, no. 3 (Fall 1987): 243–60.

Mapes, Kathleen. "'A Special Class of Labor': Mexican (Im)Migrants, Immigration Debate, and Industrial Agriculture in the Rural Midwest." *Labor: Studies in Working-Class History of the Americas* 1, no. 2 (2004): 65–88.

———. *Sweet Tyranny: Migrant Labor, Industrial Agriculture, and Imperial Politics*. Urbana: University of Illinois Press, 2009.

Márquez, Benjamin. *LULAC: The Evolution of a Mexican American Political Organization*. Austin: University of Texas Press, 1993.

Martin, Patricia Preciado. *Songs My Mother Sang to Me: An Oral History of Mexican American Women*. Tucson: University of Arizona Press, 1992.

Martinelli, Phylis Cancilla. *Undermining Race: Ethnic Identities in Arizona Copper Camps, 1880–1920*. Tucson: University of Arizona, 2009.

Martinez, John. "Mexican Emigration to the U.S., 1910–1930." PhD diss., University of California, 1957.

McBride, James D. "The Liga Protectora Latina: A Mexican American Benevolent Society in Arizona." *Journal of the West* 14, no. 4 (1975): 82–90.

McKay, R. Reynolds. "Texas Mexican Repatriation during the Great Depression." PhD diss., University of Oklahoma, 1982.

McLean, Robert N. "Mexican Workers in the United States." In *Proceedings of the National Conference of Social Work*. Chicago: University of Chicago Press, 1929.

———. *That Mexican As He Really Is, North and South of the Rio Grande*. New York: Fleming H. Revell, 1928.

McWilliams, Carey. *Factories in the Field: The Story of Migratory Farm Labor in California*. Santa Barbara, CA: Peregrine Smith, 1935.

———. *Ill Fares the Land: Migrants and Migratory Labor in the United States*. New York: Barnes and Noble Books, 1941. Reprint, 1967.

———. *North from Mexico: The Spanish-Speaking People of the United States*. Philadelphia: J. B. Lippincott, 1949.

Meeks, Eric V. *Border Citizens: The Making of Indians, Mexicans, and Anglos in Arizona*. Austin: University of Texas Press, 2007.

Meléndez, A. Gabriel. *So All Is Not Lost: The Poetics of Print in Nuevomexicano Communities, 1834–1958*. Albuquerque: University of New Mexico Press, 1997.

Melzer, Richard. "Governor Miguel Otero's War: Statehood and New Mexican Loyalty in the Spanish-American War." *Colonial Latin American Historical Review* 8, no. 1 (1999): 79–103.

——. "New Mexico in Caricature: Images of the Territory on the Eve of Statehood." *New Mexico Historical Review* 62, no. 4 (1987): 335–60.

Menchaca, Martha. "Chicano Indianism: A Historical Account of Racial Repression in the United States." *American Ethnologist* 20, no. 4 (1993): 583–603.

Merk, Frederick. *Manifest Destiny and Mission in American History: A Reinterpretation.* New York: Alfred A. Knopf, 1963.

Merry, Sally Engle. *Colonizing Hawai'i: The Cultural Power of Law.* Princeton, NJ: Princeton University Press, 2000.

Meyer, Doris. *Speaking for Themselves: Neomexicano Cultural Identity and the Spanish-Language Press, 1880–1920.* Albuquerque: University of New Mexico Press, 1996.

Meyer, Michael C., William L. Sherman, and Susan M. Deeds. *The Course of Mexican History*, 6th ed. Oxford: Oxford University Press, 1999.

Mitchell, Pablo. *Coyote Nation: Sexuality, Race, and Conquest in Modernizing New Mexico.* Chicago: University of Chicago Press, 2005.

Molina, Natalia. *Fit to Be Citizens? Public Health and Race in Los Angeles, 1879–1939.* Berkeley: University of California Press, 2006.

Montejano, David. *Anglos and Mexicans in the Making of Texas, 1836–1986.* Austin: University of Texas Press, 1987.

Montgomery, Charles. "Becoming 'Spanish-American': Race and Rhetoric in New Mexico Politics, 1880–1928." *Journal of American Ethnic History* (Summer 2001): 59–84.

——. *The Spanish Redemption: Heritage, Power, and Loss on New Mexico's Upper Rio Grande.* Berkeley: University of California Press, 2002.

Montoya, María E. *Translating Property: The Maxwell Land Grant and the Conflict over Land in the American West, 1840–1900.* Lawrence: University of Kansas Press, 2002.

Mora, Anthony P. *Border Dilemmas: Racial and National Uncertainties in New Mexico, 1848–1912.* Durham, NC: Duke University Press, 2011.

——. "Mesillaros and Gringo Mexicans: The Changing Meanings of Race, Nation, and Space in Southern New Mexico, 1848–1912." PhD diss., University of Notre Dame, 2002.

Murillo, Louis Christopher. "The Detroit Mexican Colonia from 1920 to 1932: Implications for Social and Educational Policy." PhD diss., Michigan State University, 1981.

Murrah, Erin. "Miguel Antonio Otero: Destabilizing Identity in the West." *Western American Literature* 43 (Summer 2008).

Neil, William N. "The American Territorial System since the Civil War: A Summary Analysis." *Indiana Magazine of History* 40 (September 1964): 219–40.

Nelson-Cisneros, Victor. "La clase trabajadora en Tejas, 1920–1940." *Aztlán: International Journal of Chicano Studies Research* 6, no. 2 (Summer 1975): 239–65.

Ngai, Mae M. "The Architecture of Race in American Immigration Law: A Reexamination of the Immigration Act of 1924." *Journal of American History* (June 1999): 67–92.

——. *Impossible Subjects: Illegal Aliens and the Making of Modern America.* Princeton, NJ: Princeton University Press, 2004.

Nieto-Phillips, John M. *The Language of Blood: The Making of Spanish-American Identity in New Mexico, 1880s–1930s.* Albuquerque: University of New Mexico Press, 2004.

Norris, Jim. *North for the Harvest: Mexican Workers, Growers, and the Sugar Beet Industry*. St. Paul: Minnesota Historical Press, 2009.

O'Neill, Colleen. "Domesticity Deployed: Gender, Race, and the Construction of Class Struggle in the Bisbee Deportation." *Labor History* 34, nos. 2–3 (1993): 256–73.

Onnam, G. Bromley. "The Mexican in Los Angeles from the Standpoint of the Religious Forces of the City." *Annals of the American Academy* 93 (January 1921): 130–33.

Onuf, Peter S. *Statehood and Union: A History of the Northwest Ordinance*. Urbana: University of Illinois Press, 1987.

Otero, Miguel Antonio. *My Nine Years as Governor of the Territory of New Mexico, 1897–1906*. Edited by Marion Dargan. Albuquerque: University of New Mexico Press, 1940.

———. *Otero: An Autobiographical Trilogy*. New York: Arno Press, 1974.

Padilla, Genaro M. *My History, Not Yours: The Formation of Mexican American Autobiography*. Madison: University of Wisconsin Press, 1993.

Paredes, Raymond. "The Origins of Anti-Mexican Sentiment in the United States." In David Weber, ed., *The Idea of Spanish Borderlands*. New York: Garland, 1991.

Pascoe, Peggy. "Miscegenation Law, Court Cases, and the Ideology of Race in Twentieth Century America." *Journal of American History* 83, no. 1 (June 1996): 44–69.

———. *What Comes Naturally: Miscegenation Law and the Making of Race in America*. Oxford: Oxford University Press, 2009.

Peck, Gunther. *Reinventing Free Labor: Padrones and Immigrants Workers in the North American West, 1880–1930*. New York: Cambridge University Press, 2000.

Perlmann, Joel. *Italians Then, Mexicans Now: Immigrant Origins and the Second-Generation Progress, 1890–2004*. New York: Russell Sage Publications, 2004.

Petit, Jeanne Danielle. "Building Citizens: Women, Men, and the Immigration Restriction Debates, 1890–1929." PhD diss., University of Notre Dame, 2000.

Pierri, Ettore. *Braceros: La frontera explosiva*. Mexico City: Editores Mexicanos Unidos, 1978.

Piore, Michael J. *Birds of Passage: Migrant Labor and Industrial Societies*. Cambridge: Cambridge University Press, 1979.

Pitt, Leonard. *The Decline of the Californios: A Social History of the Spanish-Speaking Californians, 1846–1890*. Berkeley: University of California Press, 1970.

Pitti, Stephen J. *The Devil in Silicon Valley: Northern California, Race, and Mexican Americans*. Princeton, NJ: Princeton University Press, 2003.

Portes, Alejandro, and Rubén G. Rumbaut. *Legacies: The Story of the Immigrant Second Generation*. Berkeley: University of California Press, 2001.

Pry, Mark E. "Arizona and the Politics of Statehood, 1889–1912." PhD diss., Arizona State University, 1995.

Ramírez, Richard Ruben. "Mexican American Repatriation during the Great *Depression*." Master's thesis, San Jose State University, 1986.

Redfield, Robert. "The Antecedents of Mexican Immigration to the United States." *American Journal of Sociology* 35 (1929–30): 433–38.

Reisler, Mark. *By the Sweat of Their Brow: Mexican Immigrant Labor in the United States, 1900–1940*. Westport, CT: Greenwood Press, 1976.

Rice, Ross R. *Carl Hayden: Builder of the American West.* Lanham, MD: University Press of America, 1994.

Rich, Adena Miller. "Case Work in the Repatriation of Immigrants." *Social Service Review* 10 (December 1936): 569–605.

Rivera, John-Michael. *The Emergence of Mexican America: Recovering Stories of Mexican Peoplehood in U.S. Culture.* New York: New York University Press, 2006.

Robinson, Cecil. *With the Ears of Strangers: The Mexican in American Literature.* Tucson: University of Arizona Press, 1963.

Romo, Ricardo. "Responses to Mexican Immigration, 1910–1930." *Aztlán: International Journal of Chicano Studies Research* 6, no. 2 (Summer 1975): 173–94.

Rosales, F. Arturo. *¡Pobre Raza!: Violence, Justice, and Mobilization among México Lindo Immigrants, 1900–1936.* Austin: University of Texas Press, 1999.

Ruiz, Vicki L. *Cannery Women/Cannery Lives: Mexican Women, Unionization, and the California Food Processing Industry, 1930–1950.* Albuquerque: University of New Mexico Press, 1987.

Rydell, Robert W. *All the World's a Fair: Visions of Empire at American International Expositions, 1876–1916.* Chicago: University of Chicago Press, 1984.

Salyer, Lucy. *Laws as Harsh as Tigers: Chinese Immigrants and the Shaping of Modern Immigration Law, 1882–1924.* Chapel Hill: University of North Carolina Press, 1995.

Sánchez, George I. *Forgotten People: A Study of New Mexicans.* Albuquerque: University of New Mexico Press, 1940.

Sánchez, George J. *Becoming Mexican American: Ethnicity, Culture, and Identity in Chicano Los Angeles, 1900–1945.* New York: Oxford University Press, 1993.

Santibañez, Enrique. *Ensayo acerca de la inmigracion mexicana en los estados unidos.* San Antonio: Clegg Co., 1930.

Saragoza, Alex M. "Recent Chicano Historiography: An Interpretive Essay." *Aztlán* 19, no. 1 (Spring 1989): 1–77.

———. "The Significance of Recent Chicano-Related Historical Writings: An Assessment." *Ethnic Affairs* 1 (Fall 1987): 24–63.

Saxton, Alexander. *The Indispensable Enemy: Labor and the Anti-Chinese Movement in California.* Berkeley: University of California Press, 1971.

Schwartz, Harry. *Seasonal Farm Labor in the United States.* New York: Columbia University Press, 1945.

Scruggs, Otey M. "The First Mexican Farm Labor Program." *Arizona and the West* 2 (Winter 1960): 319–26.

Sheridan, Clare. "Contested Citizenship: National Identity and the Mexican Immigration Debates of the 1920s." *Journal of American Ethnic History* 21, no. 3 (Spring 2002): 3–35.

Sheridan, Thomas E. *Arizona: A History.* Tucson: University of Arizona Press, 1995.

———. *Los Tucsonenses: The Mexican Community in Tucson, 1854–1941.* Tucson: University of Arizona Press, 1986.

Simon, Daniel T. "Mexican Repatriation in East Chicago, Indiana." *Journal of Ethnic Studies* 2 (Summer 1974): 11–23.

Skocpol, Theda. *Protecting Soldiers and Mothers: The Political Origins of Social Policy in the United States.* Cambridge: Harvard University Press, 1992.

Slayden, James L. "Some Observations on Mexican Immigration." *Annals of the American Academy of Political and Social Science* 93, no. 182 (January 1921): 121–26.

Smith, Rogers. *Civic Ideals: Conflicting Visions of Citizenship in U.S. History*. New Haven, CT: Yale University Press, 1997.

Sparrow, Bartholomew H. *The Insular Cases and the Emergence of American Empire*. Lawrence: University of Kansas Press, 2006.

Spickard, Paul. *Almost All Aliens: Immigration, Race and Colonialism in American History and Identity*. New York: New York University Press, 2007.

Stern, Alexandra Minna. *Eugenic Nation: Faults and Frontiers of Better Breeding in Modern America*. Berkeley: University of California Press, 2005.

———. "Eugenics beyond Borders: Science and Medicalization in Mexico and the U.S. West, 1900–1950." PhD diss., University of Chicago, 1999.

Stoler, Ann Laura, ed. *Haunted by Empire: Geographies of Intimacy in North American History*. Durham, NC: Duke University Press, 2006.

———. "Intimidations of Empire." In Ann Laura Stoler, ed., *Haunted by Empire: Geographies of Intimacy in North American History*. Durham, NC: Duke University Press, 2006, 1–22.

Stowell, Jay S. *The Near Side of the Mexican Question*. New York: George H. Doran, 1921.

Taylor, Paul S. *An American-Mexican Frontier: Nueces County, Texas*. Chapel Hill: University of North Carolina Press, 1934.

———. *Mexican Labor in the United States: Chicago and the Calumet Region*, vol. 7, no. 2. Berkeley: University of California Press, 1932.

———. *Mexican Labor in the United States: Dimmit County, Winter Garden District, South Texas*, vol. 6, no. 5. Berkeley: University of California Press, 1930.

———. *Mexican Labor in the United States: Imperial Valley*, vol. 6, no. 1. Berkeley: University of California Press, 1928.

———. *Mexican Labor in the United States: Migration Statistics*, vol. 1, no. 6. Berkeley: University of California Press, 1930.

———. *Mexican Labor in the United States: Valley of the South Platte, Colorado*, vol. 6, no. 2. Berkeley: University of California Press, 1928.

Thomas, Dana Lee. *The Story of American Statehood*. New York: Funk, 1961.

Thomson, Charles A. "Mexicans—an Interpretation." In *Proceedings of the National Conference of Social Work*. Chicago: University of Chicago Press, 1928, 499–503.

———. "Restriction of Mexican Immigration." *Journal of Applied Psychology* 11 (July–August 1927): 574–78.

Tichenor, Daniel J. *Dividing Lines: The Politics of Immigration Control in America*. Princeton, NJ: Princeton University Press, 2002.

Tinker Salas, Miguel. *In the Shadow of the Eagles: Sonora and the Transformation of the Border during the Porfiriato*. Berkeley: University of California Press, 1997.

Trevino, Roberto R. "Prensa y patria: The Spanish-Language Press and the Biculturation of the Tejano Middle Class, 1920–1940." *Western Historical Quarterly* (November 1991): 451–72.

Truett, Samuel. *Fugitive Landscapes: The Forgotten History of the U.S.-Mexico Borderlands*. New Haven, CT: Yale University Press, 2006.

Underhill, Karen Jean. "Albert J. Beveridge's Congressional Report on Arizona Territory in 1902." Master's thesis, University of Arizona, 1990.

Valdés, Dennis Nodín. "Mexican Revolutionary Nationalism and Repatriation during the Great Depression." *Mexican Studies/Estudios Mexicanos* 4 (Winter 1988): 1–23.

Valdés, Dionicio. *Mexicans in Minnesota: The People of Minnesota.* St. Paul: Minnesota Historical Society, 2005.

Vargas, Zaragosa. *Labor Rights Are Civil Rights: Mexican American Workers in Twentieth-Century America.* Princeton, NJ: Princeton University Press, 2005.

———. *Proletarians of the North: A History of Mexican Industrial Workers in Detroit and the Midwest, 1917–1933.* Berkeley: University of California Press, 1993.

Vélez-Ibáñez, Carlos G. *Border Visions: Mexican Cultures of the Southwest United States.* Tucson: University of Arizona Press, 1996.

Wagoner, Jay J. *Arizona Territory, 1863–1912: A Political History.* Tucson: University of Arizona Press, 1970.

Walker, Helen. "Mexican Immigrants and American Citizenship." *Sociology and Social Research* 13, no. 5 (1928–29): 465–71.

———. "Mexican Immigrants as Laborers." *Sociology and Social Research* 13 (1928–29): 55–62.

Waters, Lawrence Leslie. "Transient Mexican Agricultural Labor." *Southwestern Social Science Quarterly* 22 (June 1941): 49–66.

Weber, David J. *Foreigners in Their Native Land: Historical Roots of the Mexican Americans.* Albuquerque: University of New Mexico Press, 1973.

———. *The Spanish Frontier in North America.* New Haven, CT: Yale University Press, 1992.

Weber, David S. "Anglo Views of Mexican Immigrants: Popular Perceptions and Neighborhood Realities in Chicago, 1900–1940." PhD diss., Ohio State University, 1982.

Weber, Devra. *Dark Sweat, White Gold: California Farm Workers, Cotton, and the New Deal.* Berkeley: University of California Press, 1994.

Weeks, O. Douglas. "The League of United Latin-American Citizens: A Texas-Mexican Civic Organization." *Southwestern Political and Social Science Quarterly* 10, no. 3 (December 1929): 257–78.

Welsh, Cynthia Secor. "A 'Star Will Be Added': Miguel Antonio Otero and the Struggle for Statehood." *New Mexico Historical Review* (January 1992): 33–51.

Wexler, Laura. "The Fair Ensemble: Kate Chopin in St. Louis in 1904." In Ann Laura Stoler, ed., *Haunted by Empire: Geographies of Intimacy in North American History.* Durham, NC: Duke University Press, 2006, 271–96.

Wiebe, Robert H. *The Search for Order, 1877–1920.* New York: Hill and Wang, 1967.

Williams, Walter L. "United States Indian Policy and the Debate over Philippine Annexation: Implications for the Origins of American Imperialism." *Journal of American History* 66 (March 1980): 810–83.

Wyman, Mark. *Hoboes, Bindlestiffs, Fruit Tramps, and the Harvesting of the West.* New York: Hill and Wang, 2010.

———. *Round-Trip to America: The Immigrants Return to Europe, 1880–1930.* Ithaca, NY: Cornell University Press, 1996.

Zamora, Emilio, Jr. *The World of the Mexican Worker in Texas.* College Station: Texas A&M University Press, 1993.

Zelman, Donald L. "Mexican Migrants and Relief in Depression California: Grower Reaction to Public Relief Policies as They Affected Mexican Migration." *Journal of Mexican-American History* 5 (1975): 1–23.

Zolberg, Aristide R. A *Nation by Design: Immigration Policy in the Fashioning of America*. New York: Russell Sage Foundation, 2006.

Index

About the Author

Linda C. Noel is an associate professor of history at Morgan State University. She earned her PhD in history from the University of Maryland, College Park. Recently she published "'I am an American': Anglos, Mexicans, *Nativos*, and the National Debate over Arizona and New Mexico Statehood" in the *Pacific Historical Review*, which won the 2013 Michael P. Malone Award from the Western History Association.